IMAGES
of America

VILLA HILLS

I0806349

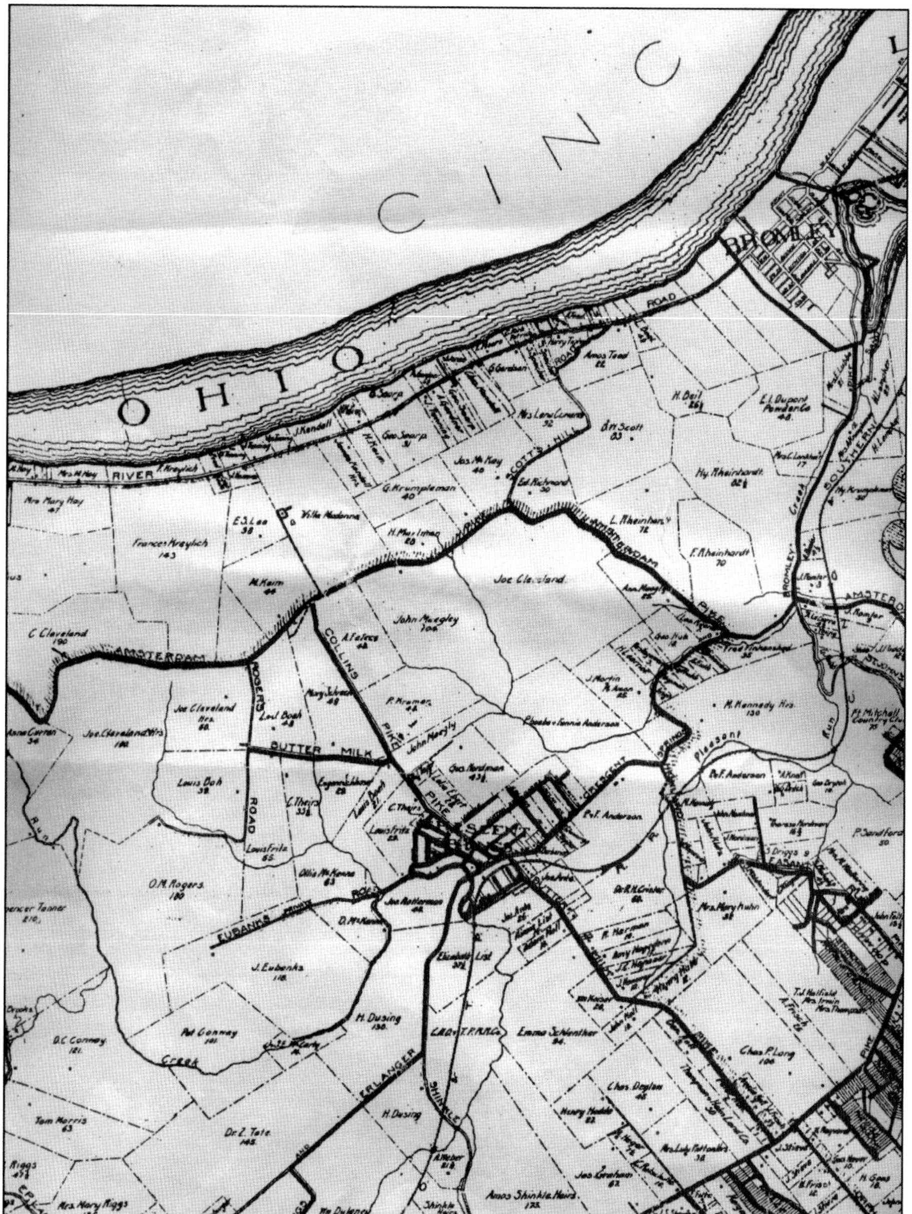

This 1914 map of Kenton County shows the area that now makes up Villa Hills and the surrounding cities. With the Ohio River, Amsterdam Road, Collins Road, and Buttermilk Pike clearly visible, it is easy to see that there were not many roads or other landmarks in the area. The property lines of each farm are apparent, and the names of the farm owners in 1914, many of whom will be seen in the pages of this book, are some of the same families who make up Villa Hills today. (Courtesy of the Kenton County Public Library.)

On the Cover: The Kremer farmers loaded up the truck after a hard day in the fields at their farm on Collins Road. In this early 1940s photograph, Urban Kremer, Ray Hansman, Frank Kremer Sr., Jerome Kremer, and Ed Lange (from left to right) show off their wares after a hard day in the fields. (Courtesy of Julie Kremer.)

IMAGES
of America

VILLA HILLS

Deborah Kohl Kremer

ARCADIA
PUBLISHING

ISBN 978-0-7385-8688-5

Published by Arcadia Publishing
Charleston, South Carolina

Printed in the United States of America

Library of Congress Control Number: 2010930144

For all general information, please contact Arcadia Publishing:
Telephone 843-853-2070
Fax 843-853-0044
E-mail sales@arcadiapublishing.com
For customer service and orders:
Toll-Free 1-888-313-2665

Visit us on the Internet at www.arcadiapublishing.com

To Nick

Contents

ACKNOWLEDGMENTS

A book like this could not come together by the work of just one person. These photographs, most of which have never been seen before in print, were donated by the kindness of the owners. Asking people to dig out photographs from 50 years prior is quite a request, so to the people who dug and then invited me over to see them, well, I truly appreciate it.

Accumulating enough photographs for a book is a tough job. Although I ran ads in several newspapers, I also called as many neighbors as I could think of, some of whom I had not seen in more than 30 years. But these people with Villa Hills roots came through, just like I knew they would.

People who donated photographs that were used in the book are acknowledged in the courtesy line following each photograph. But the following people helped me by talking to their friends and families about my quest for photographs, which led to the completion of the book.

Thank you to Judy Niewhaner, Ron Nolting, Ernie Brown, Jim Kiger, Wes Swain, Paula Abel Weber, Jeff Wendt, Dan Goodenough, Jackie Wagner, Cheryl Reynolds, Nancy Goetz Barton, Mike Sadouskas, Margie Potter Otting, Tim Grout, Andy Goetz, Scott Summe, Paul Gabis, Tim Schulte, Elaine Kuhn, Cindy Schulte Butcher, Sr. Deborah Harmeling OSB, Dominic Ruschman, Pete and Eileen Goetz, Bernie Spencer, and the *Voice of Villa Hills*.

Special thanks go to my immediate family. My parents Paul and Peg Kohl, who moved to Kenridge Drive in 1959 and were able to witness the evolution of Villa Hills right from the start. My sister, Nancy Kohl Hoffman, had photographs, as well as contacts, which were useful too. I was also lucky enough to marry into the Kremer family, who began farming on Collins Road in 1913. Aunt Julie Kremer and my sister-in-law Julie Kremer Bricking both had photographs and memories that made it into the book.

Lastly, I need to thank my husband Nick Kremer, who grew up in Villa Hills himself, and our own Villa Hills kids, Ellie Kremer and Paul Kremer. I couldn't have done this without you.

Introduction

The city of Villa Hills, which was incorporated in 1962, has roots that go back prior to Kentucky's statehood. Records show that the land was given out as payment for fighting in the Revolutionary War. And although the earliest residents left no paperwork, the large amount of arrowheads that have been found in the area tells us that the American pioneers were not the first settlers of this land that sits high atop a hill, overlooking the beautiful Ohio River.

This book in no way compares to the previous books created by the Villa Hills Millennium/ Historical Society. Those books were created to commemorate the city's birthdays, as well as the year 2000, and document exactly how Villa Hills became the city we know today. A fabulous resource, they are available at the Kenton County Library, as well as on the coffee tables of many long-time residents. The books include the names of council members, the order that subdivisions were created, and narratives by residents who actually lived this history.

This book is a photographic history of Villa Hills. Photographs from families who worked the land or created the community tell stories that are not captured in history books. They tell the stories of crops, boarding school students, and streets that were paved with gravel. If you look closely, you will see the people who took a chance to own their own home in a place that was, at the time, "way out in the country," where they could enjoy their neighbors and let their kids ride their bikes in the streets. And whenever there was something to celebrate, well, a parade was usually in order.

In the creation of this book, there were times I was asked "Why do this? Villa Hills doesn't even have a Main Street?" But I was encouraged by Loraine Braun, daughter of Villa Hills's first mayor, who said "Villa Hills never wanted a Main Street." The residential city you see today is exactly what those residents of the 1960s had in mind.

The photographs in this book span the early 1900s through the early 1980s, telling the photographic history of how Villa Hills came to be.

At the turn of the 20th century, the farmland in unincorporated Kenton County, sometimes considered part of Crescent Springs, sometimes considered Ludlow, wouldn't be known as Villa Hills for decades. Although the land was made up of farms belonging to the McCay, Cleveland, Scott, Maegley, Felice, Krumpelman, Westerman, Noll, Smith, Schreck, Boh, Eubanks, Kremer, and Summe families, among others, people lived here for generations raising families and living off the land.

Other early residents included the Benedictine Sisters. Although they had been residents of Covington since the mid-1800s, around the turn of the 20th century, the sisters decided to move out to the country for health reasons. In 1903, they purchased the 86-acre Collins farm, near the intersection of Collins and Amsterdam Roads.

Talk of becoming a city was triggered with the sale of the Boh and Schreck farms around 1955 and the subsequent creation of Kenridge Drive, Sunglow Avenue, and Mary, Frank, and Ann Streets, along with Rardin Court. The two farms, bounded by Buttermilk Pike and Rogers, Collins, and Amsterdam Roads, made up the original Villa Hills. Residents, who were afraid of being annexed by nearby Covington, began to think about incorporation. As the story goes, the founding fathers borrowed money from the Civic Club to file the incorporation papers, and on June 7, 1962, Villa Hills became a sixth-class city. Just a few days after becoming a city, Villa Hills annexed the surrounding land that roughly makes up the city's borders today.

Along with the chaos of creating a city, designing a police department, reconstructing roads, and installing a sanitary sewer system to replace septic tanks, the civic-minded residents took time to plan parades, establish football, softball, baseball, and soccer teams, and in time, create fields to play them on.

The Villa Hills Civic Club, which hosted Easter egg hunts, Christmas parties, and turkey shoots since its inception, has always been the hub of social gatherings in the city. The group purchased the club, known locally as the Lodge, as well as the surrounding lake and ball fields, from Joe and Helen Franzen in 1969. This land continues to be the site of public gatherings, and the ball fields are still leased to the city for $1 per year.

A book about Villa Hills would not be complete without a mention of nearby Crescent Springs. This small town, which most Villa Hills residents drive through each day, is a lifeline for our city. We use their churches, schools, banks, restaurants, and gas stations. At times in our history, we have shared police departments, and although our residents had always served as volunteers for the fire department, it was not until 1975 that the administrative duties were officially shared, with the creation of the Crescent-Villa Fire Authority.

Although the photographs in this book span the years 1900 through the early 1980s, Villa Hills has continued to grow and prosper since then. The late 1980s saw the development of the Thirs Dairy Farm, which is now Thirs Landing off of Buttermilk Pike. The early 1990s welcomed the opening of River Ridge Elementary School near the intersection of Amsterdam Road and Prospect Point Drive, on part of the Westerman Farm. When this school opened, it was the largest elementary school in the state of Kentucky. In the mid-1990s, the Scott family decided to sell their farm on Highwater Road, which is now the site of the Orchards Subdivision.

The pages of this book will reveal the hard-working people who have called Villa Hills home. In the captions, I have tried to capture the spirit of what it took to farm this land, build a monastery, or donate time to create our fine city. Stories of councilmen filling pot holes along the streets, the police chief using his own car for patrol, and residents donating barn space to store the city's snowplow are just small examples of what it took to get this city where it is today.

One

Patchwork Quilt of Farmland

Villa Hills started out as a farming community. Although it was not called Villa Hills until the 1960s, this portion of unincorporated Kenton County was laid out as just one farm after another. As seen in the 1914 map on page two, the area that comprises Villa Hills looks like a patchwork quilt of farmland, with Amsterdam, Collins, Buttermilk, and Rogers already in place. The sisters of St. Walburg were already the property owners of the Collins farm, but even they were running a working farm, as well as an academy for girls, on their 86-acre property. There were no businesses in the immediate area and the farmers had to travel to nearby Crescent Springs, Ft. Mitchell, Ludlow, or Erlanger for supplies.

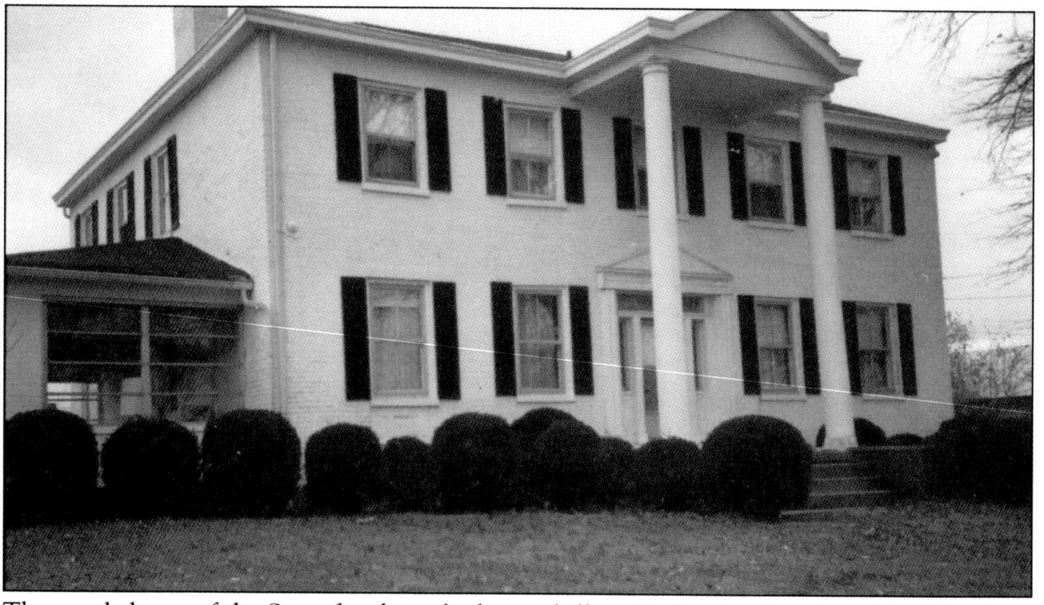

The stately home of the Scott family sat high on a hill on Highwater Road. The home, built in 1843, had been occupied by the Scott family continuously from the time of construction until it was torn down because of structural concerns in the early 2000s. Charles W. Scott, who built the home, obtained the 300 acres of land from Deborah McKay around the time of his marriage to her daughter Lucinda. The two married in 1825 and started married life in a log cabin on the property. (Courtesy of Elmira Scott.)

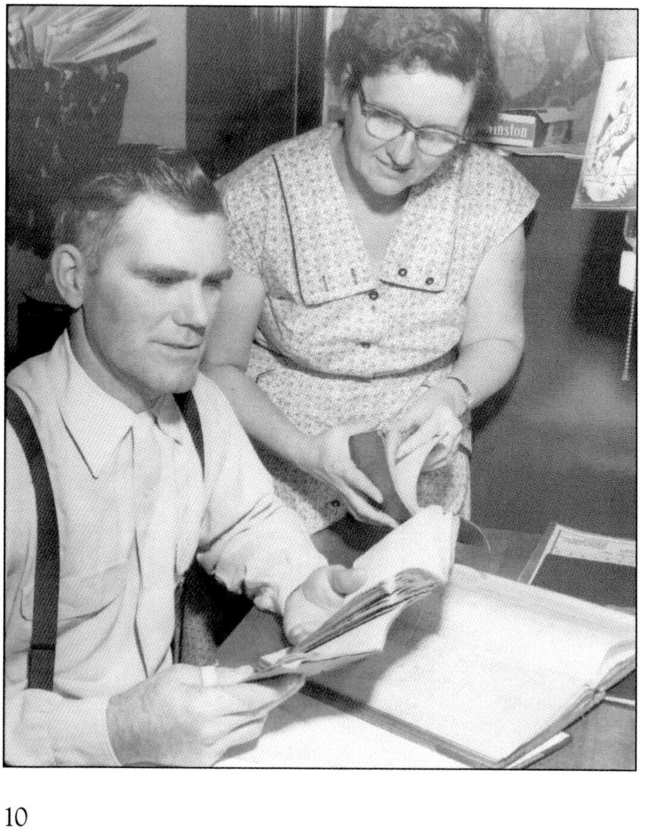

Robert Scott and his wife LaVern go over paperwork in this early 1950s photograph. The farm, which encompassed 120 acres, included an egg farm and orchards. Robert Scott was well known in the community for his years of service as a member of the Kenton County Board of Education. A graduate of the University of Kentucky, Scott valued his degree in agriculture and was a strong supporter of education issues. Kenton County Schools recognized this dedication, and in the early 1980s named the county's newest high school after him. Scott High School is in Taylor Mill, Kentucky. (Courtesy of Kay Scott Malone.)

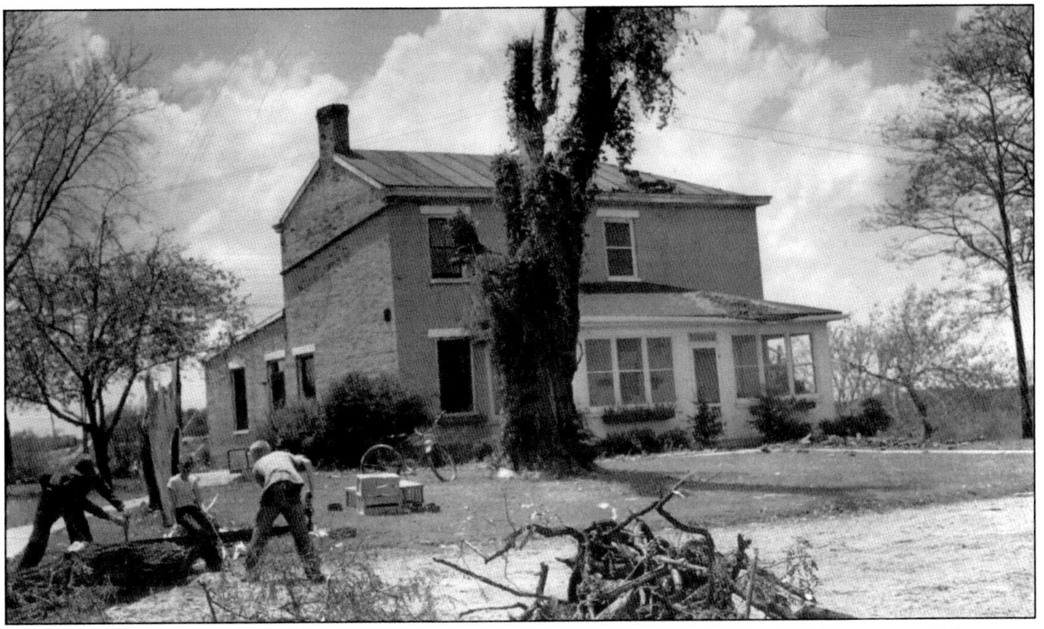

The back of the Scott home is shown in this 1948 photograph. Hail damage from a terrible storm in June of that year is visible. According to a newspaper account, Robert Scott reported golf ball–sized hail, which broke windows and tree limbs and ruined his entire crop. The storm killed more than 50 chickens, filled a lake, and caused a $10,000 loss to the Scott family. (Courtesy of Kay Scott Malone.)

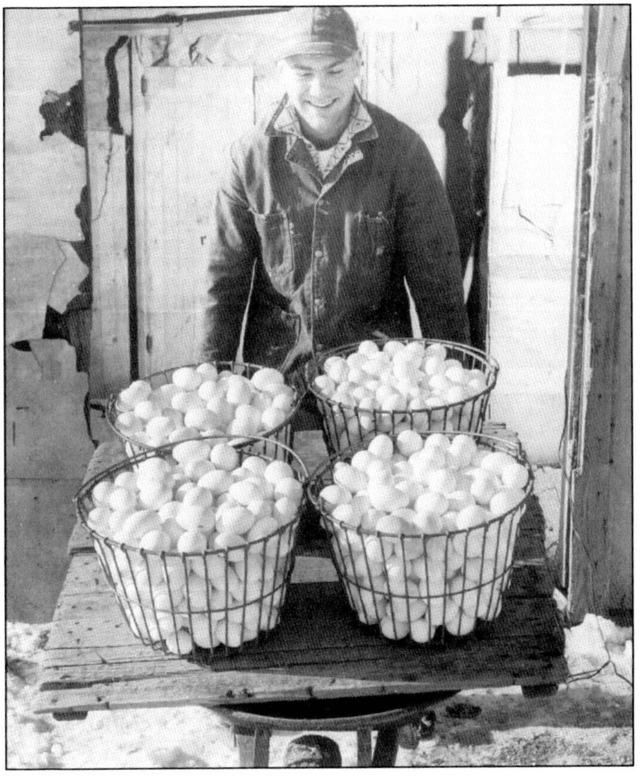

In this early 1950s photograph, Bob Scott hauls eggs from one of the family's nine chicken barns on the property. The family raised chickens strictly for their egg business. (Courtesy of Kay Scott Malone.)

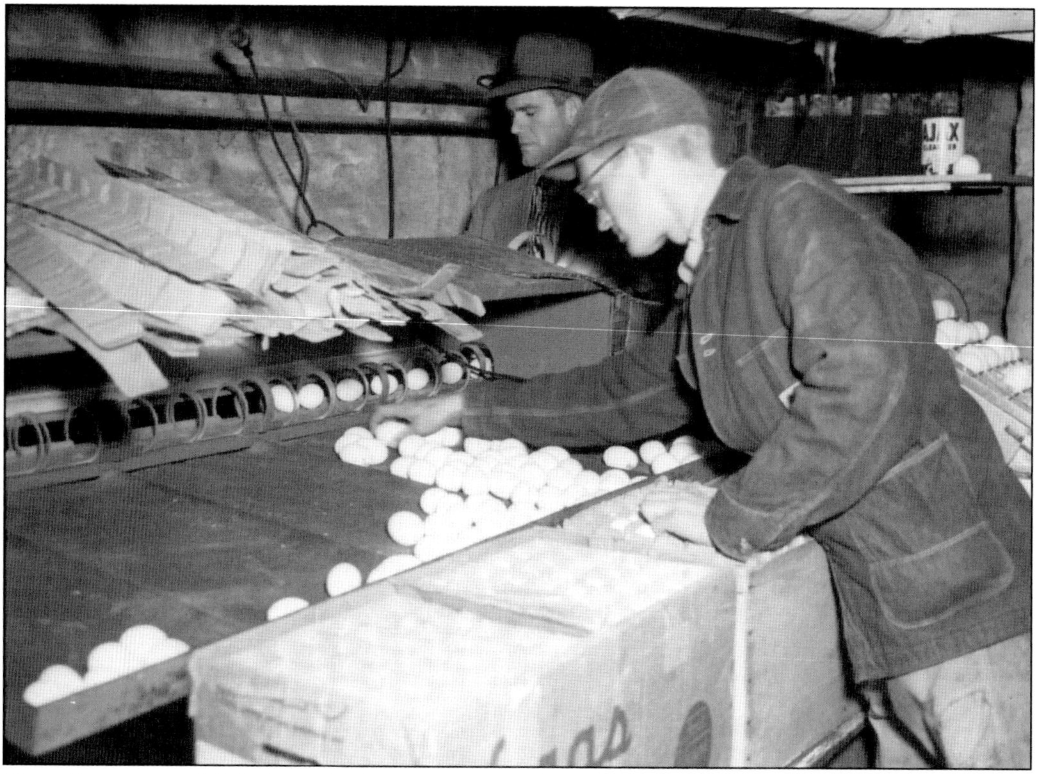

Gene Kinman and Bob Scott (right) sort eggs in the cellar of the Scott home in the early 1950s. The eggs from their 60,000 chickens were sorted daily. (Courtesy of Kay Scott Malone.)

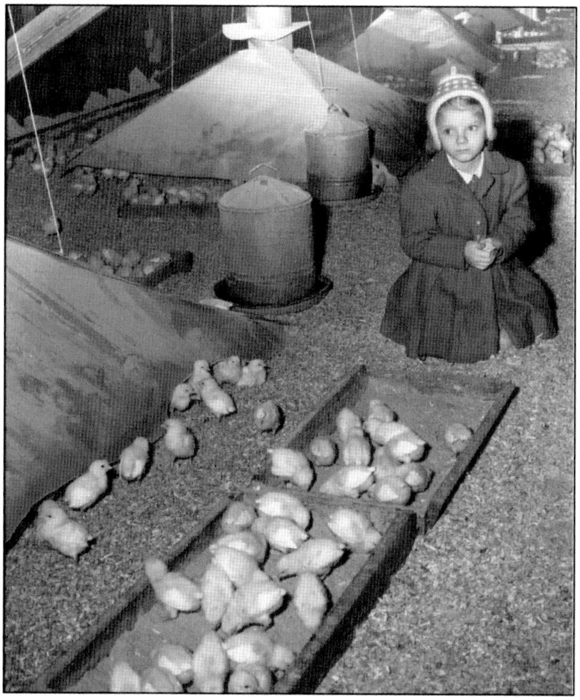

Six-year-old Kay Scott Malone plays with some baby chicks on the Highwater Road farm in 1956. The chicks huddled under the massive heaters in each barn for warmth. The Scott chicken coops had about 20,000 baby chicks at any given time. (Courtesy of Kay Scott Malone.)

The Maegly family farmed about 100 acres along the south side of Amsterdam Road in the area of current-day Palomino Drive, Woodchuck Street, North Oak Drive, Woodstone Way, and Squire Oaks Drive. In this 1935 photograph, Stanley and Matilda Maegley stand with their daughters June (Kinsler) and Alma (Moore) in front of their milk house and cow barn. This photograph was taken in the area of where North Oak Drive is today. (Courtesy of the Earl Maegly family.)

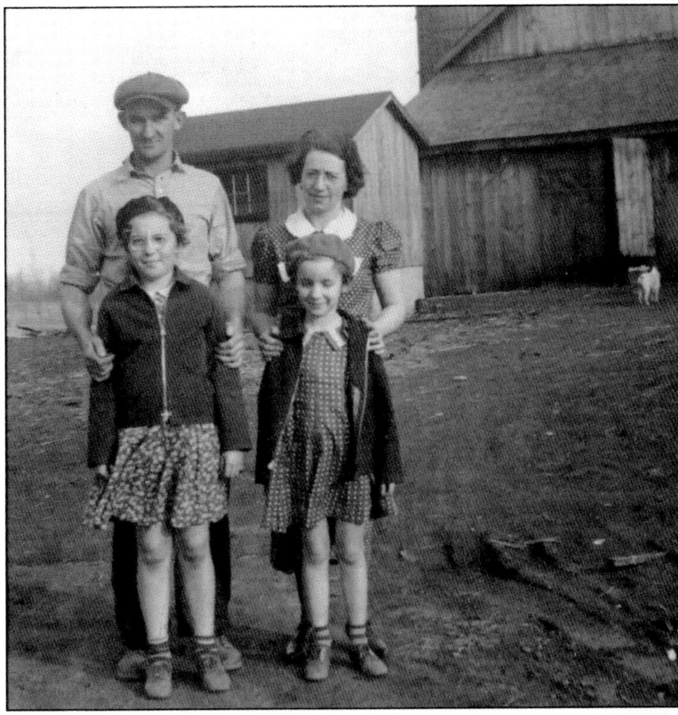

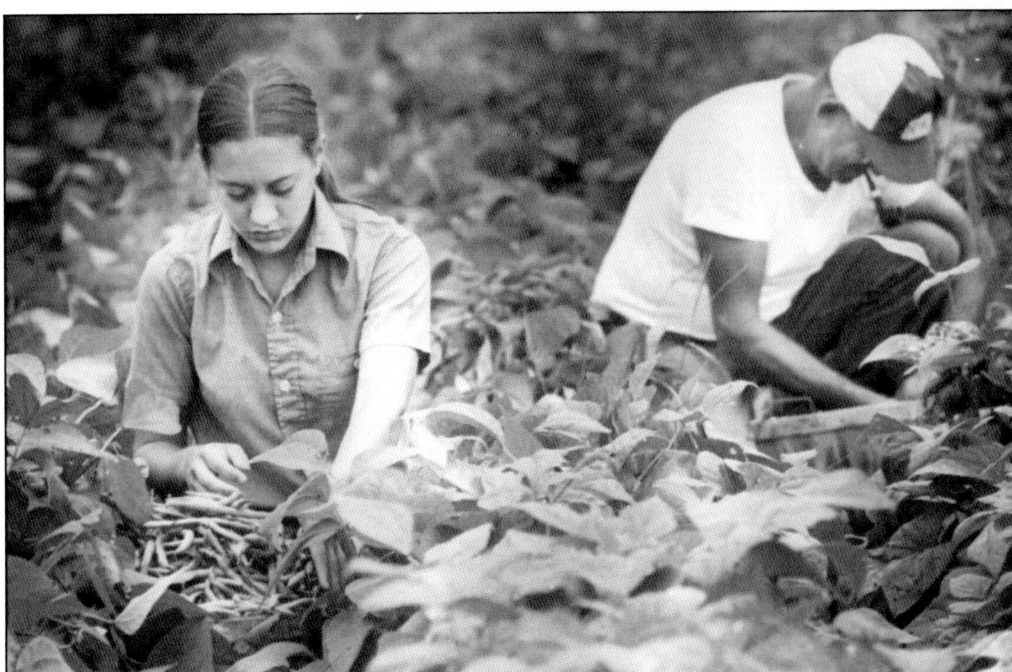

The Maegly farm grew all kinds of fruits and vegetables, like peaches, apples, strawberries, and corn, and its production of poultry and eggs was also well known in the area. In this early-1970 photograph, Earl Maegly and Judy Schewe pick green beans on the family's 100 acres. The farm was sold in the mid-1970s and became the Del Mar Meadows subdivision and part of Country Squire Estates. (Courtesy of the Earl Maegly family.)

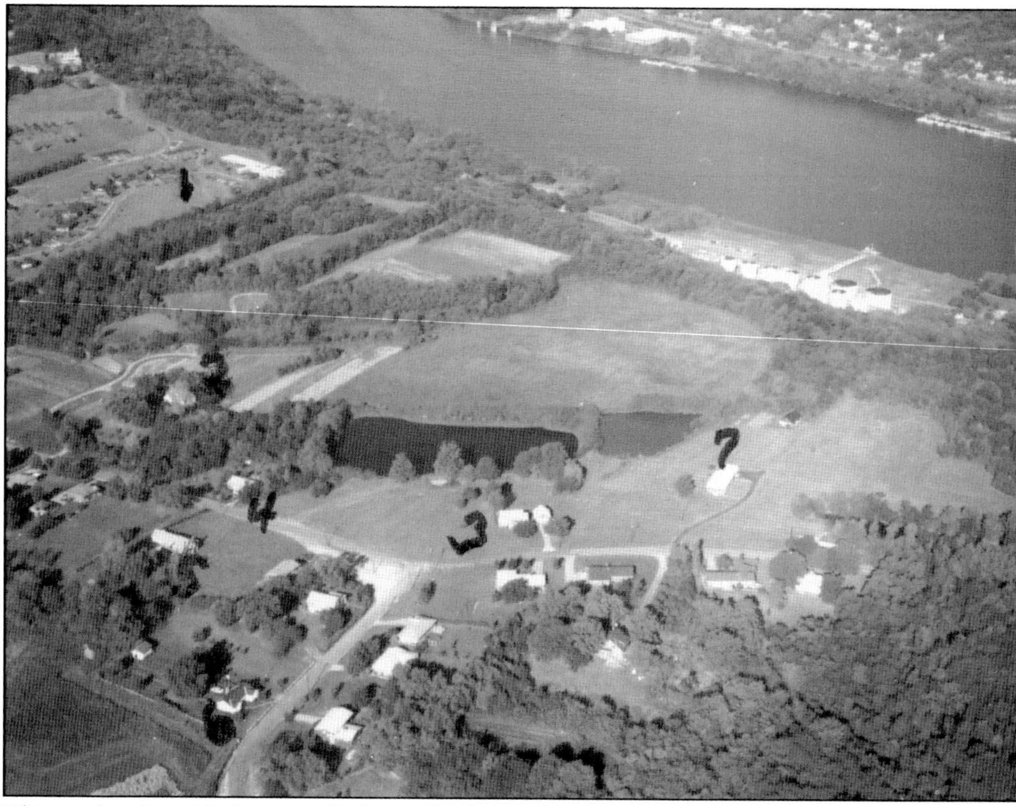

This undated aerial photograph shows the farms along Amsterdam Road and Highwater Road. Amsterdam Road makes a sharp turn in the middle, where it descends the hill into Crescent Springs. The Ohio River is along the top. Madonna Manor Nursing Home is along the left, with the Krumpelman farm adjacent. Other farm owners whose property is shown were the Kinnard, Reckner, Graven, Eubank, and Reinhard families. (Courtesy of Stan and Linda Krumpelman.)

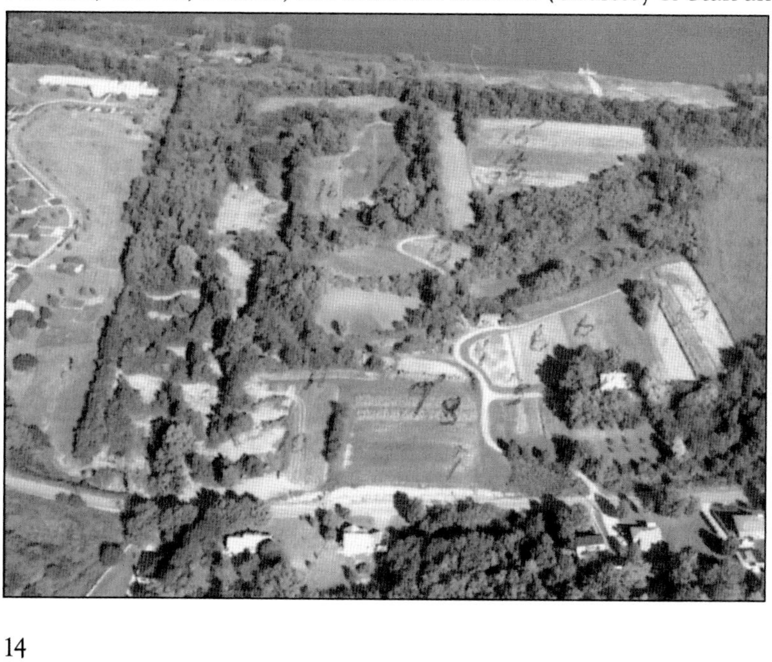

This aerial photograph, taken in 1978, shows the Krumpelman farm on Amsterdam Road. Amsterdam Road runs from left to right, across the bottom. On the left is Madonna Manor Nursing Home. (Courtesy of Stan and Linda Krumpelman.)

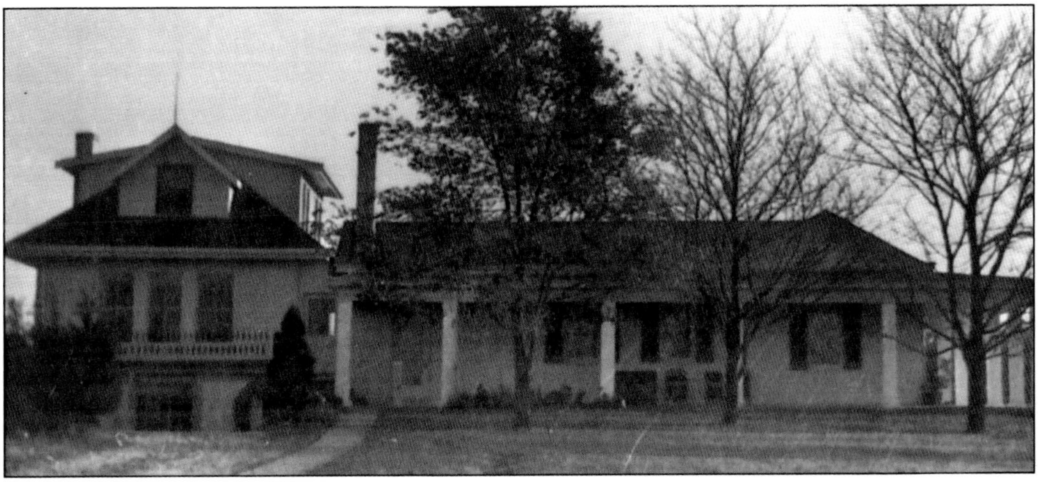

This photograph shows the Krumpelman homestead on Amsterdam Road. The farm was turned into a subdivision in the late 1970s and named George Anne Heights. The streets in the neighborhood were named for Krumpelman relatives. Doriel Drive was named for Dorothy and Daniel Krumpelman. Crestbern Drive was named for Crescentia and Bernard Krumpleman, and Armella Drive was named for Armella Krumpleman. (Courtesy of Stan and Linda Krumpelman.)

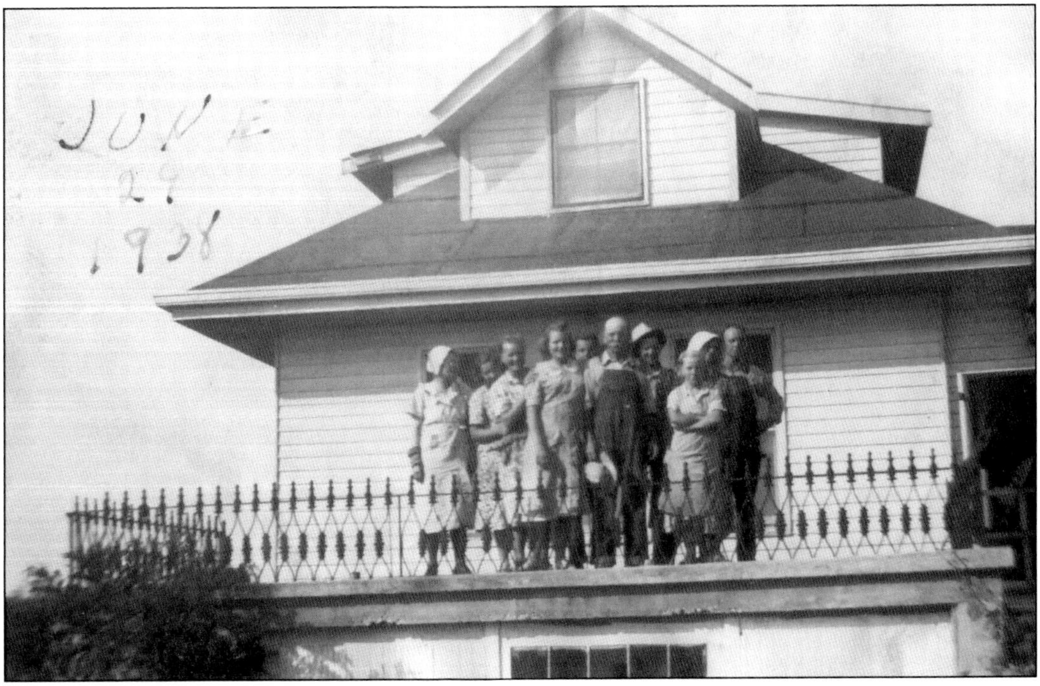

Standing on the balcony of the farmhouse in 1938 are the Krumpelman family and friends. From Left to right are Josephine Lankheit, unidentified, and then Dorothy, Melly, Ben, George, Dan, Cenny, Ann, and Bill Krumpelman. (Courtesy of Carol Noll.)

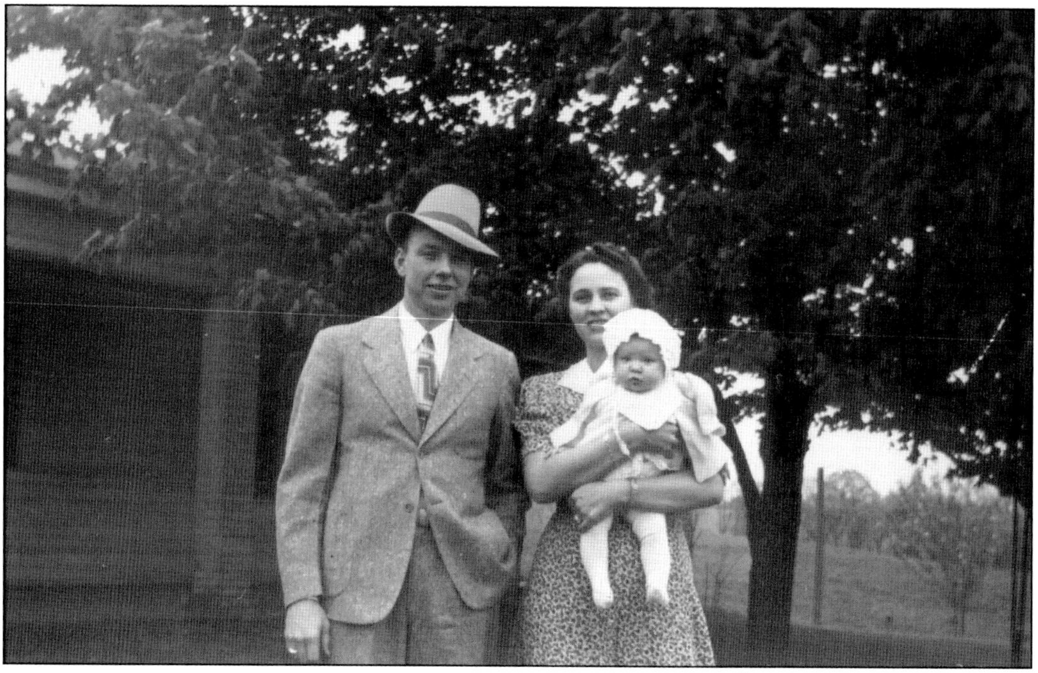

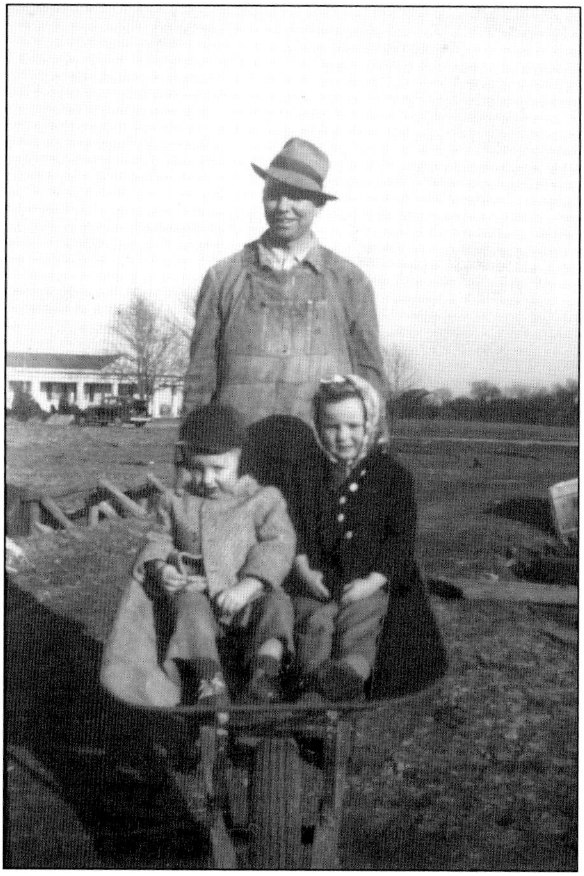

Here are Bill and Marie Krumpelman holding their daughter Carol in 1942. Bill Krumpelman and his family began building houses on the family farm in the late 1970s. They named the neighborhood George Anne Heights, in honor of Bill's parents, George and Anne. (Courtesy of Carol Noll.)

Here is Bill Krumpelman on the family farm with his children Charlie and Carol in 1946. Bill Krumpelman was a home builder who, along with his brother Ben and eventually his sons and grandsons, built many homes on Kenridge Drive, Sunglow Drive, Cecilia Drive, and Orchid Lane and in the neighborhood called George Anne Heights, which was built where he is shown standing here. (Courtesy of Carol Noll.)

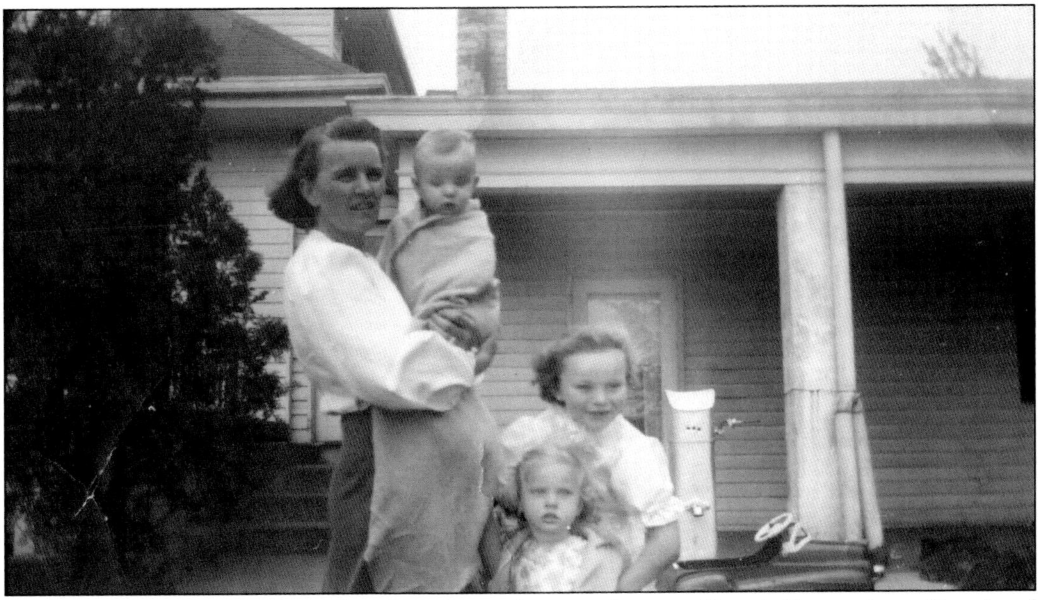

Dorothy Krumpelman holds nephew Ken Krumpelman with nieces Connie Krumpelman (front) and Carol Krumpelman in this 1948 photograph. The photograph was taken outside the Krumpelman family home. (Courtesy of Carol Noll.)

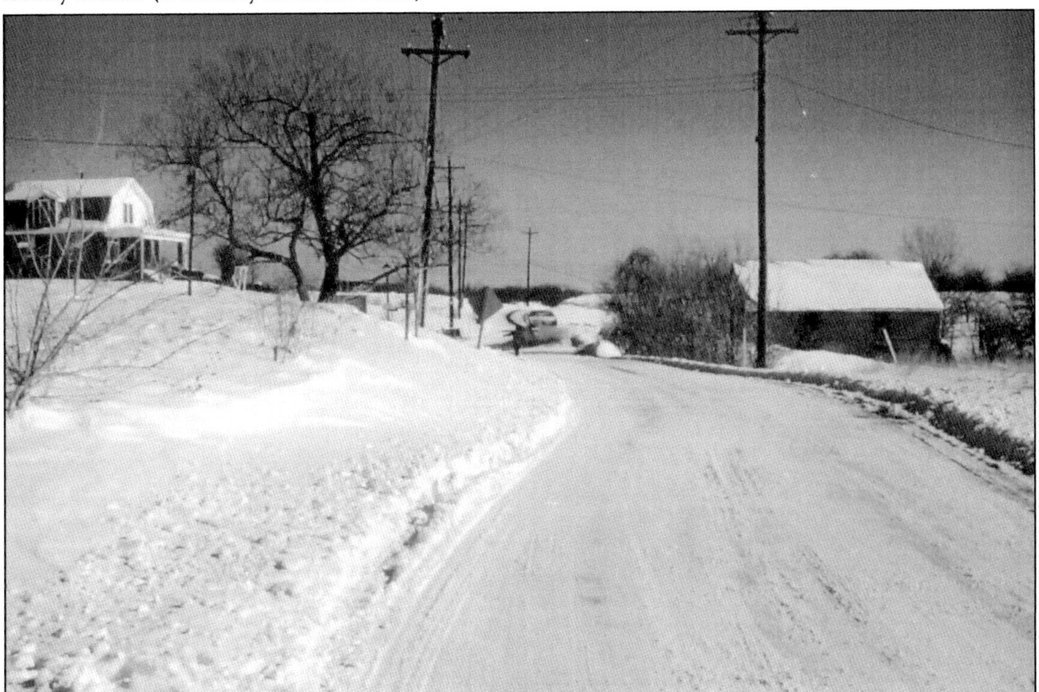

The Westerman farm, located at 2728 Amsterdam Road, was established in 1916. The Westerman farm grew fruits and vegetables and also produced eggs. This snowstorm photograph from the 1970s was taken near the intersection of Amsterdam Road and what is now Valley Trails. The Westerman home, on the left, sat near the entrance to Radio Road, which leads to the radio towers and is now the entrance to Prospect Point. (Courtesy of Lida Smith McClure.)

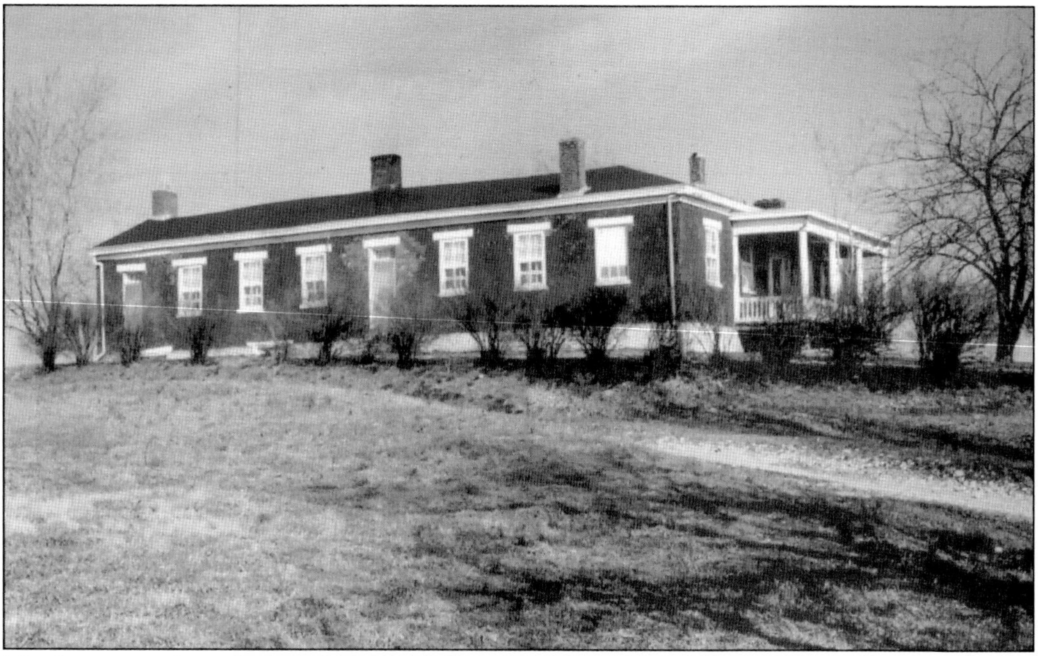

This home, which was built in the 1860s, belonged to the Smith family. It was located on Amsterdam Road, near what is now the entrance to Prospect Point. The bricks, which were made on site, created sturdy walls, which were three-bricks thick. The home was torn down in the 1980s to make way for the Smith Ridge subdivision. (Courtesy of Lida Smith McClure.)

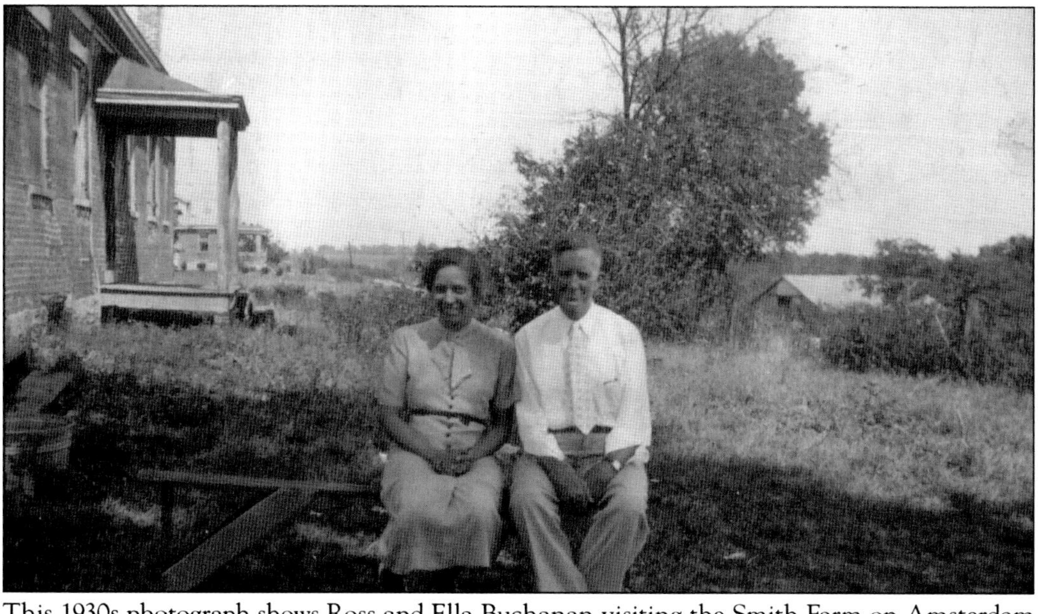

This 1930s photograph shows Ross and Ella Buchanan visiting the Smith Farm on Amsterdam Road. The 32-acre farm raised chickens as well as cherry, apple, and plum trees and had a grape arbor. The farm was near the intersection of Amsterdam Road and Prospect Point Drive. (Courtesy of Lida Smith McClure.)

Cousins Warren Smith (left) and William Smith haul apples from the orchards at the Smith Farm in the spring of 1941. (Courtesy of Lida Smith McClure.)

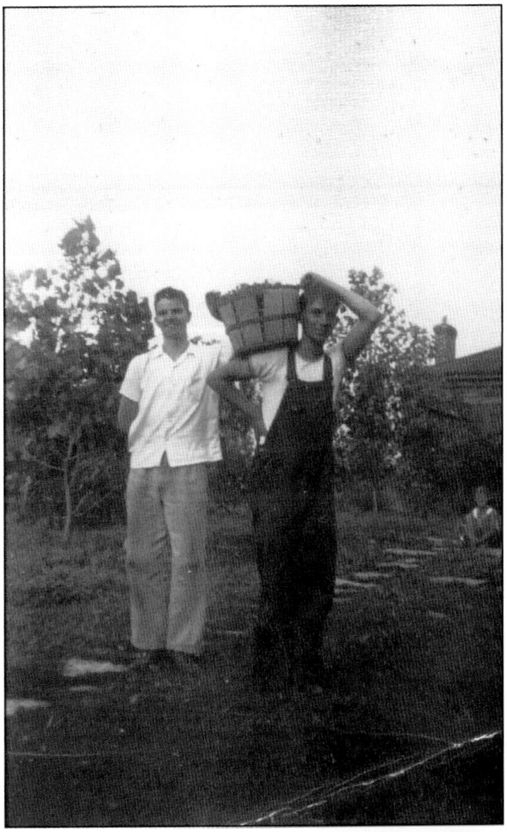

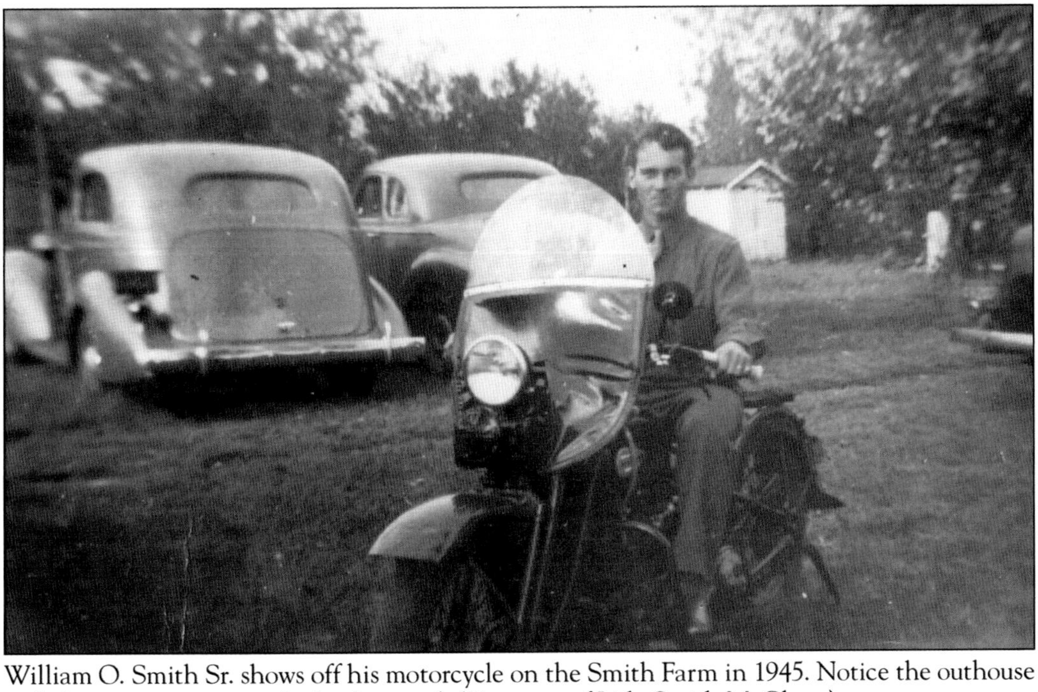

William O. Smith Sr. shows off his motorcycle on the Smith Farm in 1945. Notice the outhouse and the cistern pump in the background. (Courtesy of Lida Smith McClure.)

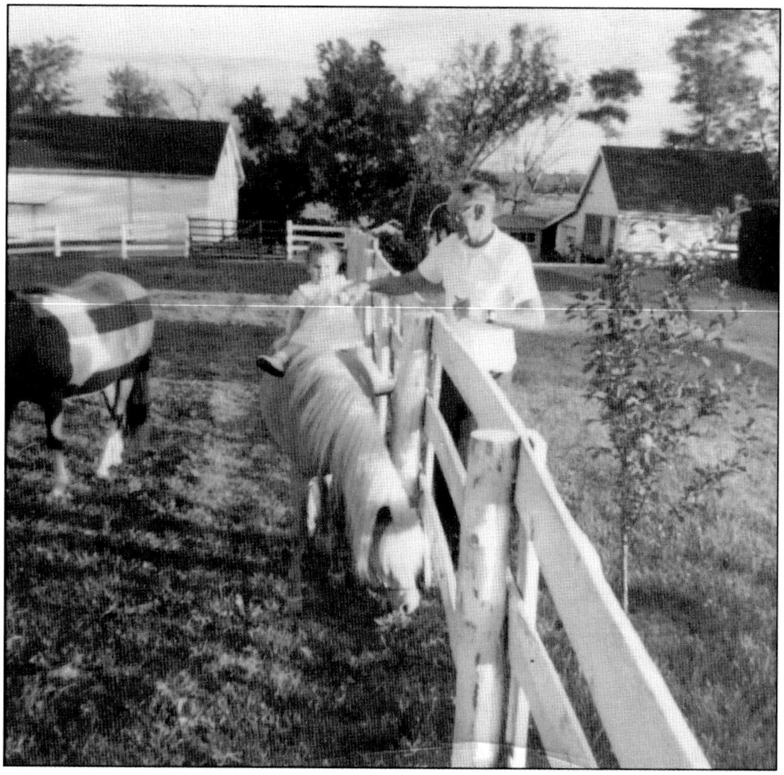

Young Barbie Cooney gets a pony ride with the help of her grandfather Jerry Lohre in this 1967 photograph. The ponies were kept on the Rich Eubank farm, near the corner of Buttermilk Pike and Meadowood Drive. (Courtesy of Barb Cooney Bailey.)

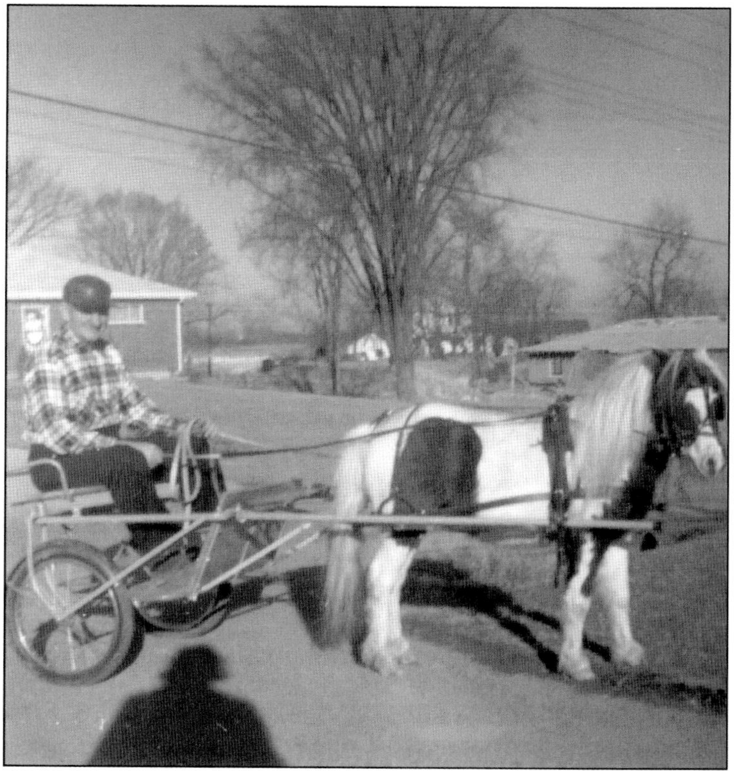

Rich Eubanks takes a spin in his pony cart in this 1959 photograph, taken in his driveway on Buttermilk Pike near the entrance to Villa Hills. (Courtesy of Barb Lohre Cooney.)

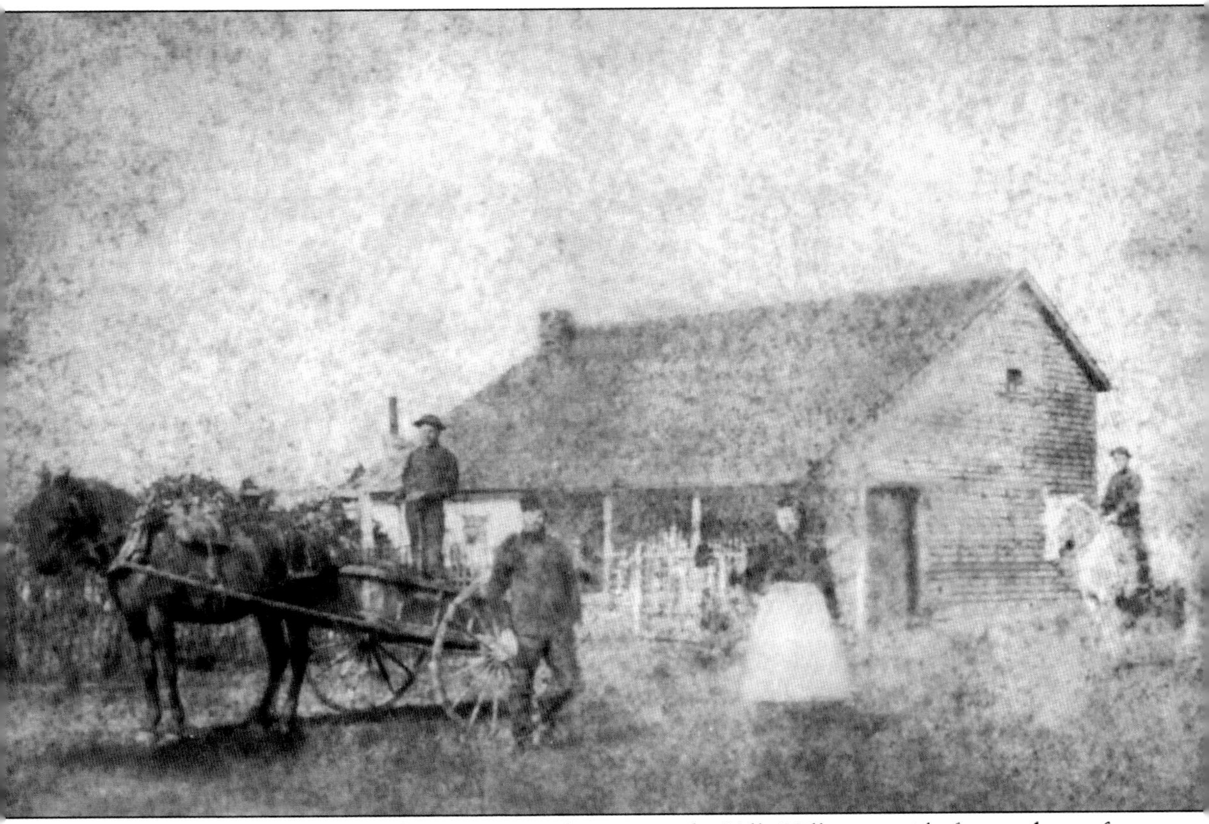

Karl and Henrietta Thirs put down roots in what is now the Villa Hills area with the purchase of 25 acres of land near Dry Creek on September 5, 1883. The family name is pronounced "tears," rhyming with "Sears," although people often mistakenly pronounce it "thurs," as in "Thursday." This photograph from the late 1800s shows the Thirs family on their early homestead. Due to the age of the photograph, the quality is poor, but the home and several family members can be seen. The Thirs had three children, Charles, Hugo, and Anna. Charles married Lillian Maegley in 1874, and they also lived on the farm, where they raised a third generation of Thirs family members, Irma, Anna, Bertha, Hilda, Carl, Robert, George, Walter, and Paul. The youngest children, Walter and Paul, never married and ran the farm and dairy business until selling the property to Arlinghaus Builders in 1992. (Courtesy of Julie Kremer Bricking.)

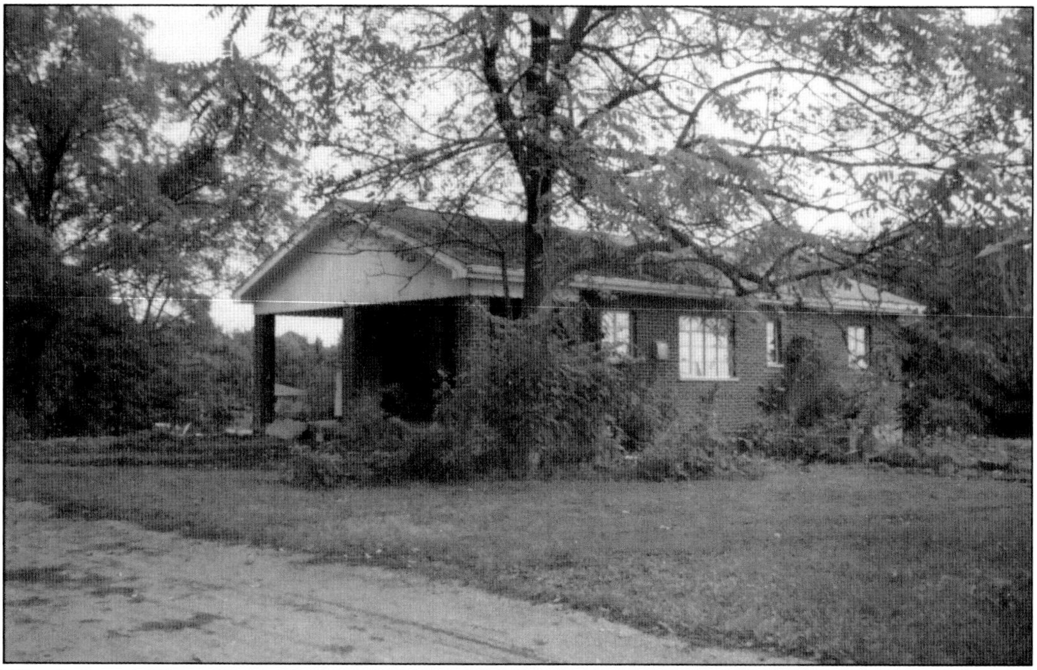

This home, built in the 1950s, was home to the Thirs boys, Robert, Walter, and Paul. Although the three bachelors lived long lives, everyone in Villa Hills always referred to them as the Thirs "boys." (Courtesy of Eileen Thirs Dunavan.)

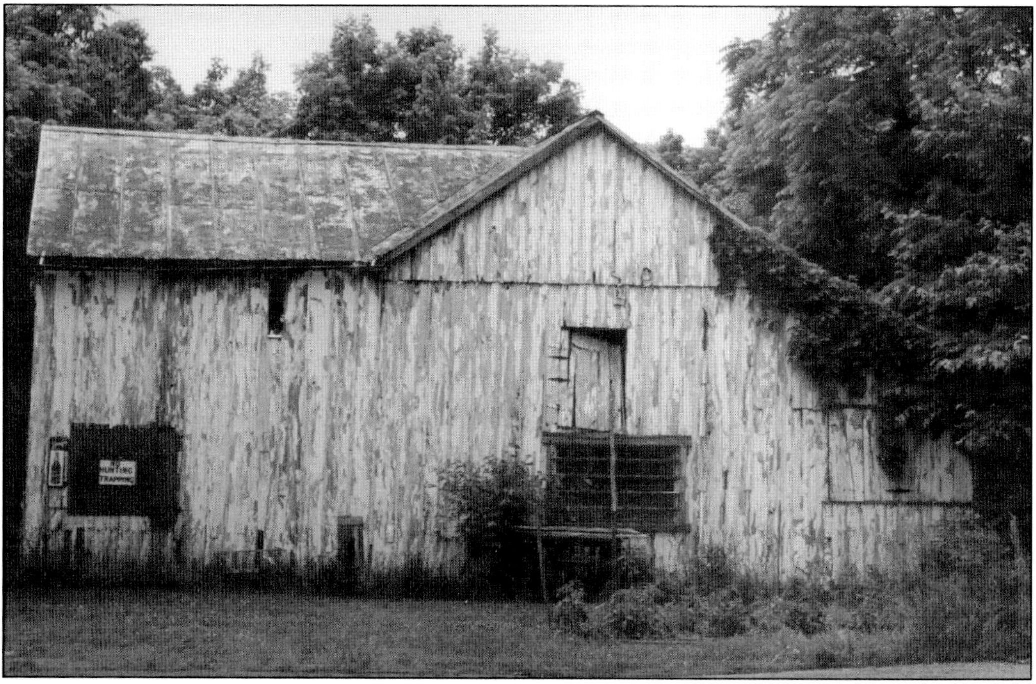

This barn stood proudly at the end of the Thirs farm driveway that was off of Buttermilk Pike, near Kenridge Drive. This photograph was taken in the early 1980s, but the barn had been there long before. (Courtesy of Jenny Voskuhl Canipe.)

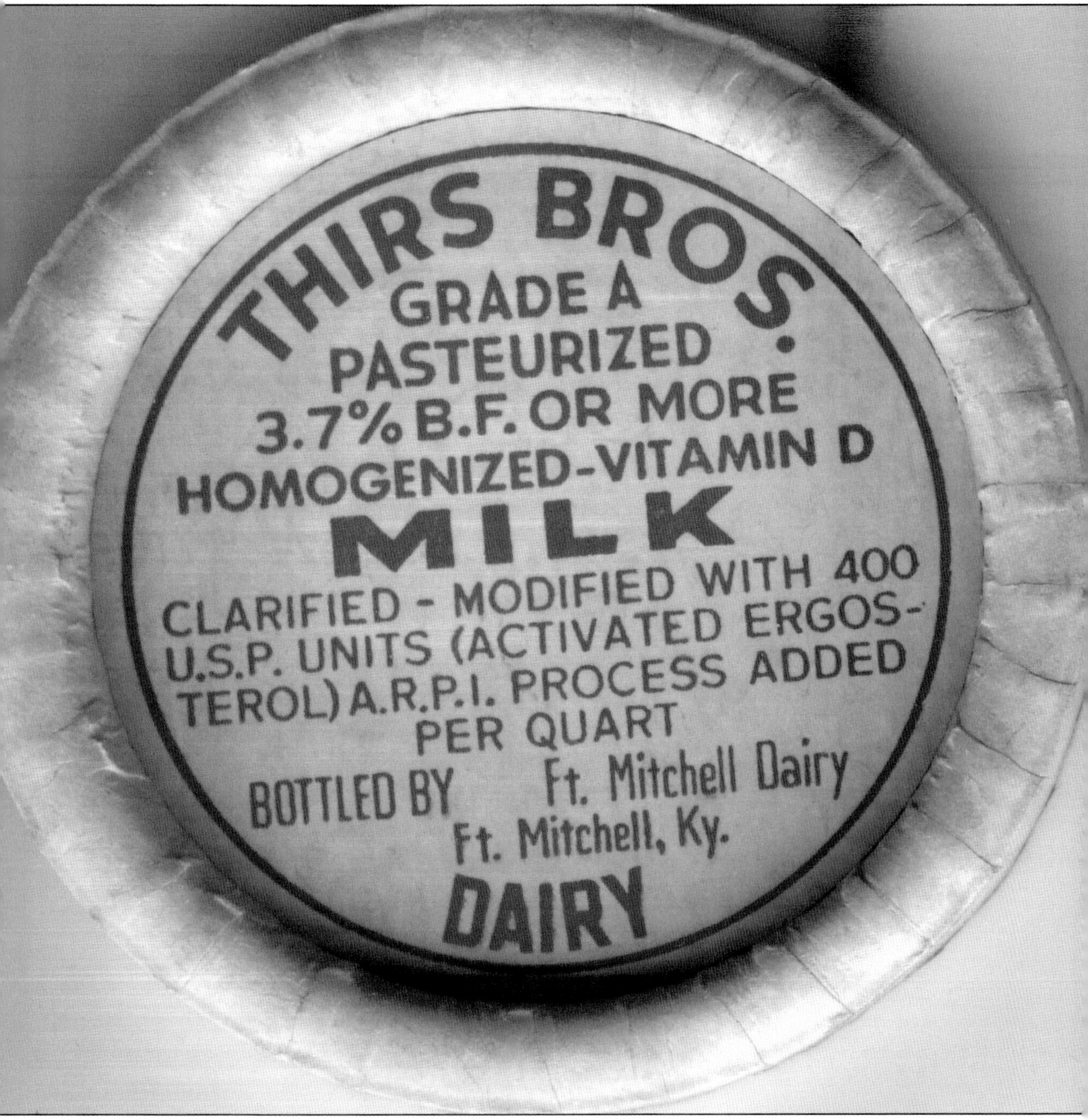

The Thirs family, who first established roots in the Villa Hills area after the Civil War, were dairy farmers. The farm, which is now a subdivision called Thirs Landing, was on the south side of Buttermilk Pike, across the street from Kenridge Drive and Sunglow Drive. This photograph is of the familiar cardboard lid that covered the gallon bottles. Young Villa Hills families were raised on this milk, and many families have stories of children carrying the heavy bottles all the way home, only to have them crash together or drop in the driveway, resulting in broken glass and gallons of spilled milk. The dairy farm evolved into a community gathering place, as the Thirs brothers usually knew all the local news and loved to share it with everyone who stopped by. The farm itself sloped downhill, along Buttermilk Pike. This hill was usually full of local sled riders whenever there was an accumulation of snow. (Courtesy of Nick Kremer.)

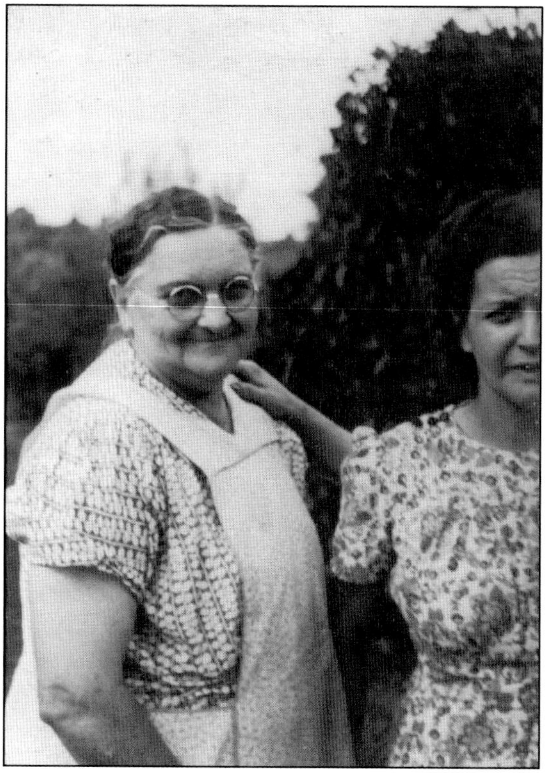

Lillian Thirs (left) with Bertie Thirs Cuthbert are seen here on the Thirs farm in the 1940s. Lillian was honored decades later when a street in the Thirs Landing subdivision was named in her honor. (Courtesy of Eileen Thirs Dunavan.)

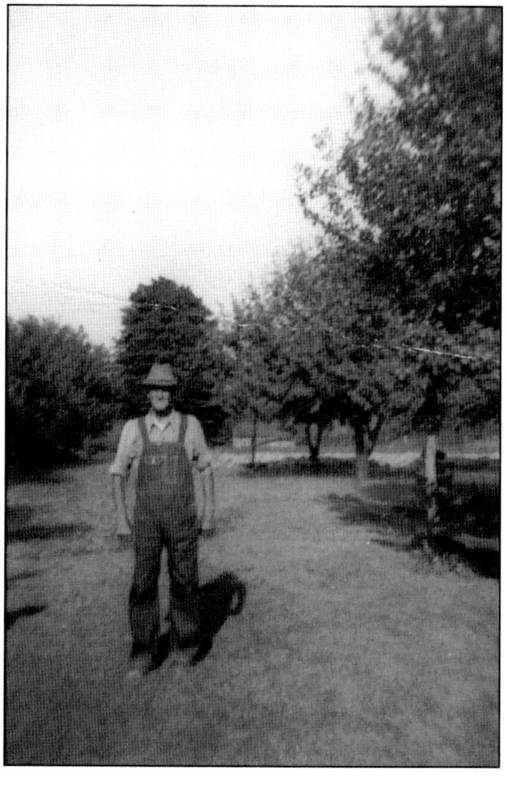

Hugo Thirs, second son of Karl and Henrietta, is seen in this 1930s photograph. After reaching adulthood, he lived alone in a small cabin on the Thirs property until he died in 1958. (Courtesy of Eileen Thirs Dunavan.)

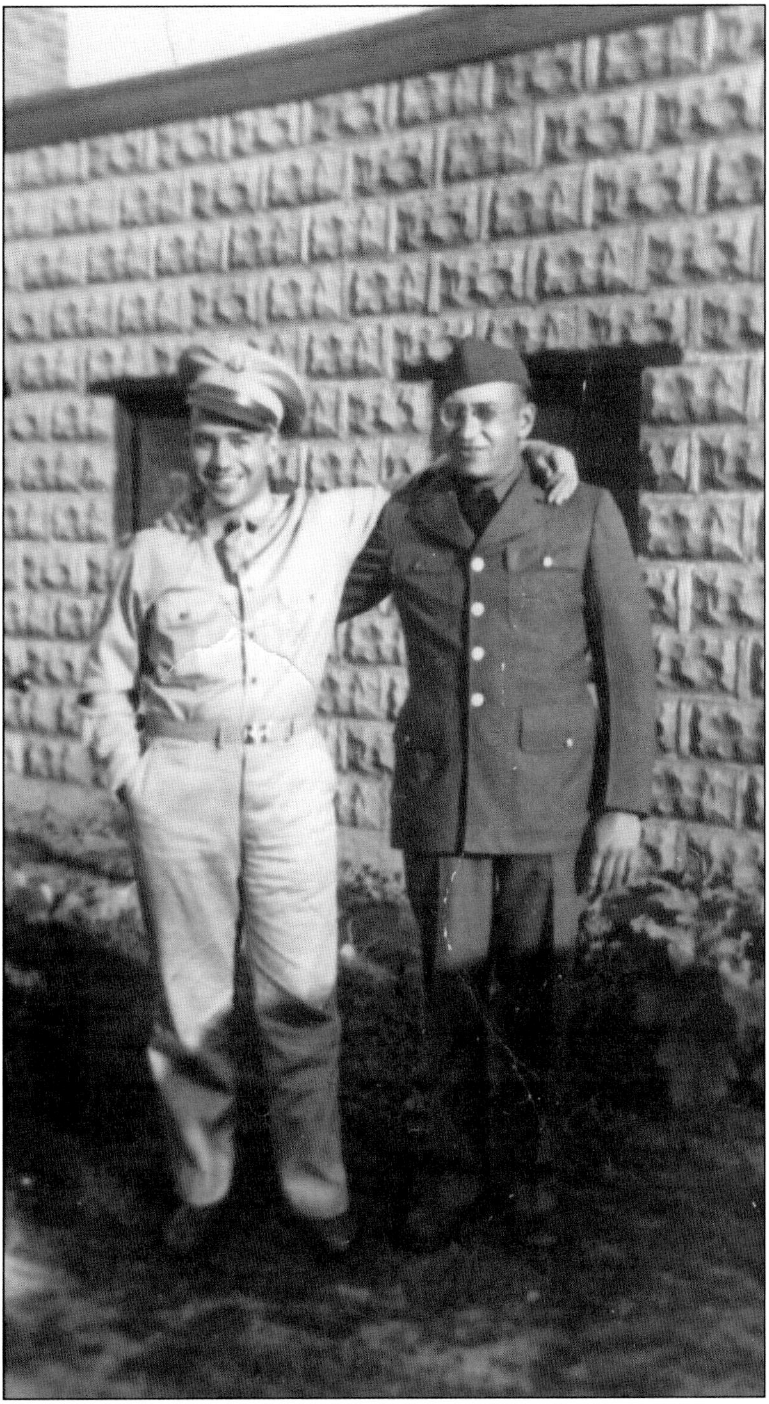

Walter Thirs (left) and his brother Bob Thirs pose next to the milk house of their dairy farm before heading off to war in the early 1940s. Walter was a survivor of the Bataan Death March. This brutal, 70-mile march of 75,000 American and Filipino prisoners of war across the Philippines to a prison camp resulted in about 20,000 deaths. Both brothers thankfully returned to their Villa Hills farm after the war. (Courtesy of Eileen Thirs Dunavan.)

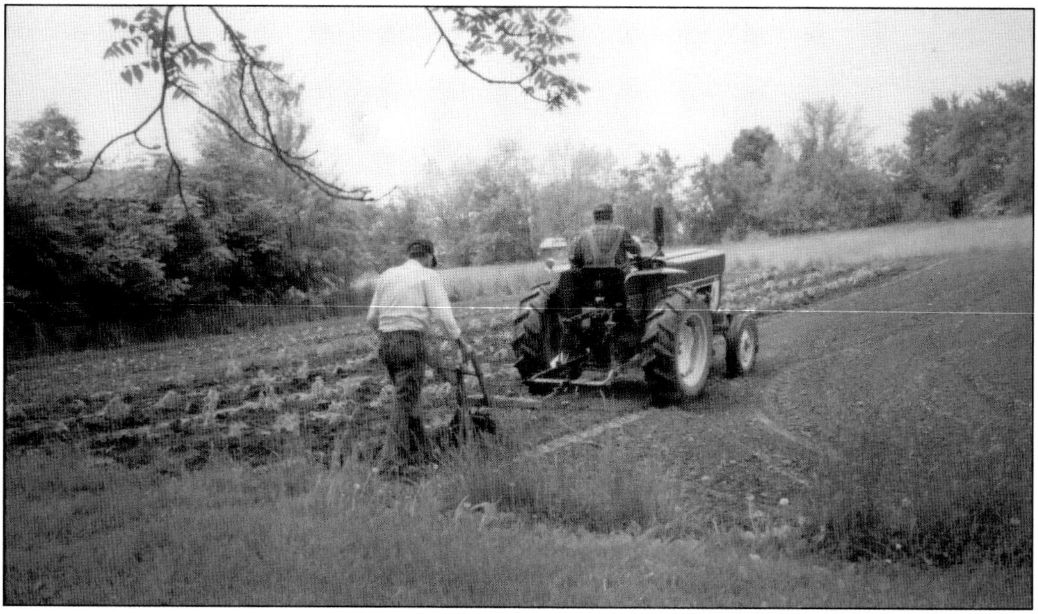

Paul Thirs (left) and his brother Walter Thirs plow the fields in this early 1980s photograph. This field was on the right side of the driveway, near the parking area for the dairy business. The brothers grew all kinds of produce but, in later years, specialized in tomatoes and green onions. (Courtesy of Eileen Thirs Dunavan.)

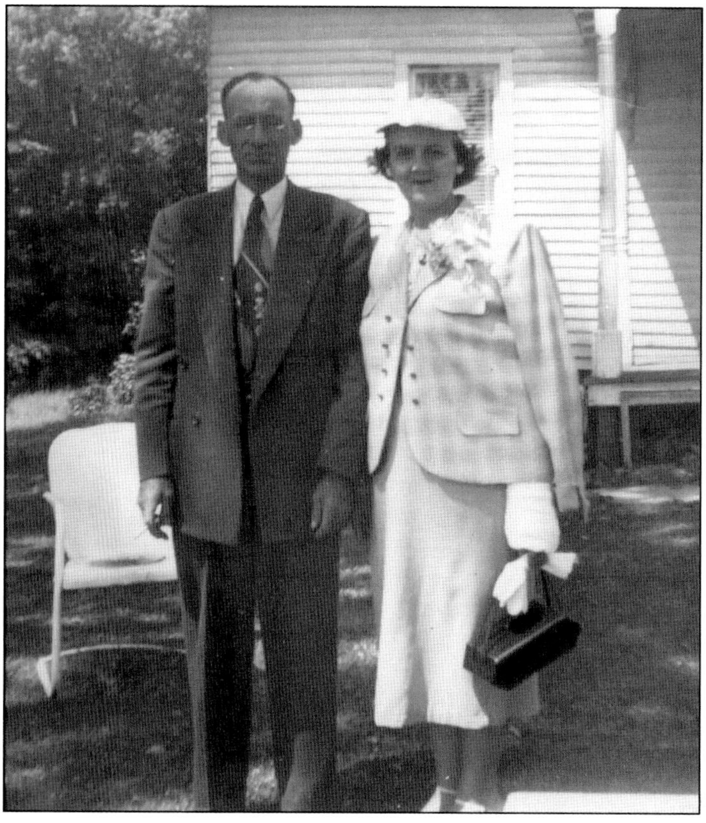

Jerry and Henrietta Herrmann Lohre stand in front of their home on the Schreck-Lohre farm in 1953. The home sat between Buttermilk Pike and what is now Frank Street. The home was torn down in 1956. Family friend Joe Franzen, of Rogers Road, took it apart piece by piece and, in the early 1960s, used the wood to construct a building on his property. He turned this building into a bar, known as Franzen's. In the late 1960s, an organized group of residents purchased the building, and it is today known as the Villa Hills Civic Club. (Courtesy of Barb Lohre Cooney.)

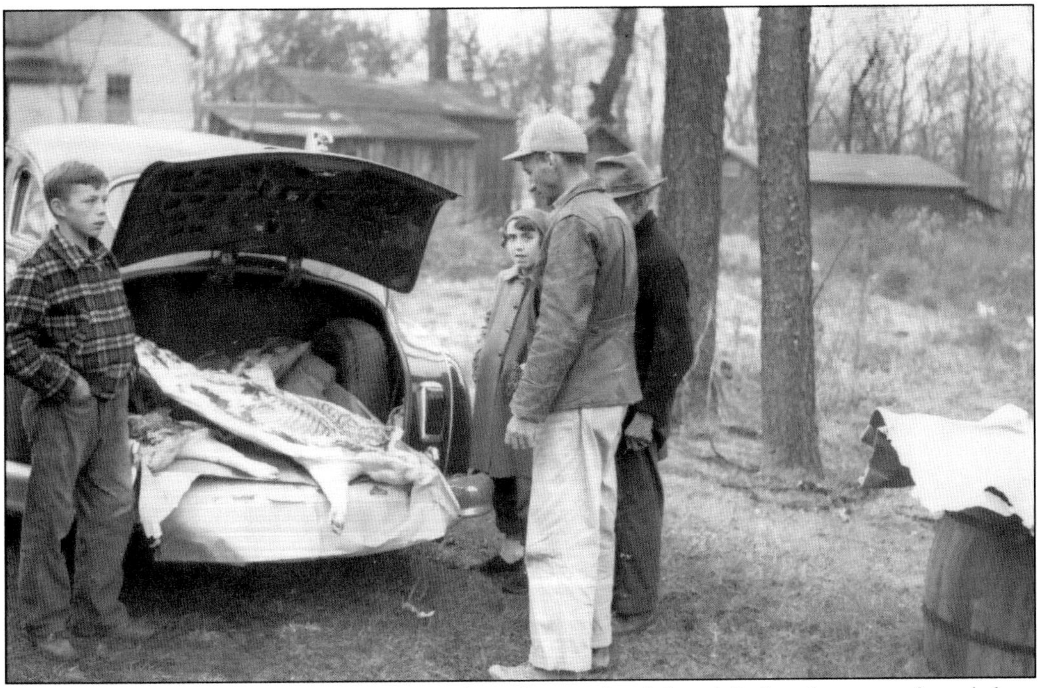

Getting ready to butcher a hog in the early 1950s on the Schreck-Lohre farm are, from left to right, Jerry Hellmann, Jerry Lohre, Ed Schreck, and Barb Lohre Cooney. The farm spanned the west side of present-day Collins Road, and the current location of Mary, Frank, and Ann Streets, and Rardin Court. Those streets were all named for members of the Schreck family; however, Rardin Court was named for a man who died in a bulldozer accident while building in the area. (Courtesy of Barb Lohre Cooney.)

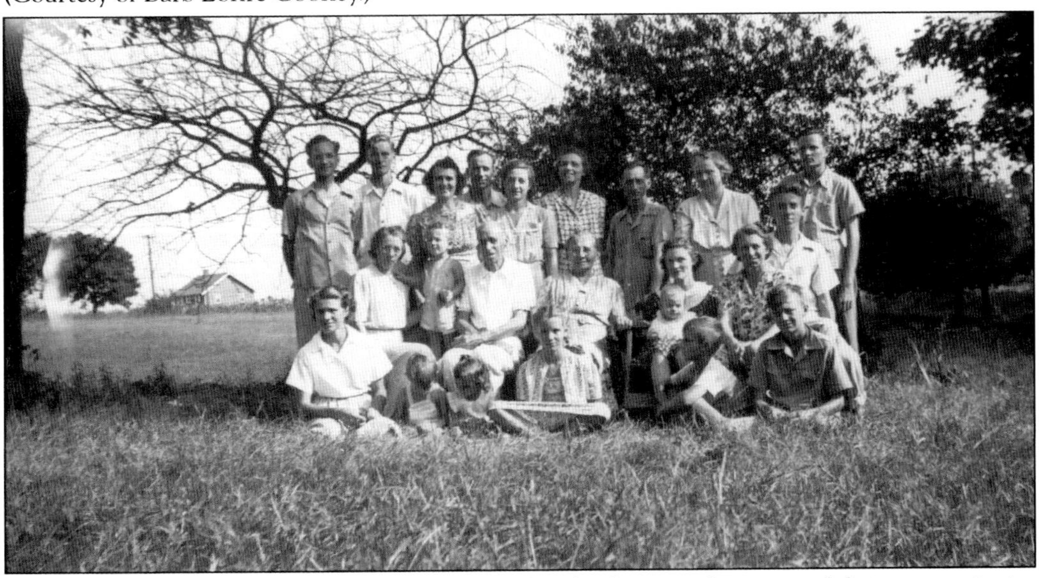

Scheck and Lohre family members gather for a family photograph at one of their many picnics on their 50-acre farm. This 1940s photograph was taken somewhere in the vicinity of what is now Rardin Court. When the property was sold, the subdivision was called Woodlawn Acres. (Courtesy of Barb Lohre Cooney.)

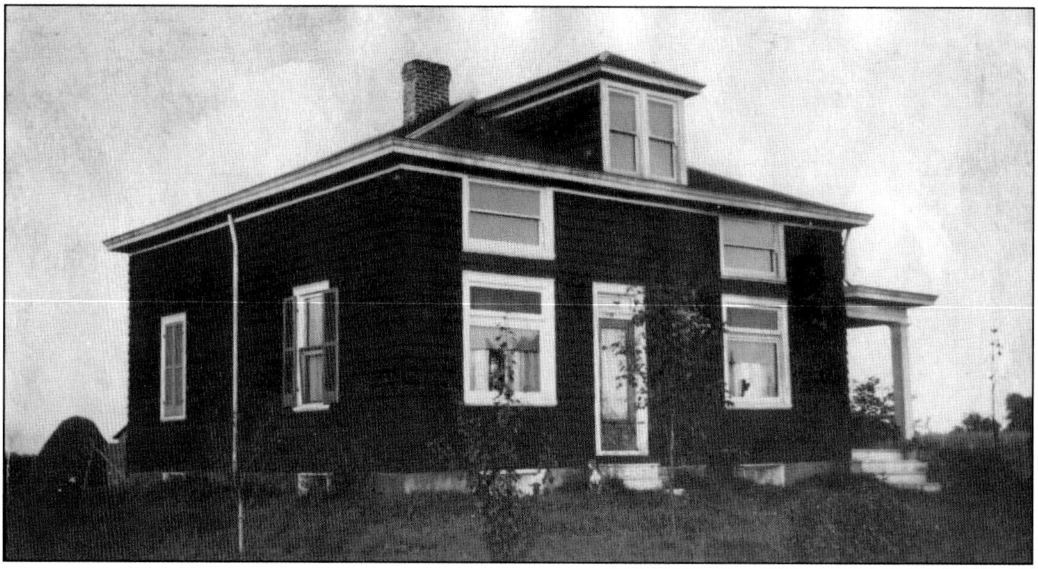

The photograph above is of the Kremer home, which currently sits at 818 Collins Road. Frank Kremer built it in 1913. He and his wife Julia had six children, Urban, Art, Frank, Julie, Jerome, and Matthew. Matthew passed away as a baby. The photograph below, taken in the winter of 1943, shows the same house looking much as it does today. In the 1940s, the family added a second floor and a porch and painted the exterior a lighter color. (Courtesy of Julie Kremer.)

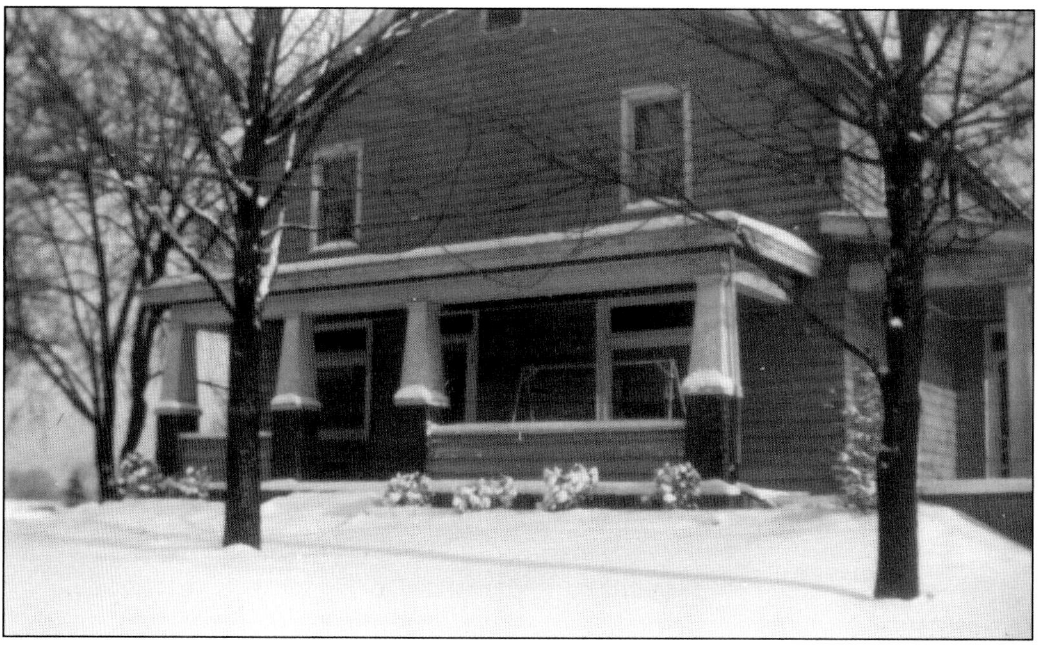

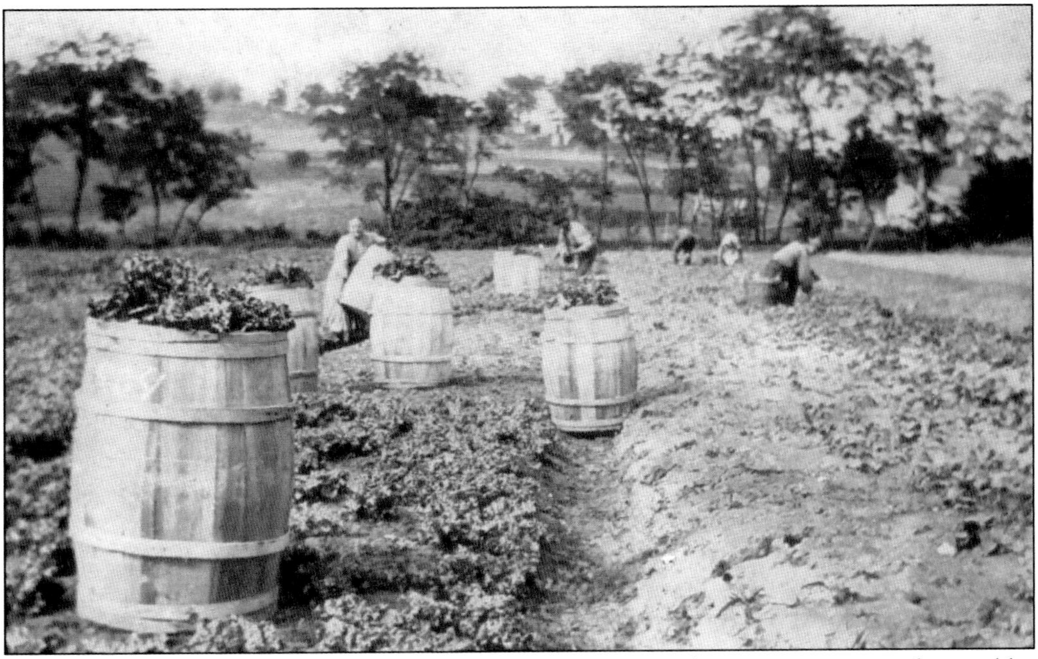

The Kremer family, of 818 Collins Road, were truck farmers. They grew a variety of vegetables that were sold at wholesale markets in Cincinnati. These markets were located along the river at the foot of downtown. Known as "the Bottoms," this area was comprised of commission houses that bought from farmers and sold to grocery stores and restaurants. In the photograph above, taken prior to the 1920s, the family cuts leaf lettuce and packs it in wooden barrels. These fields are in the area of where Kremer Lane is today. The photograph below shows the wagon packed with lettuce barrels, which are on their way to Cincinnati to be sold. The family purchased their first truck in 1920, which made the trip to Cincinnati much easier than using this horse and wagon. (Courtesy of Julie Kremer.)

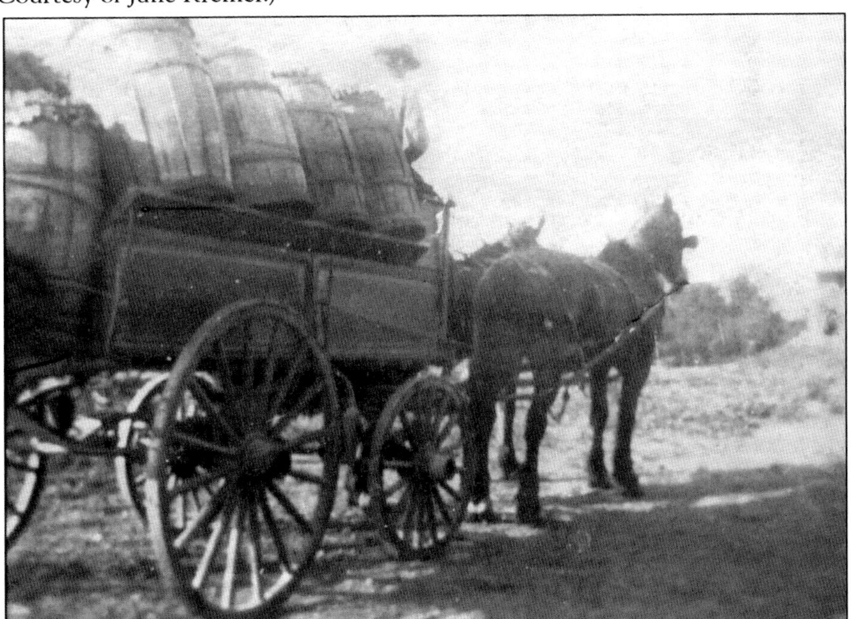

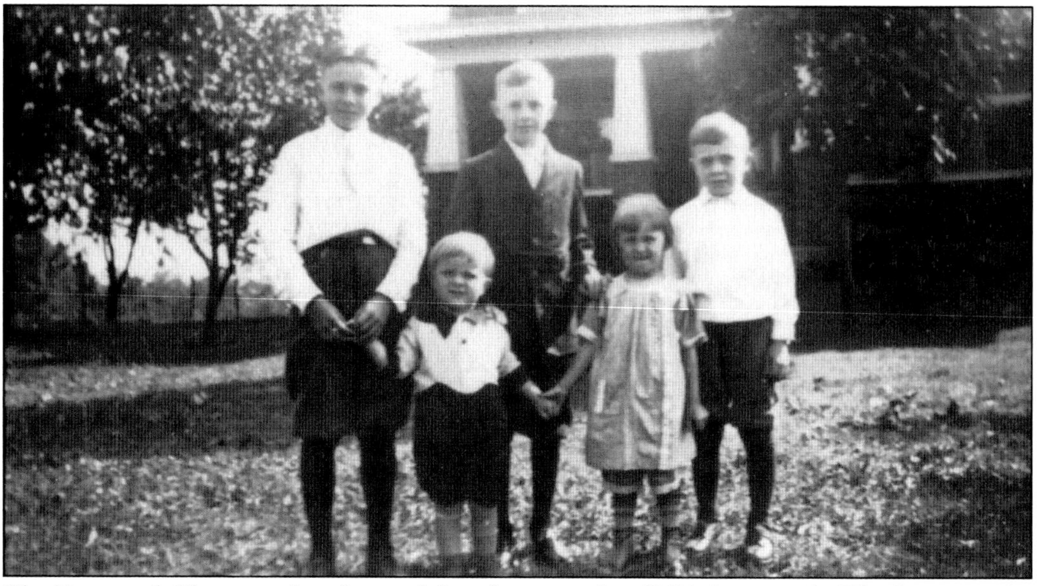

The Kremer children stand in front of their home in this 1927 photograph. The house in the background is the same house as on page 28. The children are, from left to right, Urban, Jerome, Art, Julie, and Frank. This photograph is believed to have been taken in honor of Art Kremer's confirmation, as he is wearing a suit. (Courtesy of Julie Kremer.)

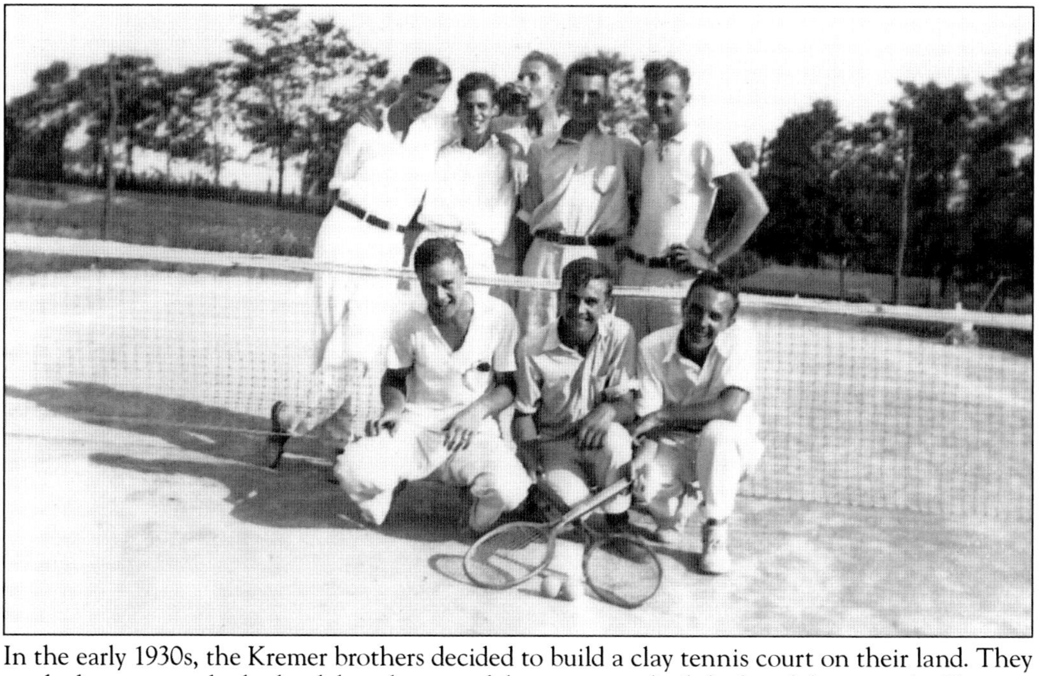

In the early 1930s, the Kremer brothers decided to build a clay tennis court on their land. They used a horse to grade the land, but the rest of the court was built by hand, because the Kremers did not have a tractor at that time. This 1938 photograph shows some players gathering for the Kremers' annual tennis tournament, which was held each Labor Day. The court ran parallel with Collins Road, and the camera is looking toward Crescent Springs. The players are, from left to right, (front row) John Saalfeld, Frank Kremer, and unidentified; (second row) Ed Busse, Ray Huelfeld, Norb Saalfeld, Urb Kremer, and Art Kremer. (Courtesy of Julie Kremer.)

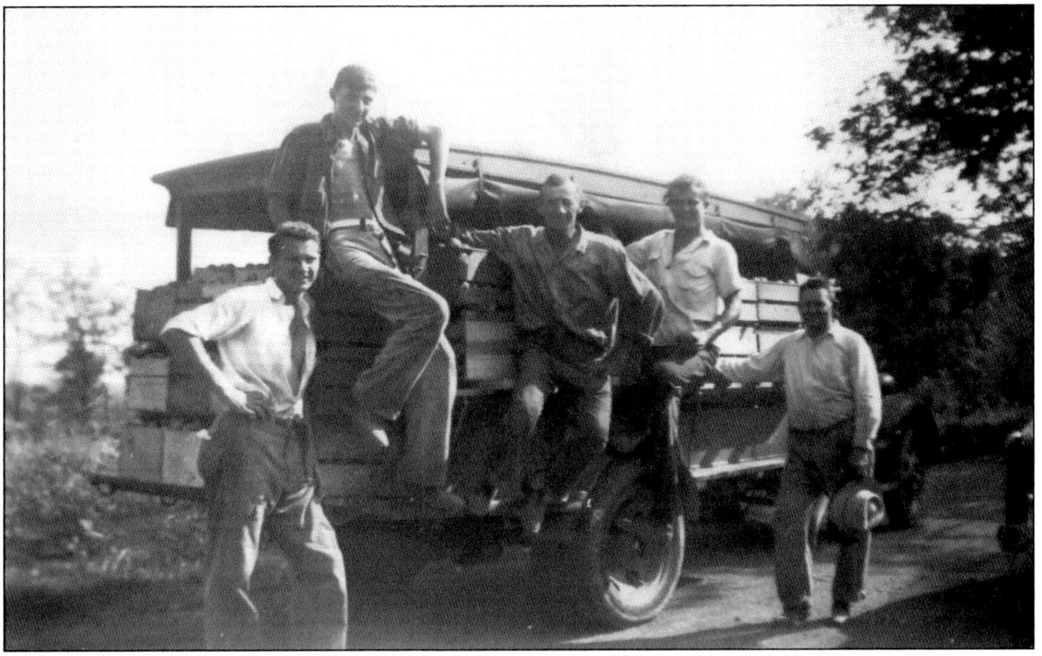

Here the Kremer farmers load up the truck after a hard day in the fields at their farm on Collins Road. In this early-1940s photograph, Urban Kremer, Ray Hansman, Frank Kremer Sr., Jerome Kremer, and Ed Lange, from left to right, show off their wares after a hard day in the fields. During World War II, area farmers began working on Sundays, which was not a common practice at the time. By doing so, they could get their goods to market on Sunday night, so the produce would be available to the wholesale customers on Monday morning. (Courtesy of Julie Kremer.)

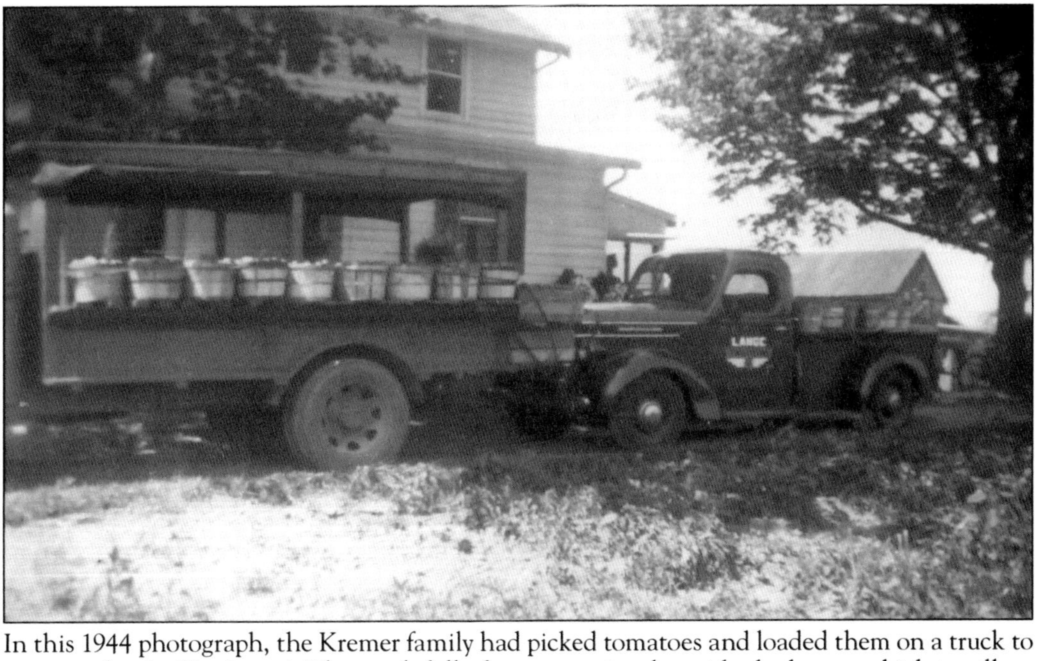

In this 1944 photograph, the Kremer family had picked tomatoes and loaded them on a truck to go to market in Cincinnati. The truck full of tomatoes sits alongside the house, which is still on the property. (Courtesy of Julie Kremer.)

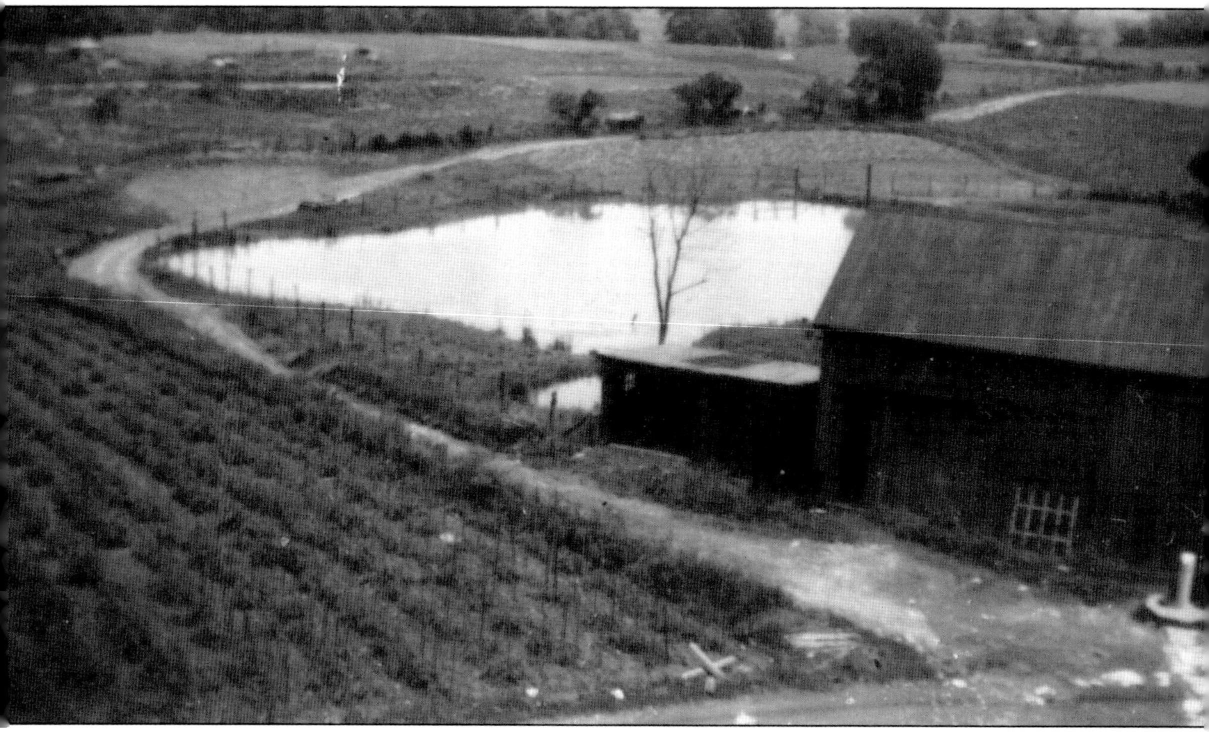

This 1942 photograph was taken from the roof of the home at 818 Collins Road, looking out over the Kremer farm. The family began farming in 1913 and grew vegetables. The fields and lake are now the site of Kremer Lane. The small line of trees next to the tractor path was the dividing line between Pete Kremer's farm and his brother Frank Kremer's farm. The Pete Kremer farm is now known as Cecilia Drive. (Courtesy of Julie Kremer.)

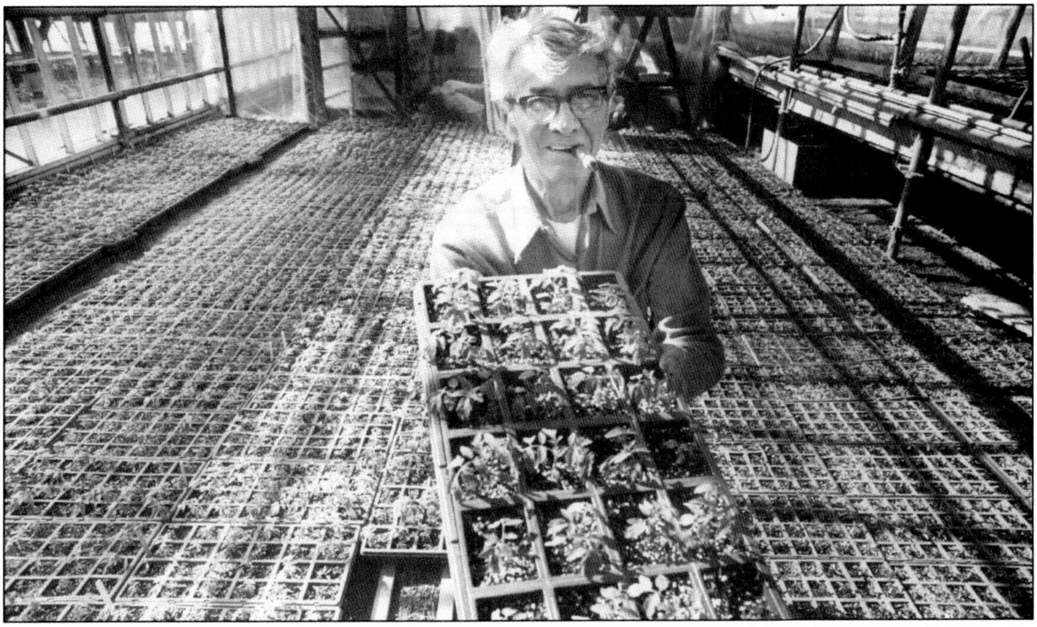

The Kremers, who had several greenhouses on their farm, grew vegetables, plants, and flowers. In this 1980 photograph, Urban Kremer proudly displays his young tomato plants. The farm became known for its tomatoes and Bibb lettuce. A restaurant in San Francisco, California, enjoyed Kremer's Bibb lettuce so much, it would order it from Urban, who would take it to the airport and ship it directly to them. (Courtesy of the Kenton County Library.)

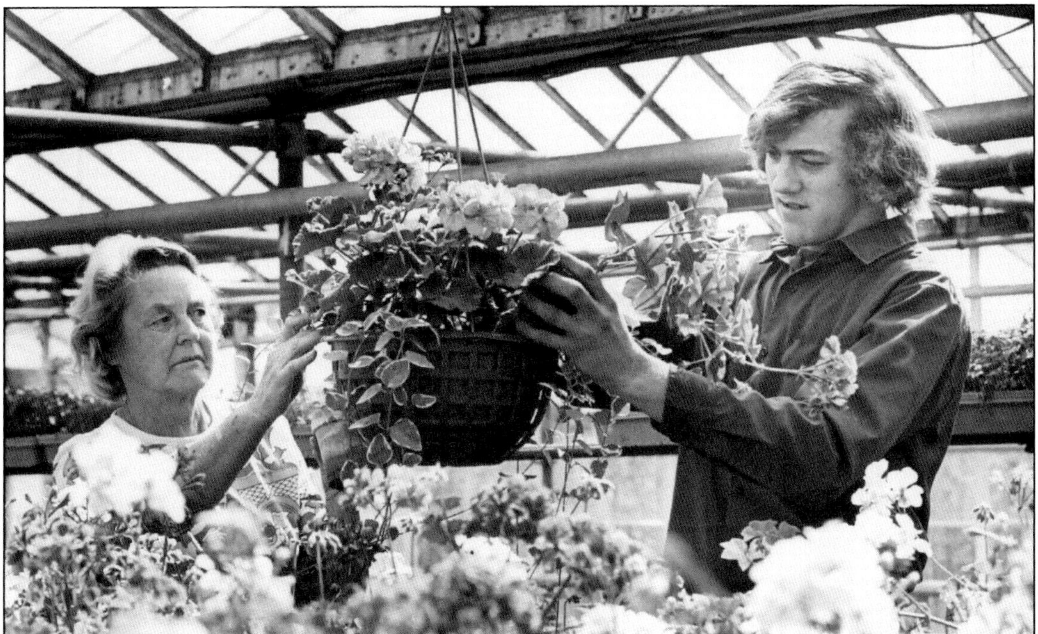

The greenhouses on the Kremer property housed vegetables and bedding plants. The Kremers would grow annuals like geraniums, marigolds, and petunias and sell them individually or in mixed baskets. In this 1974 photograph, Loraine Kremer and her son Kevin work together in the greenhouse to create one of the hundreds of hanging baskets they sold each spring. (Courtesy of the Kenton County Library.)

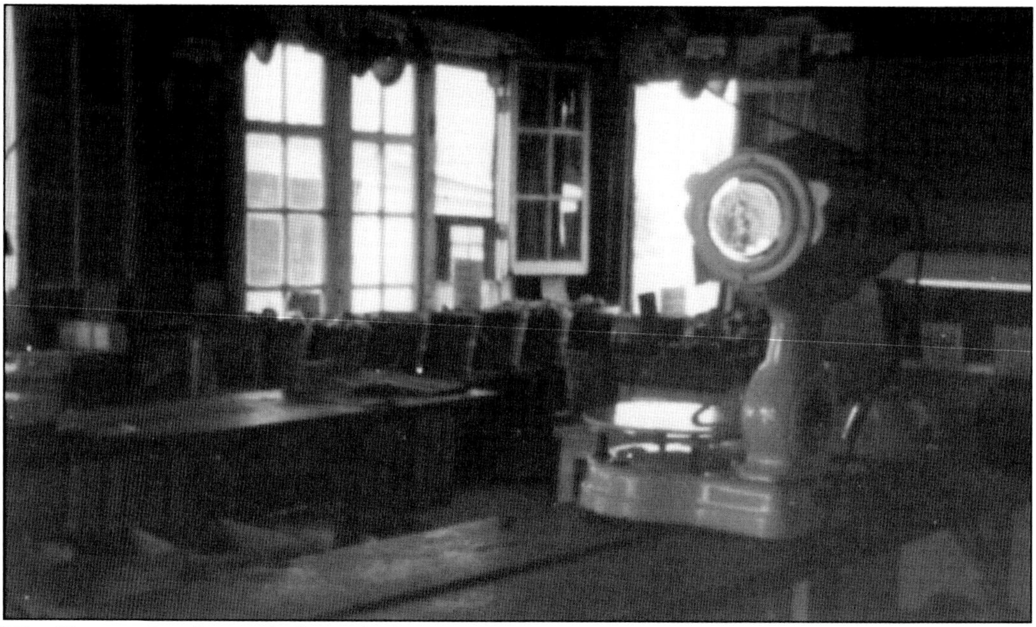

The Kremer family regularly took their fresh produce to market, but in the 1940s, more and more people came directly to the farm to buy the freshly pulled corn, crisp leaf lettuce, and the homegrown tomatoes that the Kremer farm was becoming well known for. The family set up this market shed inside a barn on the property. The business had no set hours and people showed up at all times of day to buy produce. This early-1970s photograph shows how they displayed their merchandise in bushel baskets. In the early 1980s, the family moved their produce market to Crescent Springs. (Courtesy of Nancy Kohl Hoffman.)

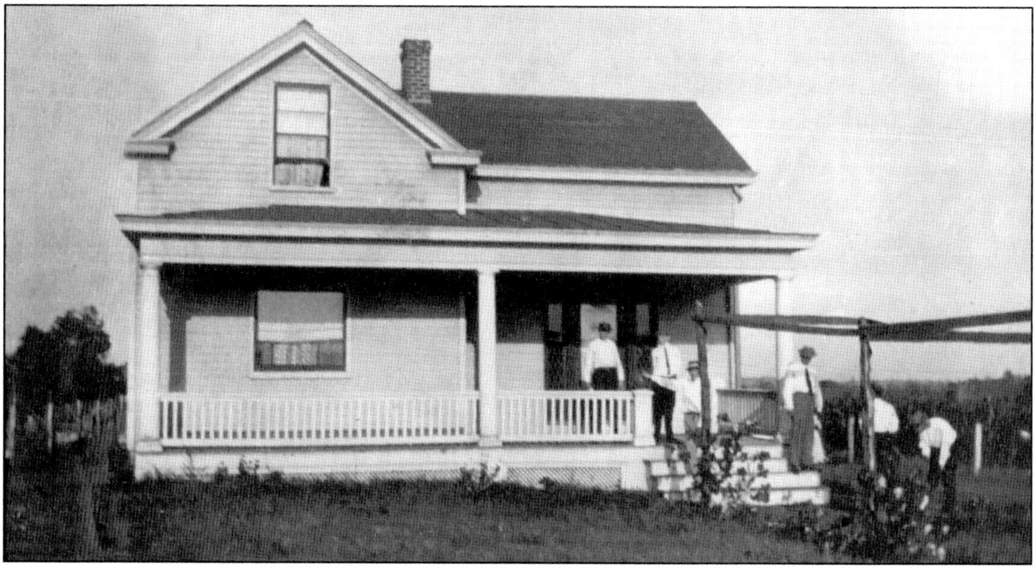

The house in this 1915 photograph sat on Collins Road, near the intersection of Collins and what is Cecilia Drive today. Pete Kremer, whose land was adjacent to his brother Frank Kremer's farm, owned the house. The farm grew sweet potatoes and a variety of vegetables in small lots. Pete had three daughters, Elizabeth, Cecilia, and Teresa. When the land was sold for development in the early 1970s, the first street was named Cecilia Drive in honor of Pete's daughter. (Courtesy of Julie Kremer.)

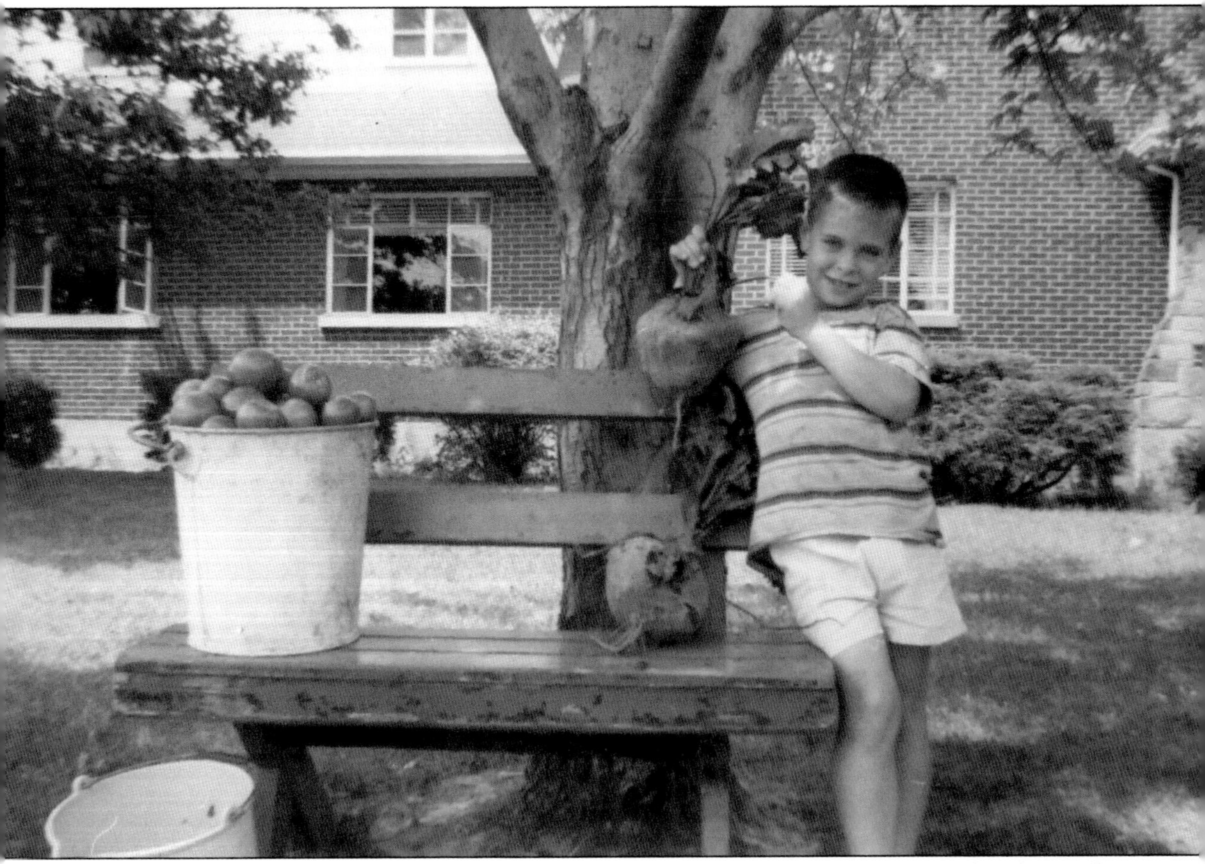

Tony Noll displays his huge beet on the Noll farm in this late-1950s photograph. The Noll farm was located on Amsterdam Road west of the Collins Road intersection. During the 1960s and 1970s, it was frequently the location for Villa Hills festivals and turkey shoots. (Courtesy of Carol Noll.)

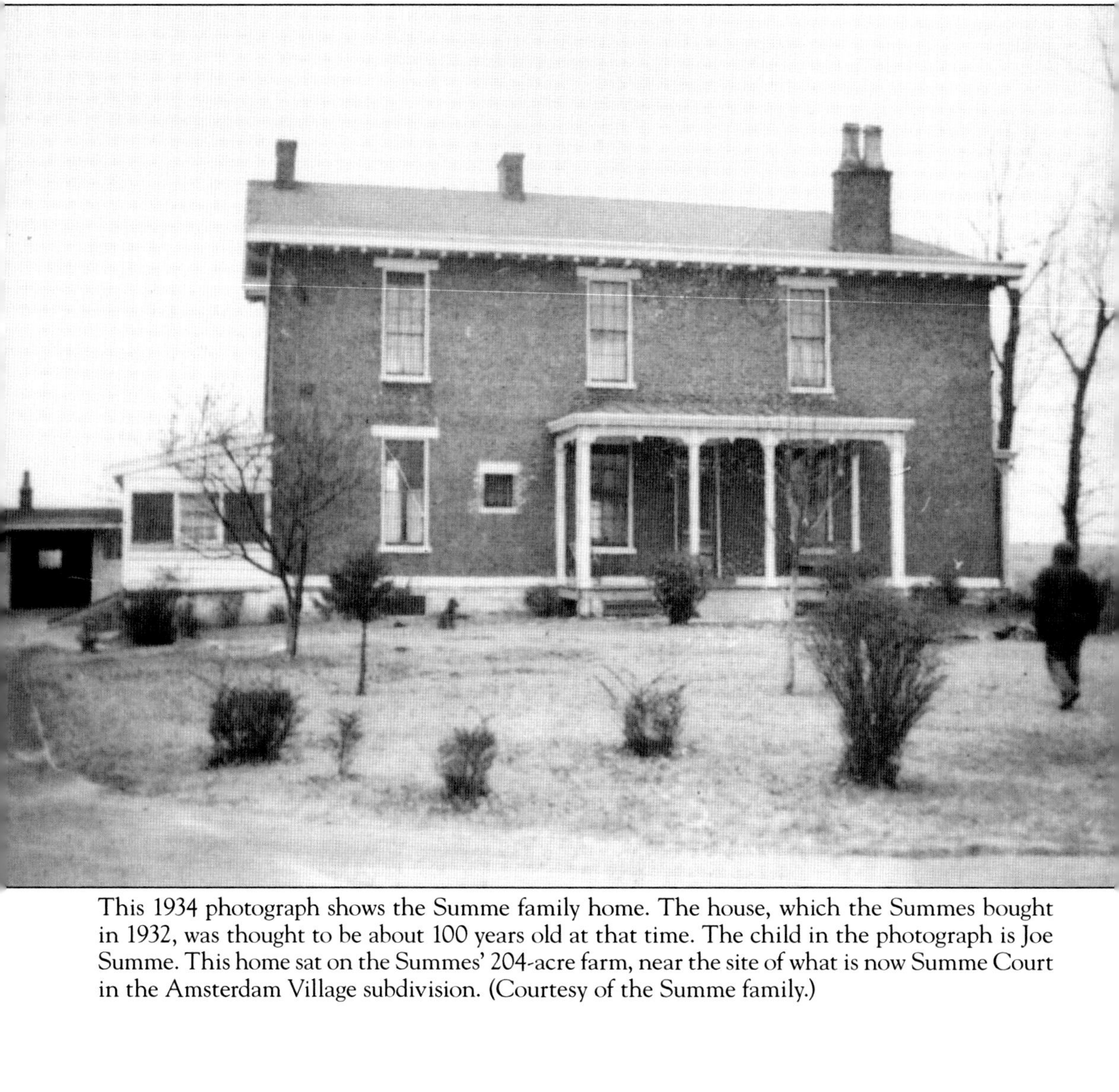

This 1934 photograph shows the Summe family home. The house, which the Summes bought in 1932, was thought to be about 100 years old at that time. The child in the photograph is Joe Summe. This home sat on the Summes' 204-acre farm, near the site of what is now Summe Court in the Amsterdam Village subdivision. (Courtesy of the Summe family.)

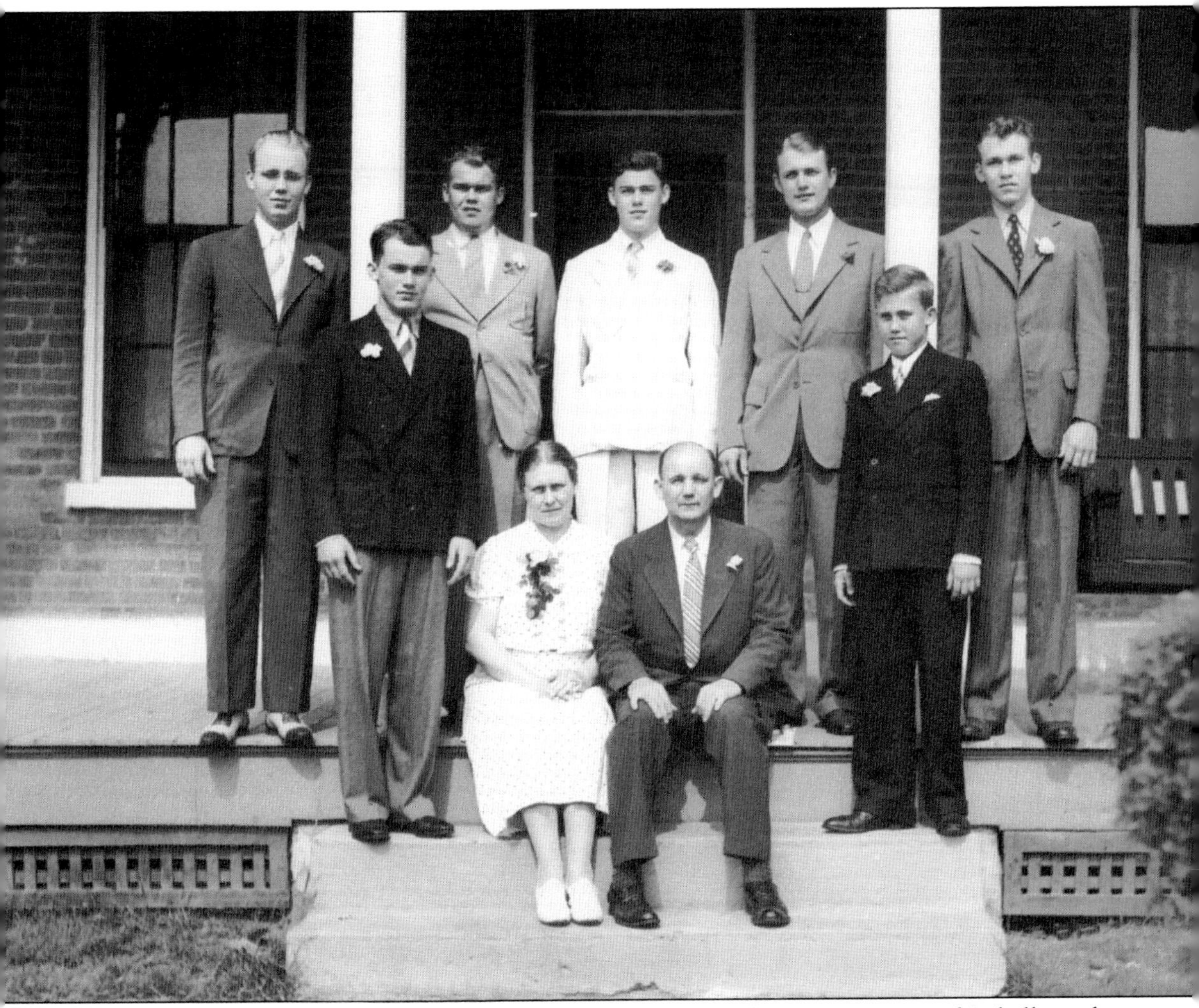

This 1939 or 1940 photograph commemorates the 25th wedding anniversary of Isabelle and Frank Summe, sitting. Posing with the Summes are their seven sons. Standing on the porch are, from left to right, John, Frank, Joe, Paul, Ed, and standing on the top step are Jim and Charlie. (Courtesy of the Summe family.)

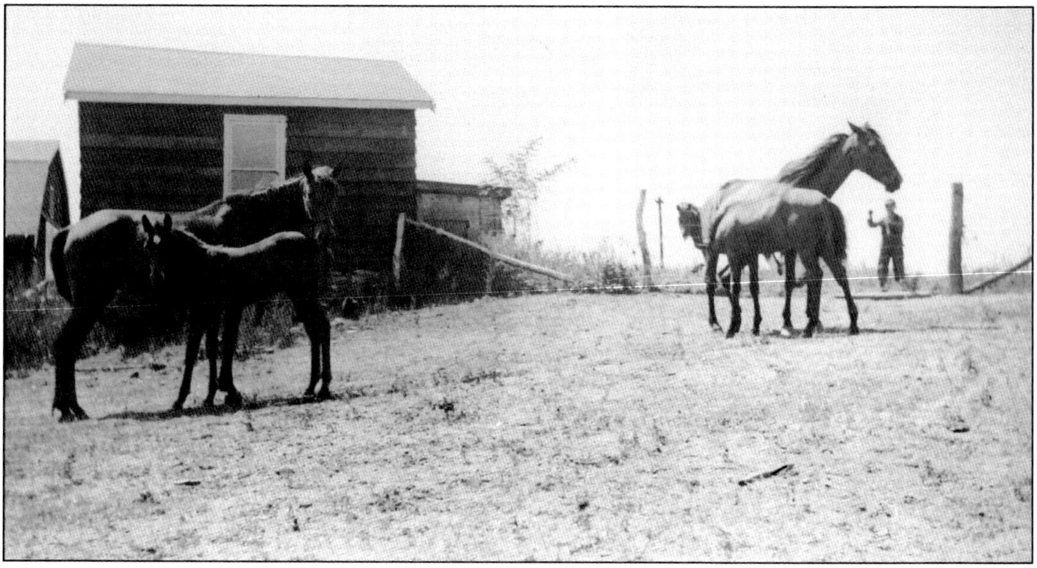

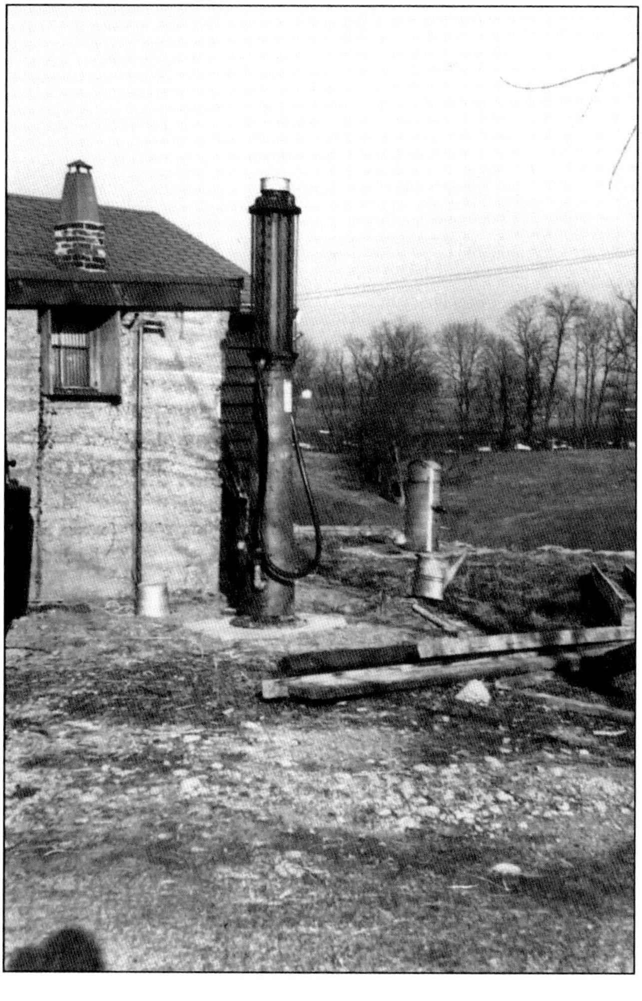

The Summe family raised sheep, beef cattle, and trotting horses, as seen in this 1933 photograph. Their large barn can barely be seen at far left. Another smaller barn, behind the two horses at left, was actually built with leftover wood from the large barn. The Summe children used the small barn as a playhouse. It had a cellar underneath, which the family used to store potatoes. On the right, the concrete ice storage house can be seen. (Courtesy of the Summe family.)

The Summe farm had a gasoline pump, as seen in this 1940s photograph. During World War II, farmers received stamps allowing them to purchase and store gas for their farms. The pump had to be physically cranked to fill the glass tank on top with gas, which would then come out of the hose with the help of gravity. To the right of the gas pump is a cistern water pump. (Courtesy of the Summe family.)

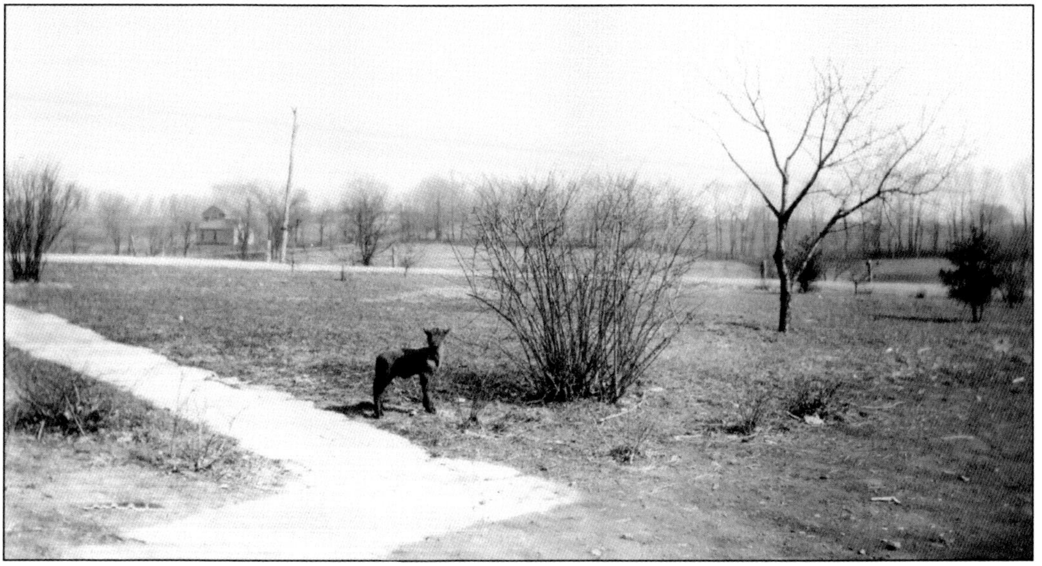

Looking out of the Summe home, the road that crosses the photograph is actually the family driveway. The house in the distance belonged to a neighbor. A waterway was located in the valley that was later dammed up to create the current Lake Leen. Along the tree line in the distance is Rogers Road. Although it was a dirt road, the county maintained it, and Frank Summe gave the road crews extra money to clean it well, since Summe family members were its primary users. (Courtesy of the Summe family.)

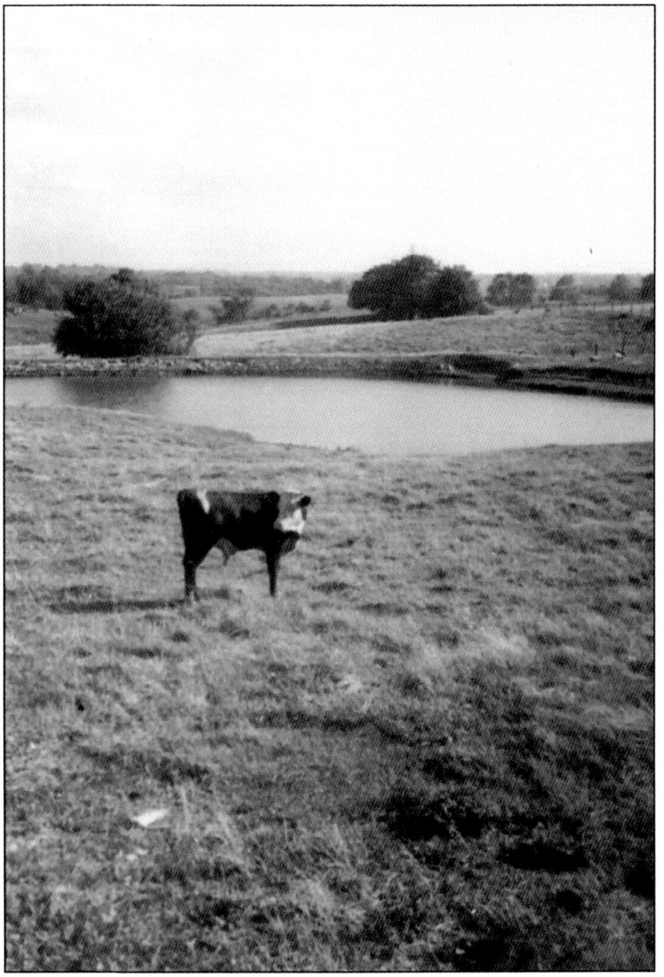

Looking south toward the Steenken farm on Rogers Road is the Summe farm lake. In the event of a dry spell, the Summes, as well as other farmers in the area, were able to purchase water from the Benedictine Sisters of St. Walburg, who had paid to have a waterline installed from Fort Mitchell in 1930. (Courtesy of the Summe family.)

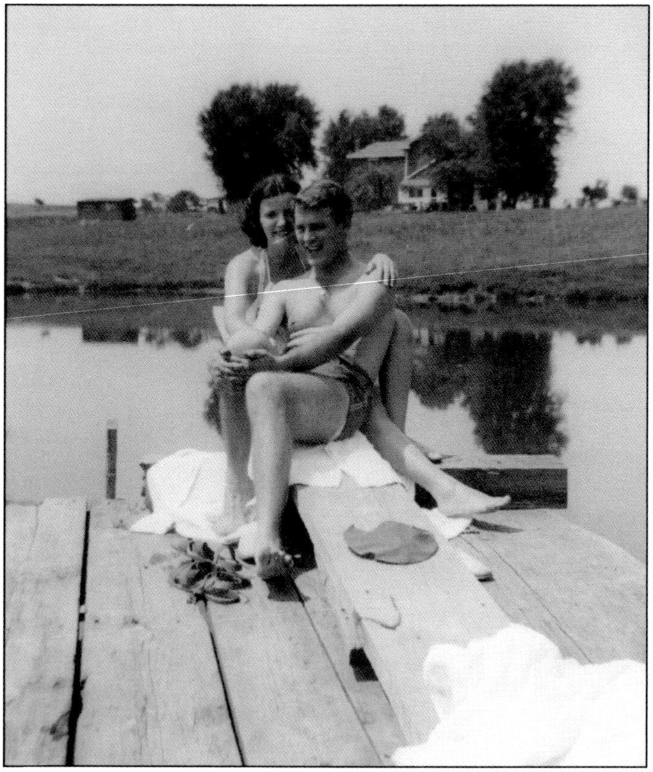

In this 1939 photograph, Paul and Mary Boone Summe take a swim in the Summe farm lake. The home in the background was the Summe homestead. Although this photograph was taken near the current Lake Leen, the lake pictured was completely drained when the Summe farm was sold in the late 1960s. (Courtesy of the Summe family.)

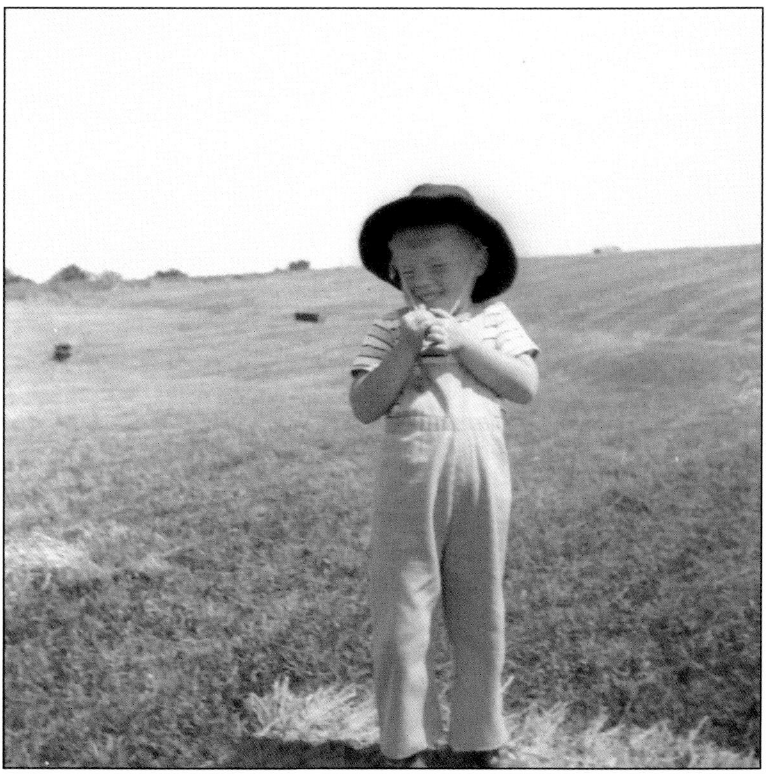

Young John Summe Jr. stands in the family's 30-acre hay field in this 1942 photograph. The top of the hill is Niewhaner Drive today. (Courtesy of the Summe family.)

In this 1970 photograph, Frank Burdick stands with his grandfather Robert Stephenson in Stephenson's backyard at 908 Kenridge Drive. This photograph is looking west. Beyond the backyard is the Summe farm, which is now the subdivision of Amsterdam Village.

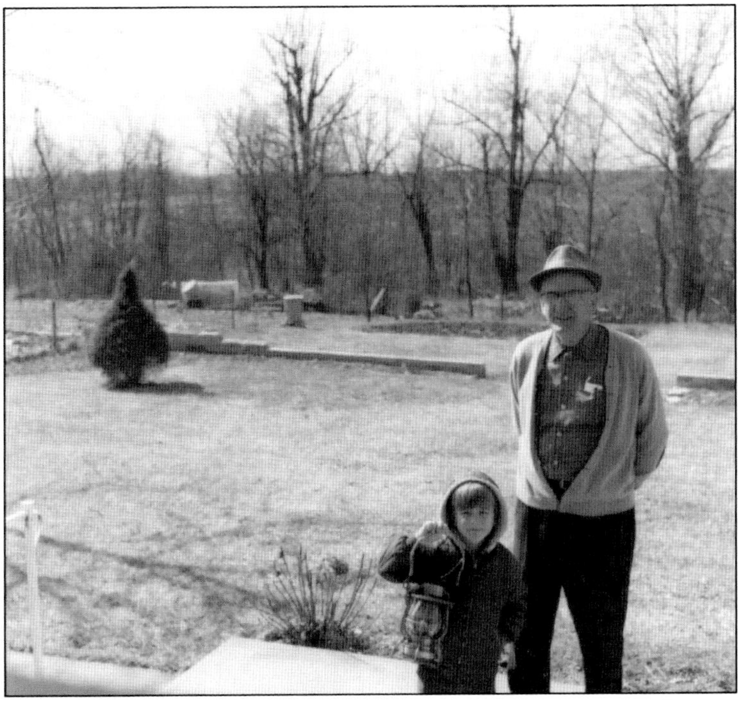

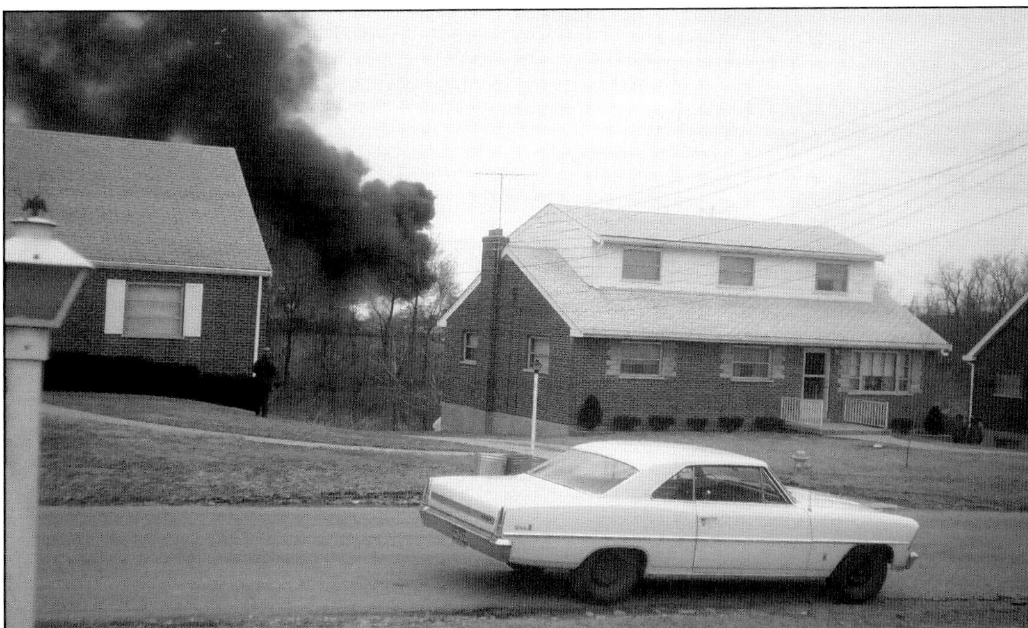

The Summe children had moved off the farm by the late 1960s, but the brothers who still lived nearby returned to the farm each day to feed 30 to 40 cows and tend to the farm, which was primarily growing hay at that time. In 1969, the barn on the property went up in flames. Although no one was ever charged, it was considered arson and the cause was suspected to be kids playing with fire. No people were hurt, but about five cows died. The financial loss was around $100,000, and this was the deciding factor for the family to sell the farm. This photograph was taken from Kenridge Drive, but the smoke could be seen for miles. (Courtesy of Paul and Peg Kohl.)

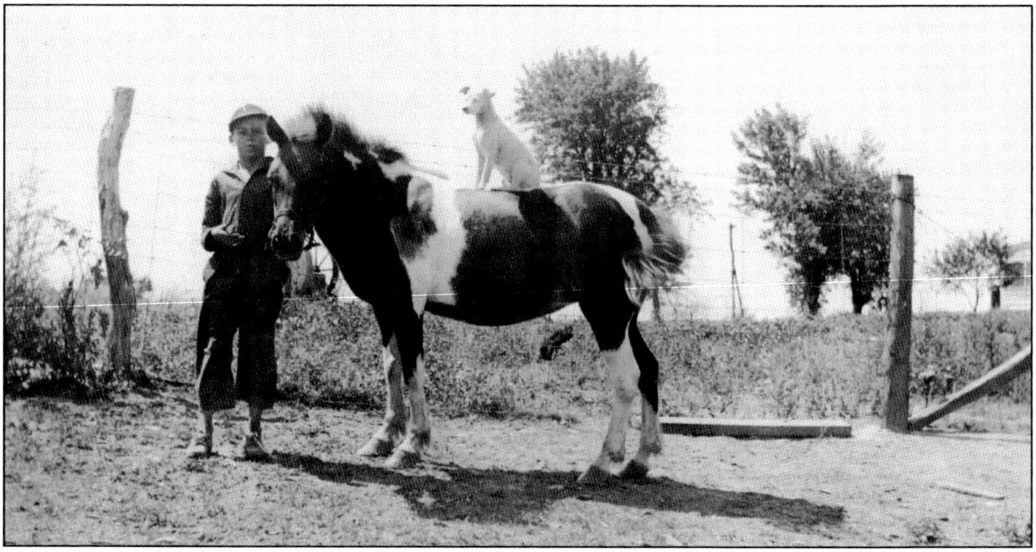

Joseph Summe stands outside the Summe family home in this 1933 photograph with his horse Fanny and dog Queenie. The family farm covered the area that makes up Amsterdam Village subdivision today, bounded by Rogers Road on the east and Amsterdam Road on the north. The family bought the farm in 1932, and sold it in the late 1960s to the Drees Company. (Courtesy of the Summe family.)

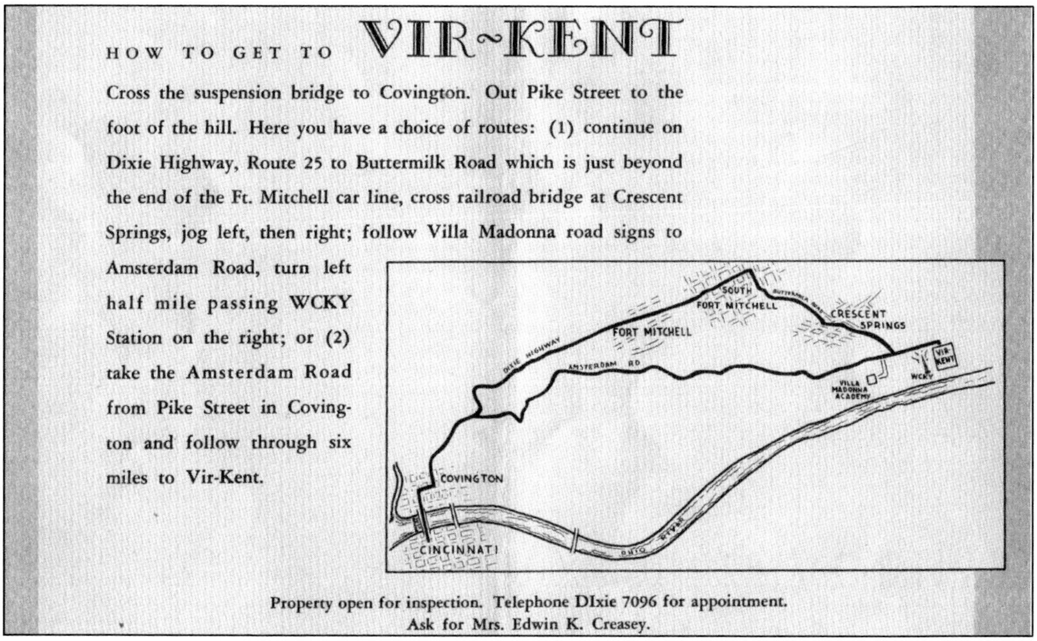

HOW TO GET TO VIR-KENT

Cross the suspension bridge to Covington. Out Pike Street to the foot of the hill. Here you have a choice of routes: (1) continue on Dixie Highway, Route 25 to Buttermilk Road which is just beyond the end of the Ft. Mitchell car line, cross railroad bridge at Crescent Springs, jog left, then right; follow Villa Madonna road signs to Amsterdam Road, turn left half mile passing WCKY Station on the right; or (2) take the Amsterdam Road from Pike Street in Covington and follow through six miles to Vir-Kent.

Property open for inspection. Telephone DIxie 7096 for appointment.
Ask for Mrs. Edwin K. Creasey.

This is the back page of a brochure advertising acreage for sale along Amsterdam Road. The land, which encompassed about 100 acres, was perfect for farming and offered a "view of the Anderson Ferry." The Creasy family offered the land for sale sometime in the late 1930s or early 1940s. Since the location was a bit remote, this map and directions were included. William and Alberta (Remke) Hausman purchased the farm and owned it until 1964, when they sold it to the Drees Company. The area was eventually the site of the condominiums and apartments of Prospect Point. (Courtesy of Marilyn Remke Smain.)

Two

The Benedictine Sisters of St. Walburg Monastery

The story of the Villa Madonna property starts in 1859, when three Benedictine nuns from Erie, Pennsylvania, arrived in Covington to teach German immigrants. They had no idea they would be the catalysts for an elementary school, high school, boarding school, nursing home, Montessori school, and, even, the naming of a town.

They established a school and monastery on Twelfth Street in Covington and grew their community for about 50 years. In the early 20th century, when faced with diseases from the inner city, the sisters searched the area for a country location and purchased the 86-acre Collins farm near the small town of Crescent Springs. A local priest suggested the name Villa Madonna, which means "country seat of Our Lady," and the sisters agreed.

By September 1904, Villa Madonna Academy established its school inside the former Collins home and transferred the ten boarding students and day students from St. Walburg Academy to the new school.

The Sisters built several buildings on the property over the years, including the academy building, which was completed in 1907; the monastery building, completed in 1937; and a high school building, which opened in 1958. In the mid-1960s the sisters created a nursing home on the property.

It was in the early 1960s when surrounding farms began to sell, and the sisters began getting new neighbors in the form of young families moving into the subdivisions.

As Villa Hills established a Civic Club and a city, the name of Villa Madonna was incorporated. Neighborhoods like Madonna Acres, Villa Vista, and Villa Heights, as well as the name of Villa Hills itself are all reflections of their ties to Villa Madonna.

The Benedictine Sisters of St. Walburg Monastery have been good neighbors. Their schools and day care facilities have educated many Villa Hills residents. Madonna Manor nursing home has been home to many of Villa Hills's elderly residents as well. Their beautiful grounds, overlooking the scenic Ohio River, are welcoming for Villa Hills joggers, walkers, and bike riders. And although all of these things have touched the lives of many residents, it is the leasing of the ball fields that sit on 20 acres of their property that has affected the most people. It is impossible to count how many of our residents played their first soccer game or hit their first baseball on the fields the sisters have shared with the city since the early 1970s.

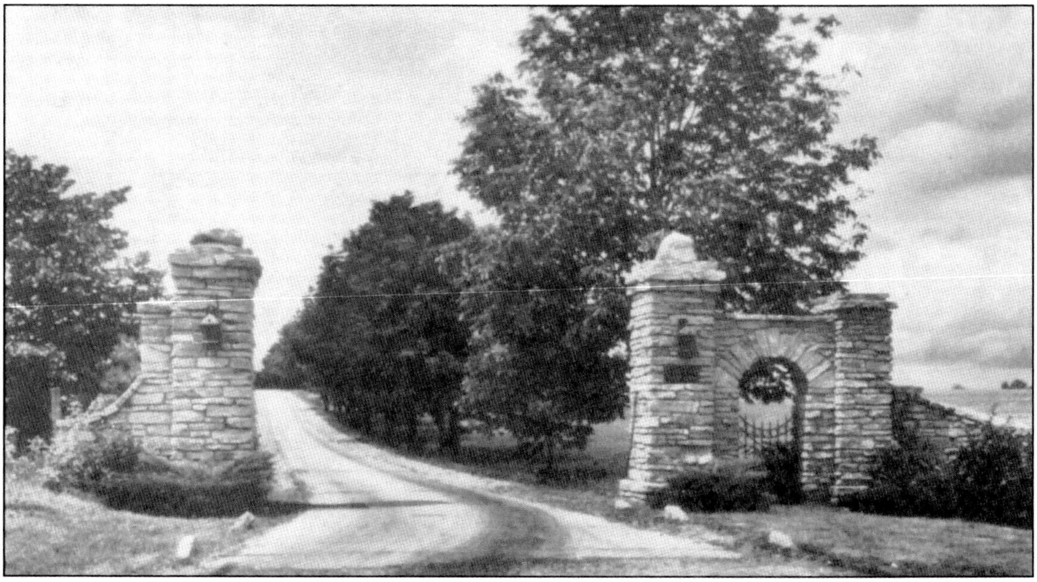

While prioress in the 1930s, Sr. Margaret Hugenberg is credited with beautifying the property. As an artist, she added features like gardens and the stone villa gates, seen in this photograph, which were built in 1931. (Courtesy of www.nkyviews.com.)

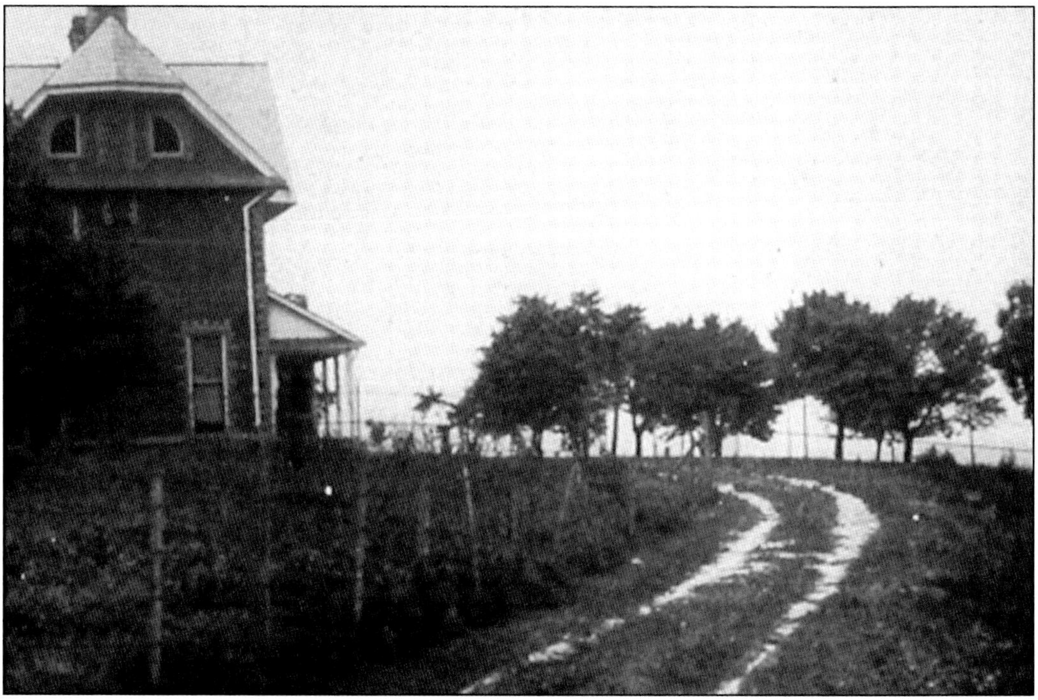

This house, which stands next to the original academy building, was built for the Collins family just after the Civil War. The Collins family sold the property to the Sisters of St. Walburg in 1903, and the sisters used it for classrooms while the school building was under construction. After the academy was built, the home was also used as a dormitory for the junior and senior girls who were boarding at the school. (Courtesy of the Benedictine Sisters of St. Walburg Monastery.)

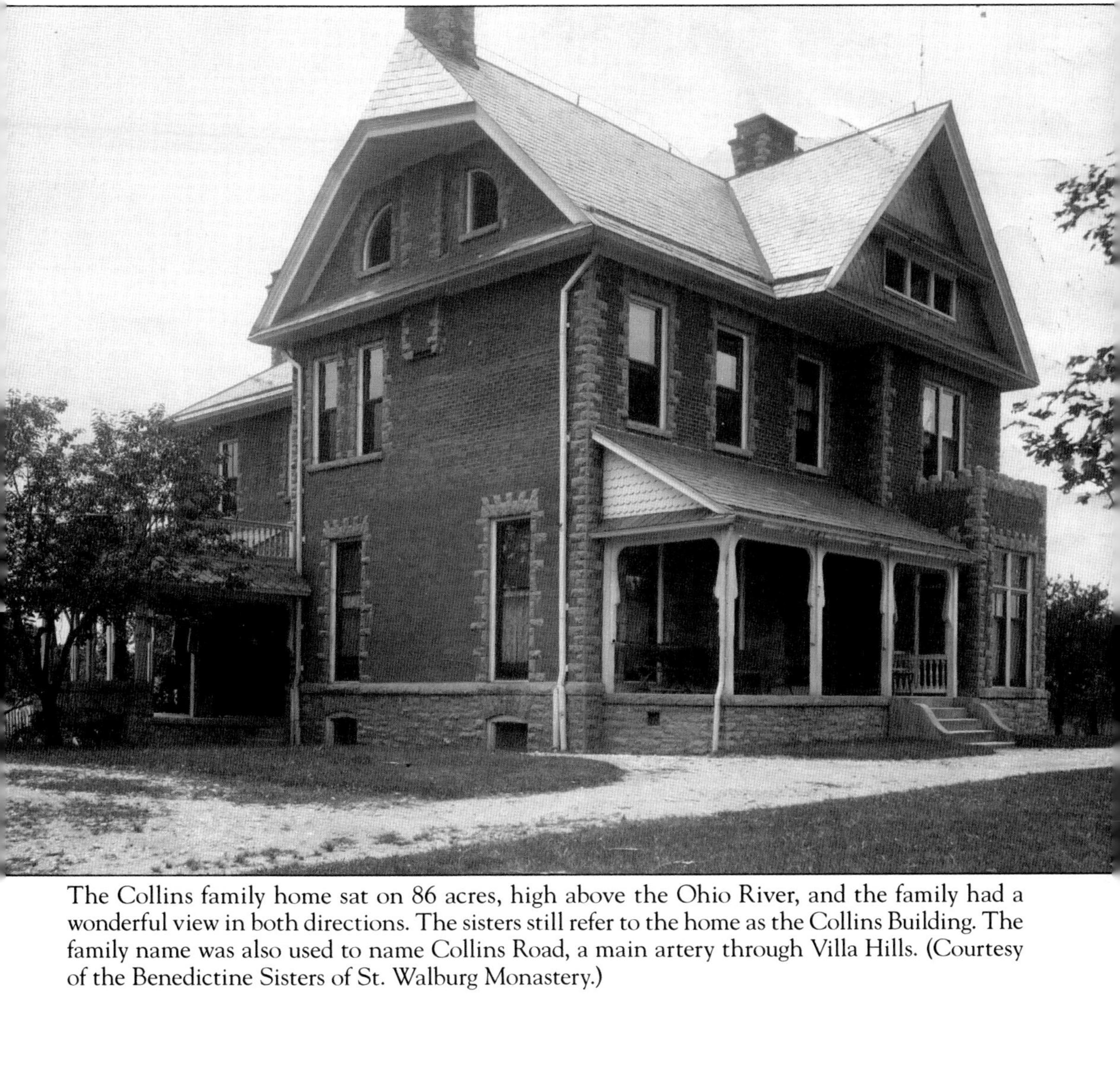

The Collins family home sat on 86 acres, high above the Ohio River, and the family had a wonderful view in both directions. The sisters still refer to the home as the Collins Building. The family name was also used to name Collins Road, a main artery through Villa Hills. (Courtesy of the Benedictine Sisters of St. Walburg Monastery.)

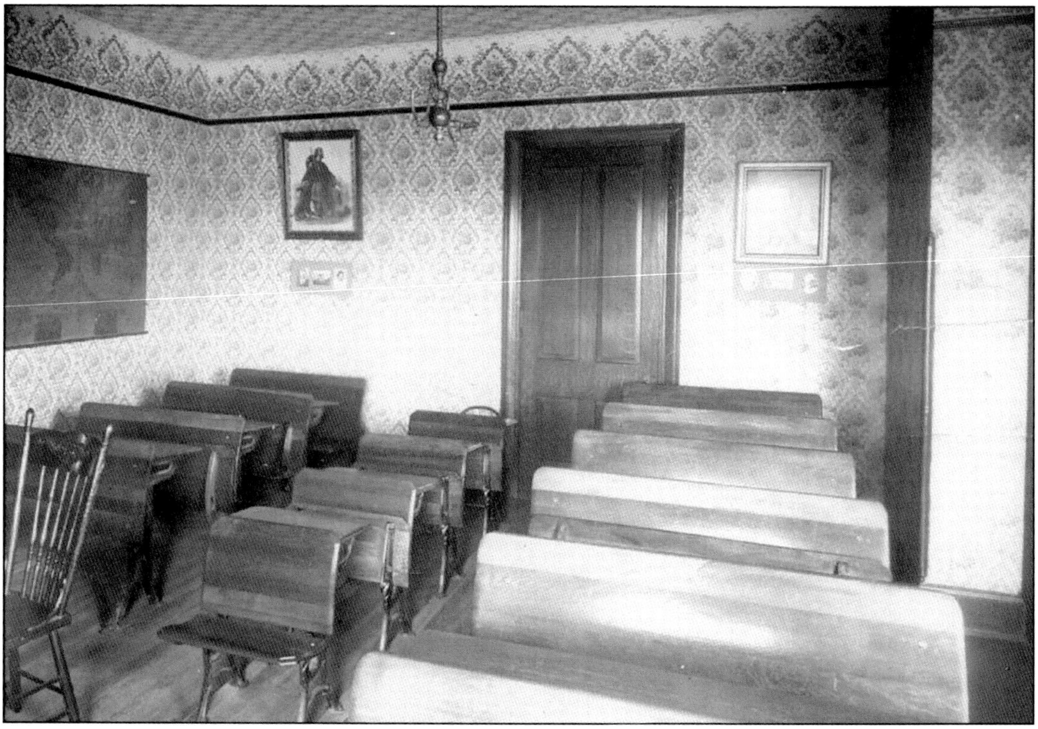

Another use of the Collins House was for classrooms. The large home had room for four classrooms and a chapel on the first floor. The second floor was the students' living quarters, and the sisters who taught at the school resided on the third floor. (Courtesy of the Benedictine Sisters of St. Walburg Monastery.)

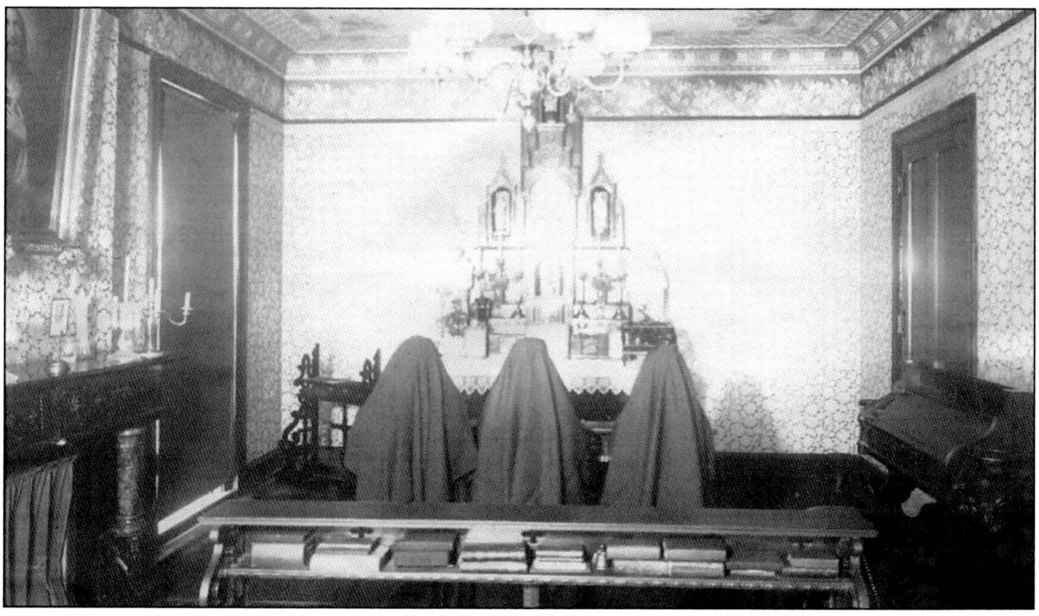

The Collins Home served many purposes over the years. This photograph, which was probably taken around 1903, shows how a room was transformed into a chapel. This chapel was used until the school chapel was complete. (Courtesy of the Benedictine Sisters of St. Walburg Monastery.)

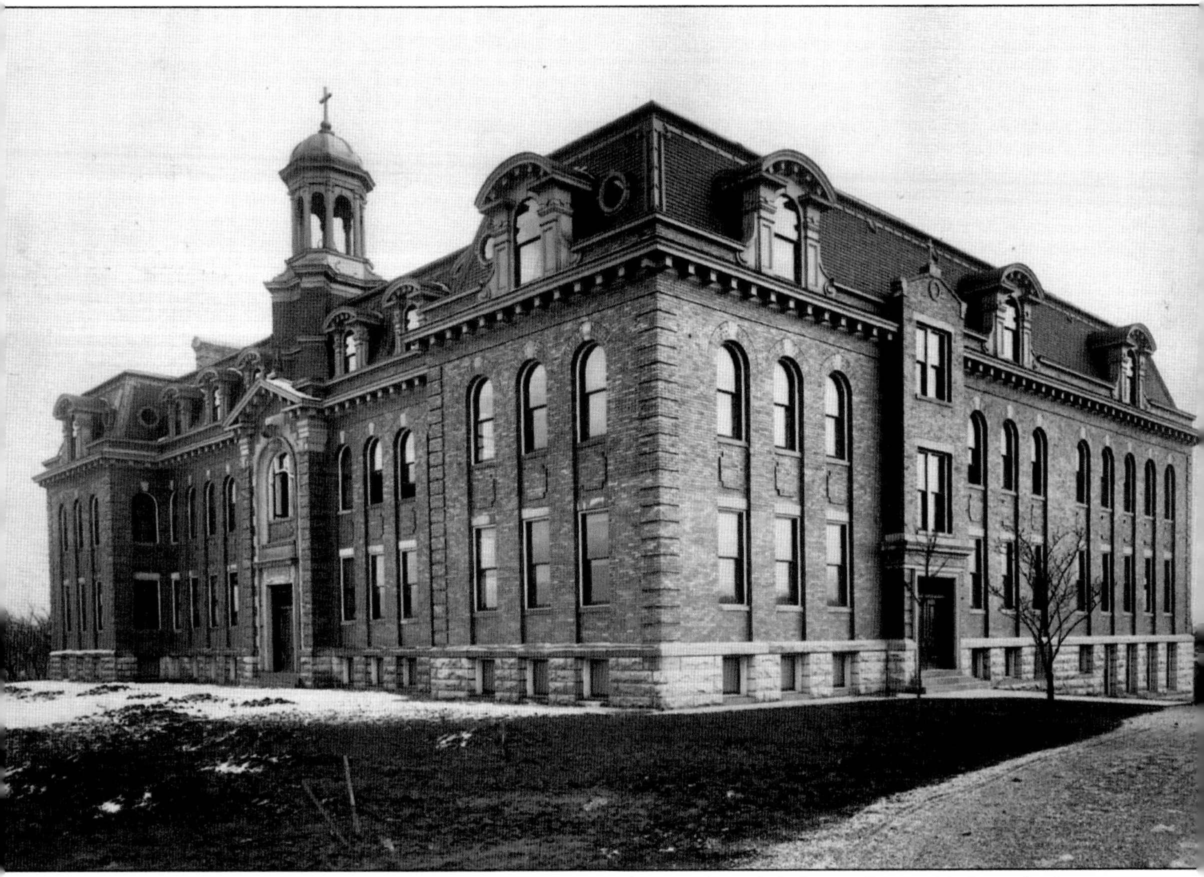

The Villa Madonna Academy building was competed in 1907 and dedicated in 1908. It took about two years to build. The building included classrooms, a chapel, and a cafeteria. The third floor was used for dormitories for the boarding students. The bell atop the roof can be seen from many spots in Northern Kentucky, as well as from across the river on the western side of Cincinnati. The building was also home to Villa Madonna College, which was established in 1921 and remained on the campus until 1929. This college is now known as Thomas More College. (Courtesy of the Benedictine Sisters of St. Walburg Monastery.)

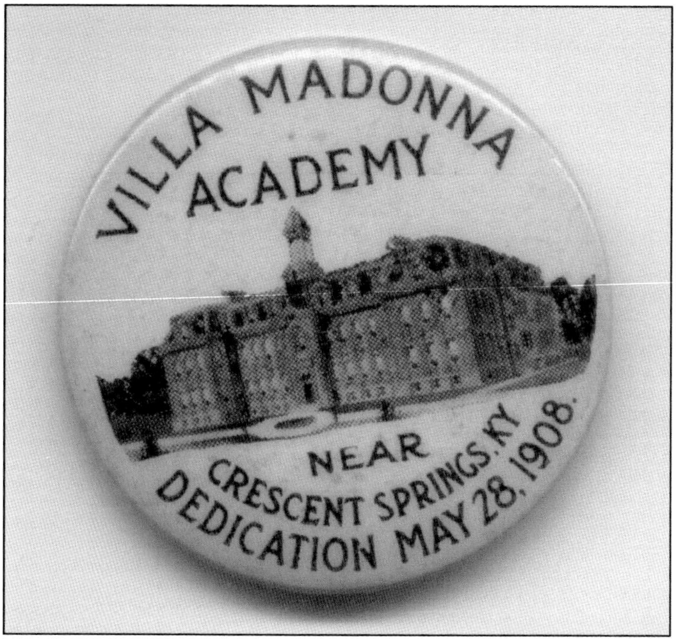

The dedication of Villa Madonna Academy took place on May 28, 1908. These pins were distributed to those who came to the dedication. At the time, Villa Hills was not yet a city, so the button says "Near Crescent Springs." The building was officially completed in 1907, but this event was the official dedication of the building and chapel and the blessing of the bell atop the building by Bishop Camillus Mays, bishop of Covington. (Courtesy of the Benedictine Sisters of St. Walburg Monastery.)

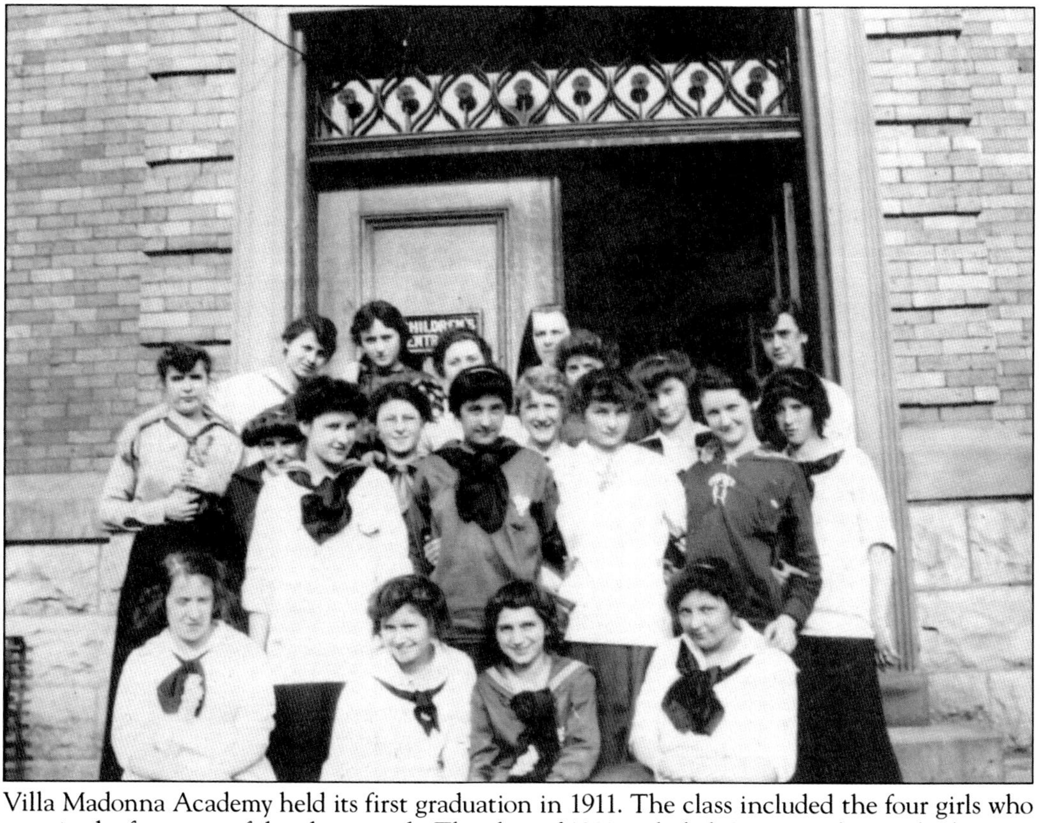

Villa Madonna Academy held its first graduation in 1911. The class included the four girls who were in the front row of the photograph. The class of 1911 included Katrine Adams, who became Sr. Miriam Annunciata, OSB, and Villa's second directress from 1929 to 1961. (Courtesy of the Benedictine Sisters of St. Walburg Monastery.)

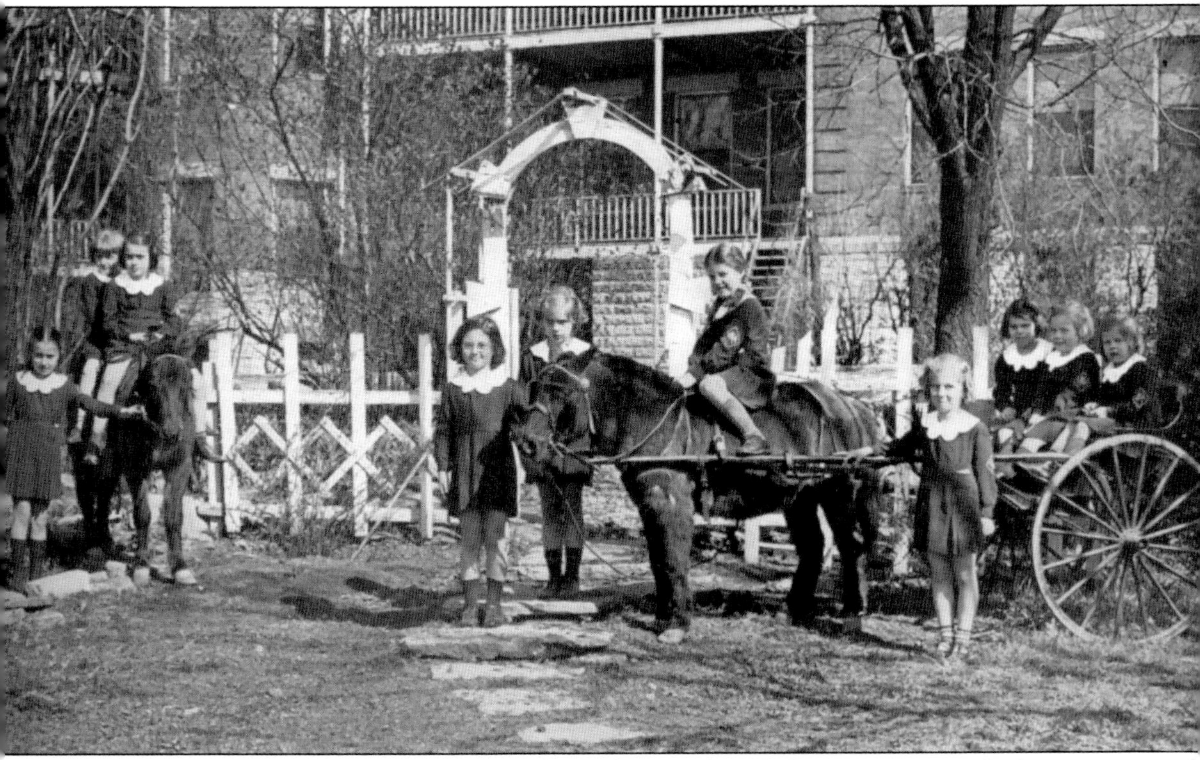

In this 1939 photograph, the elementary students play outside with their new ponies, which were a gift to the school. The ponies were used for recreation. This photograph was taken in the back of the 1907 Academy Building. (Courtesy of the Benedictine Sisters of St. Walburg Monastery.)

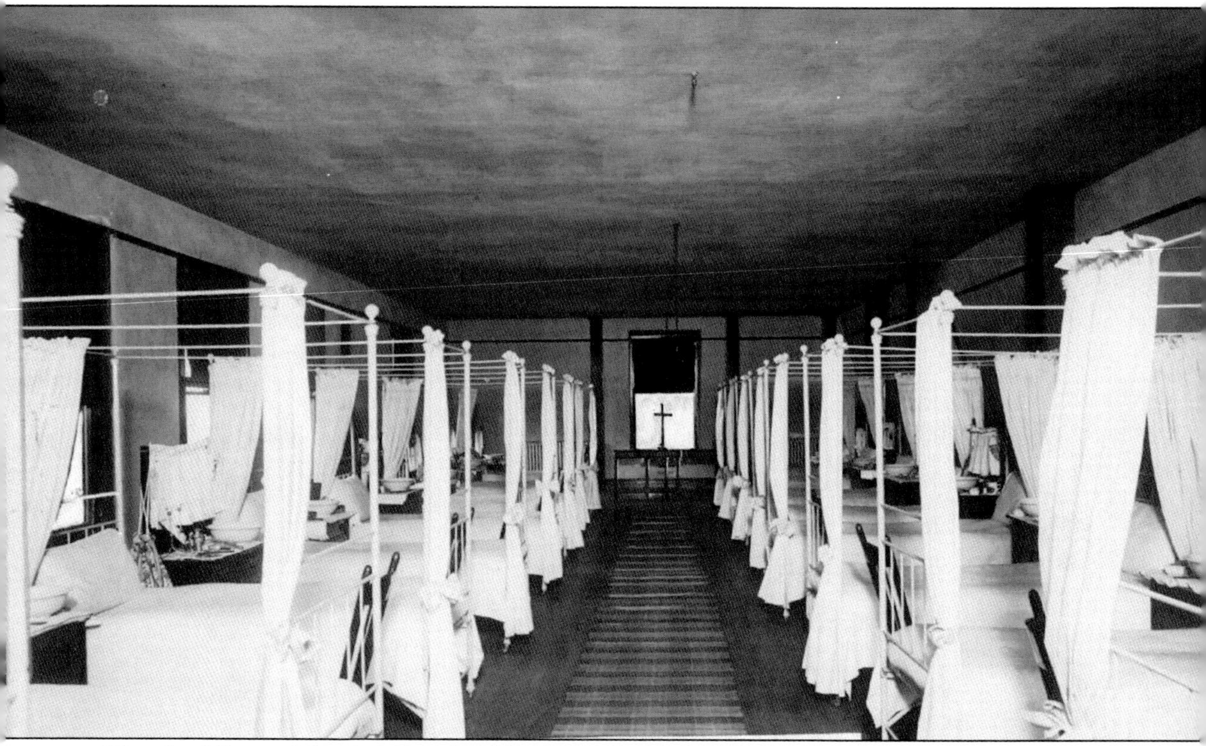

The third floor of the Academy Building was used as living quarters for the boarding students. There were four rooms like the one pictured here. The students typically had a curtained iron bed and a wardrobe with washstand for their use. Female students of all ages came from other states, as well as countries like Hong Kong, Guatemala, Cuba, Germany, and Saudi Arabia. The boarding school was discontinued in 1979. (Courtesy of the Benedictine Sisters of St. Walburg Monastery.)

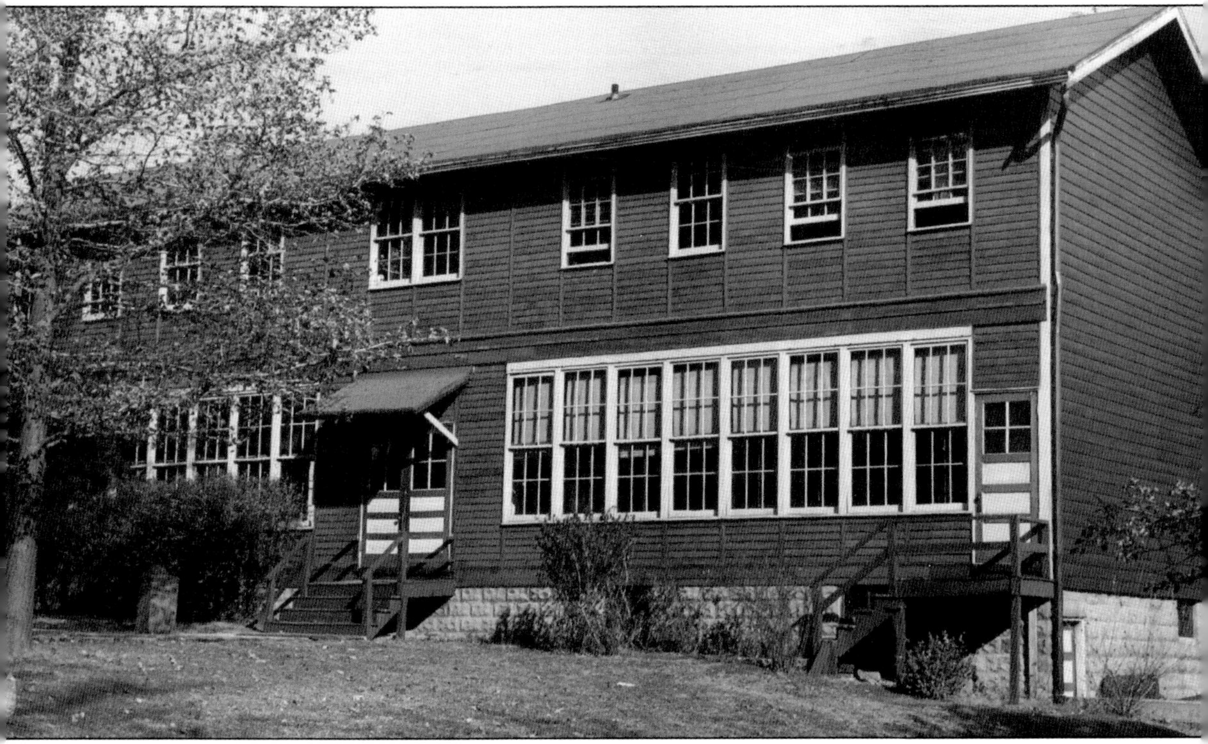

Due to crowded classrooms, the sisters added a pre-fabricated four-room building, ordered from the Sears-Robuck Company, to the property. Known as the Brown House, it was located on the east side of the academy, near the school's tennis courts. It was used for elementary classes from 1921 to 1957. The building was a gift from the school's librarian. (Courtesy of the Benedictine Sisters of St. Walburg Monastery.)

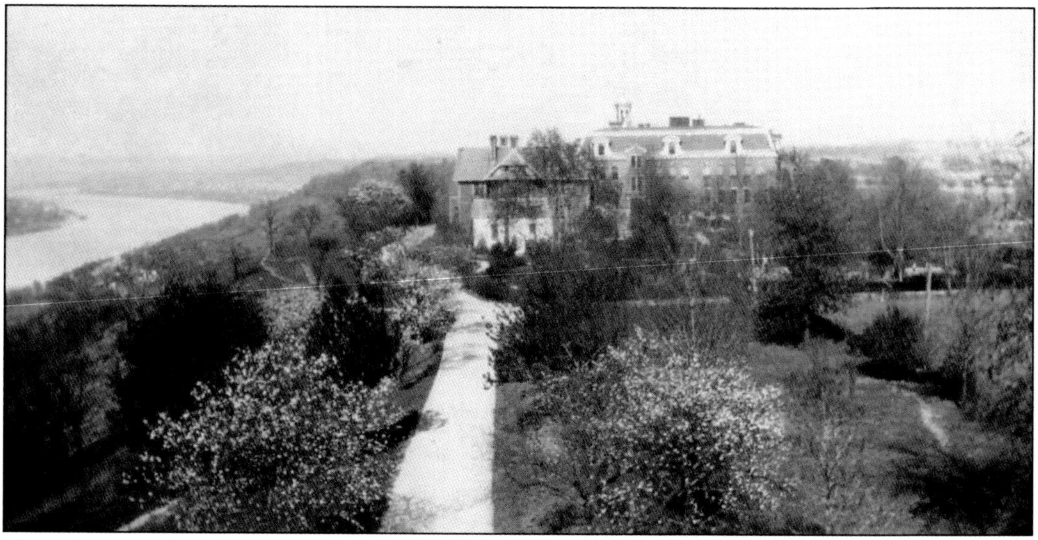

This photograph was taken from the third floor of the Lee Home, which the sisters purchased around 1910. It shows side views of the 1907 Academy Building and the Collins Home and a wonderful view of the Ohio River. In 1916, the sisters voted to transfer the administration of the monastery and the novitiate to the Lee House. At the time of this photograph, the monastery was still located in Covington. (Courtesy of the Benedictine Sisters of St. Walburg Monastery.)

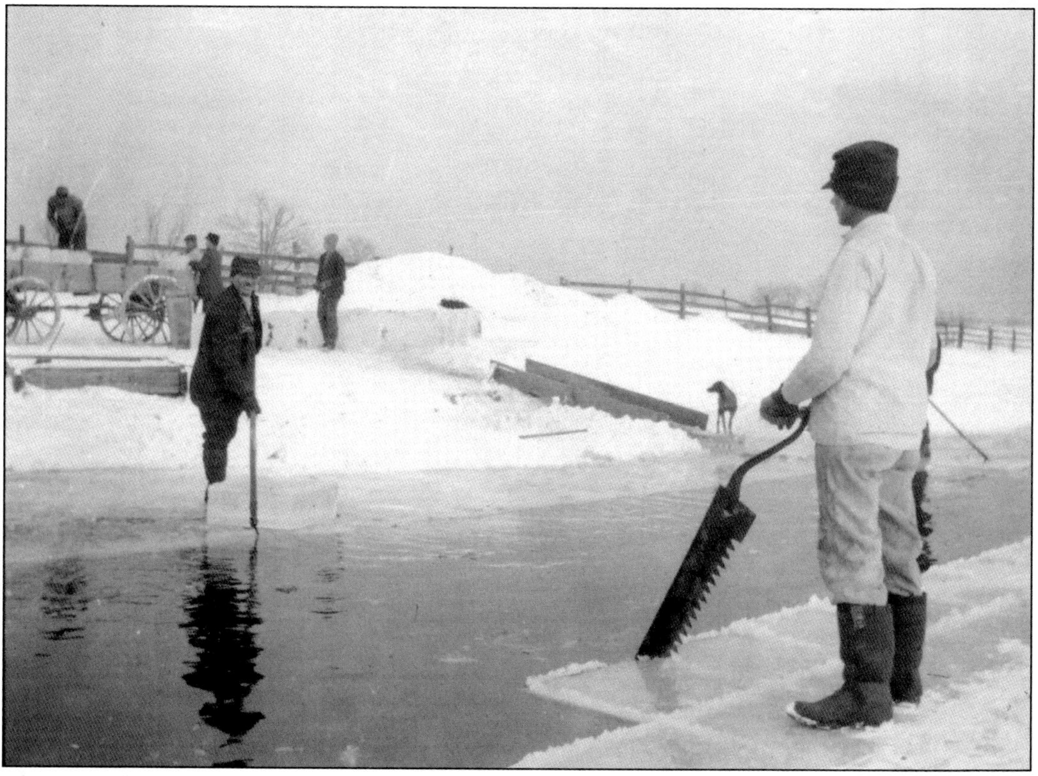

This 1916 photograph shows how ice was cut from the lakes on the property for use in the monastery and academy. The ice was stored in an icehouse on the property until the sisters got electricity in 1917. (Courtesy of the Benedictine Sisters of St. Walburg Monastery.)

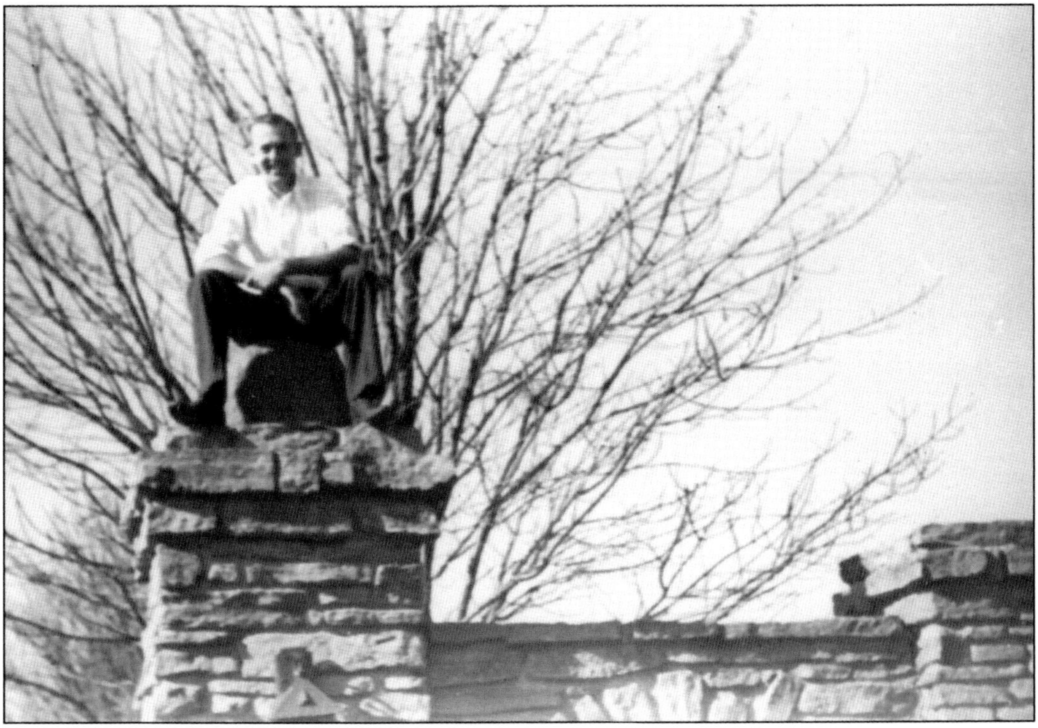

In this 1940s photograph, Earl Foltz, of Crescent Springs, sits high atop a stone pillar, part of the Villa gates. Built in 1931, the gates, which were never actually used as gates, sit proudly at the entrance to the St. Walburg property. (Courtesy of Judy Foltz Whelan.)

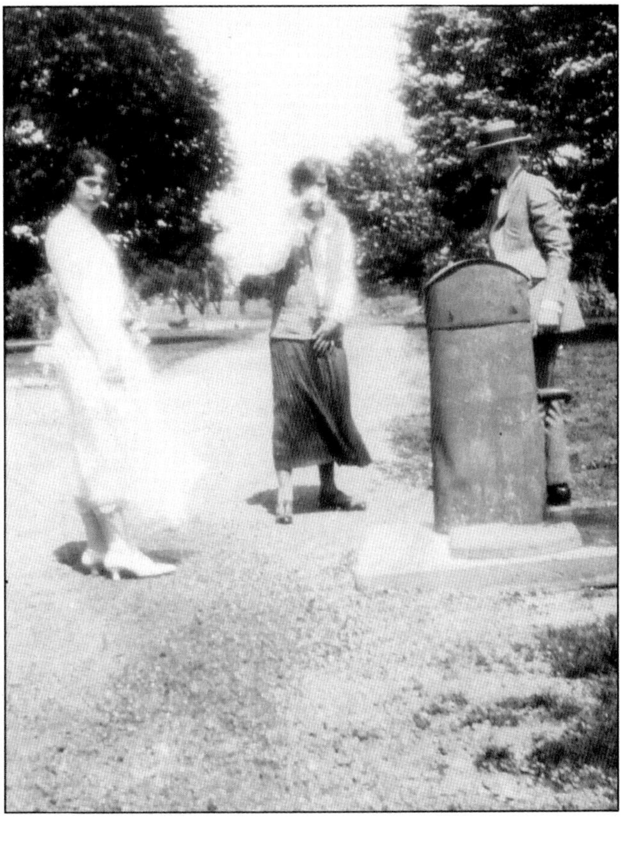

This water pump, which was located between the Collins Home and the 1907 Academy Building, was a gathering spot for students and sisters. After an extremely dry year in 1929, Prioress Sr. Margaret Hugenberg had a waterline installed, bringing in city water from Fort Mitchell. Although the sisters and students now had access to water, the sisters encouraged using lake water whenever possible. The sisters' city water was also sold to local farmers during dry periods. (Courtesy of the Benedictine Sisters of St. Walburg Monastery.)

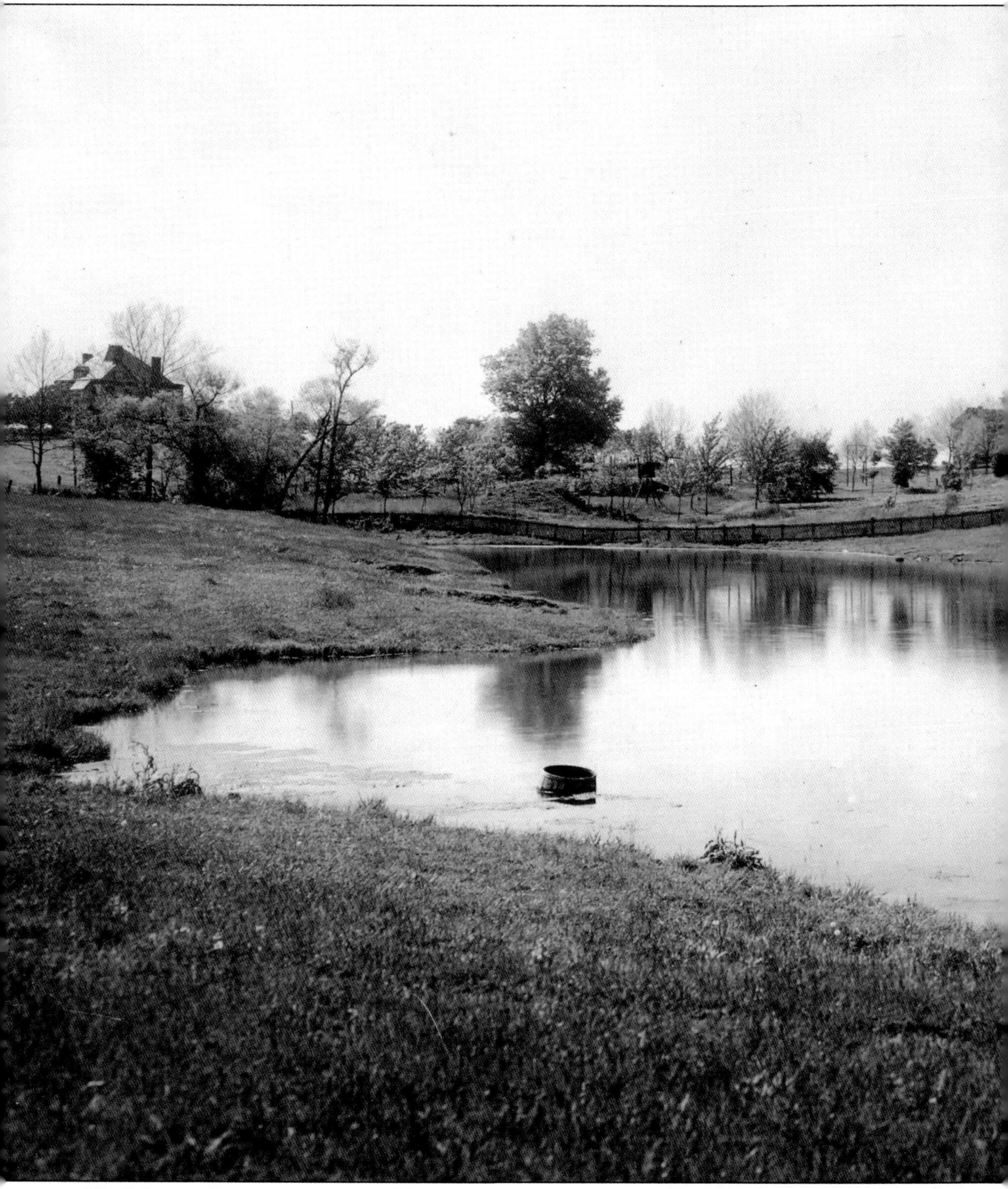

The lakes on the property were used for many purposes, as seen in this 1913 photograph. Although the sisters and the students used it for boating in the summer and ice-skating in the winter, the

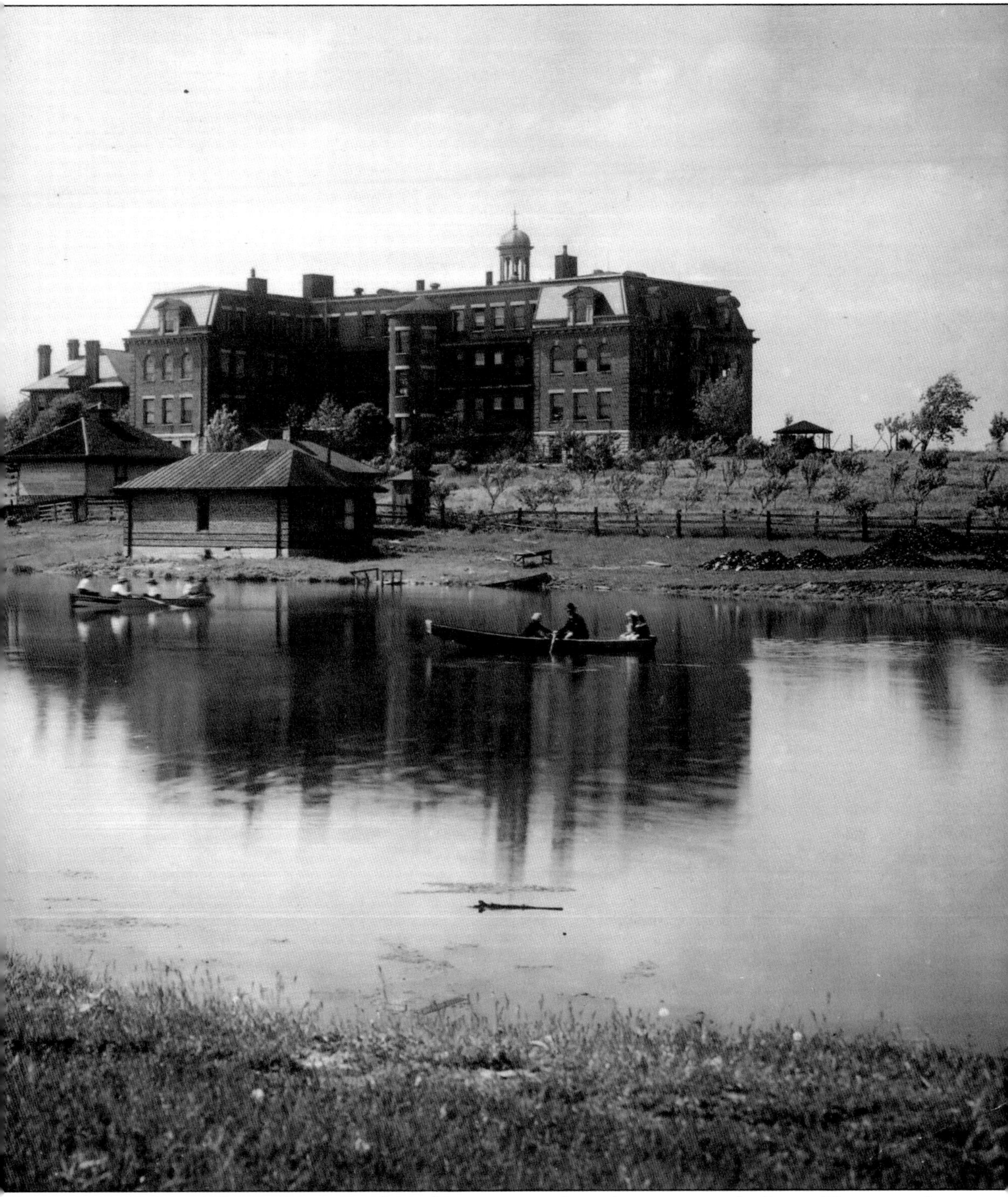

sisters suspected the students would sneak in a swim when they were not looking. (Courtesy of the Benedictine Sisters of St. Walburg Monastery.)

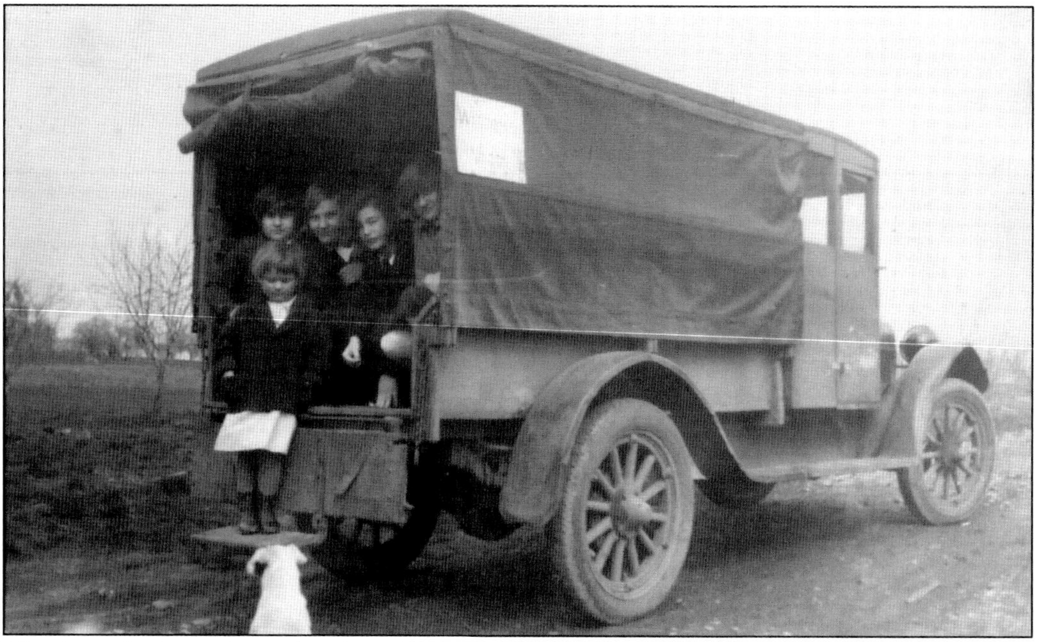

This bus, which was lovingly referred to as the Wisdom Wagon, was actually an old truck fitted with bench seats. It was used to transport academy students from the streetcar line in Fort Mitchell to school. (Courtesy of the Benedictine Sisters of St. Walburg Monastery.)

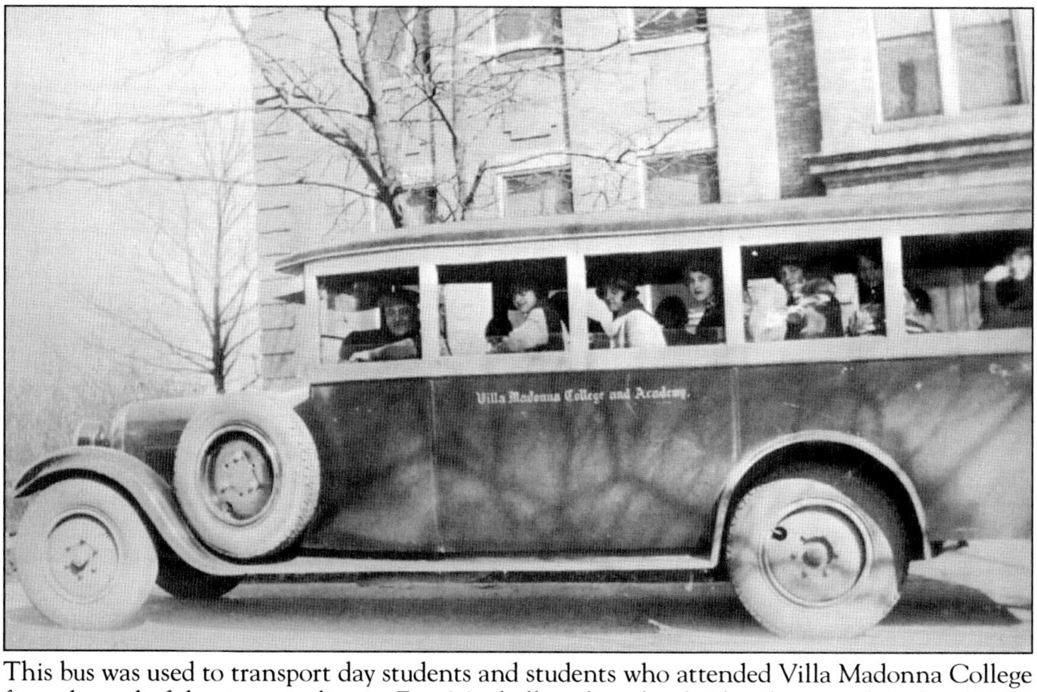

This bus was used to transport day students and students who attended Villa Madonna College from the end of the streetcar line in Fort Mitchell to the school. The photograph is dated 1927. (Courtesy of the Benedictine Sisters of St. Walburg Monastery.)

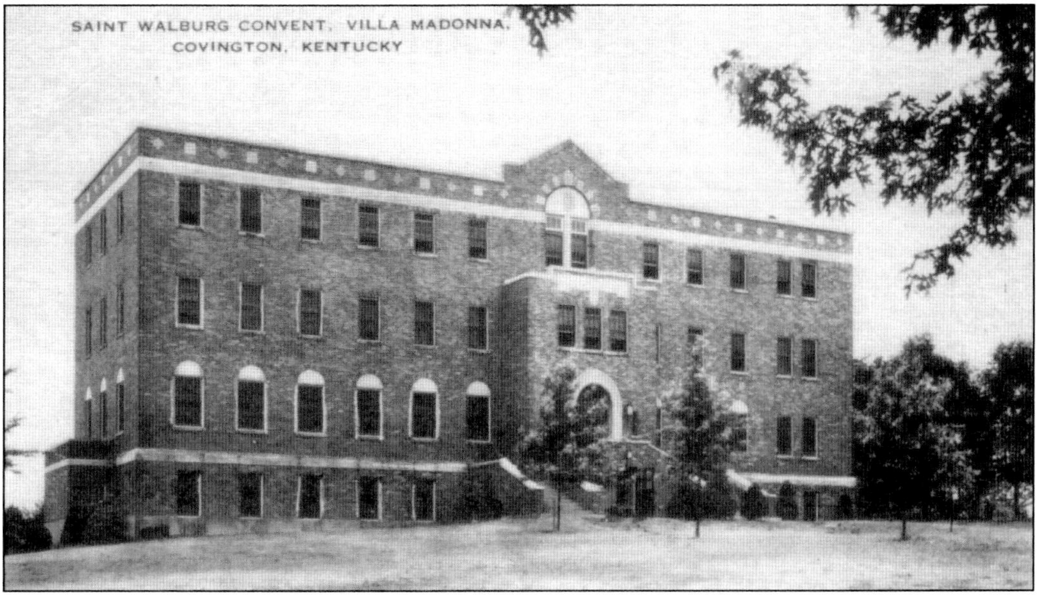

St. Walburg Convent building was completed in 1937. When it opened it had 47 tiny bedrooms for sisters and two bedrooms for guests. The postulants and novices were assigned to 24 cubicles. Although the building was always intended to be the motherhouse for the convent, the whole community could never reside there at the same time. Sisters were assigned to schools and hospitals, which is where they lived most of the time. When the whole congregation did need to gather, they usually did so in the summer, so the non-resident sisters could lodge in the dormitories in the Academy Building. In 1961, the monastery's most populous year, there were 271 Benedictine Sisters affiliated with St. Walburg Monastery. The sisters used the third floor as the infirmary, but in 1968 an infirmary wing, with 32 rooms, was added to the south side of the building. This wing also included a large meeting room, which could hold the entire membership of the community. (Courtesy of www.nkyviews.com.)

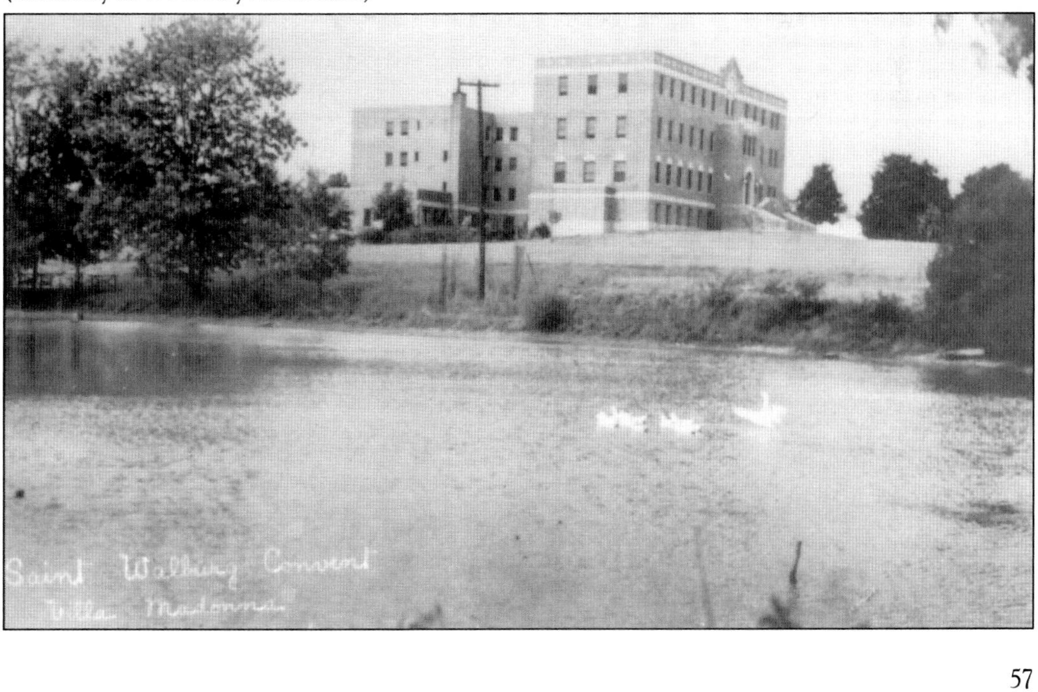

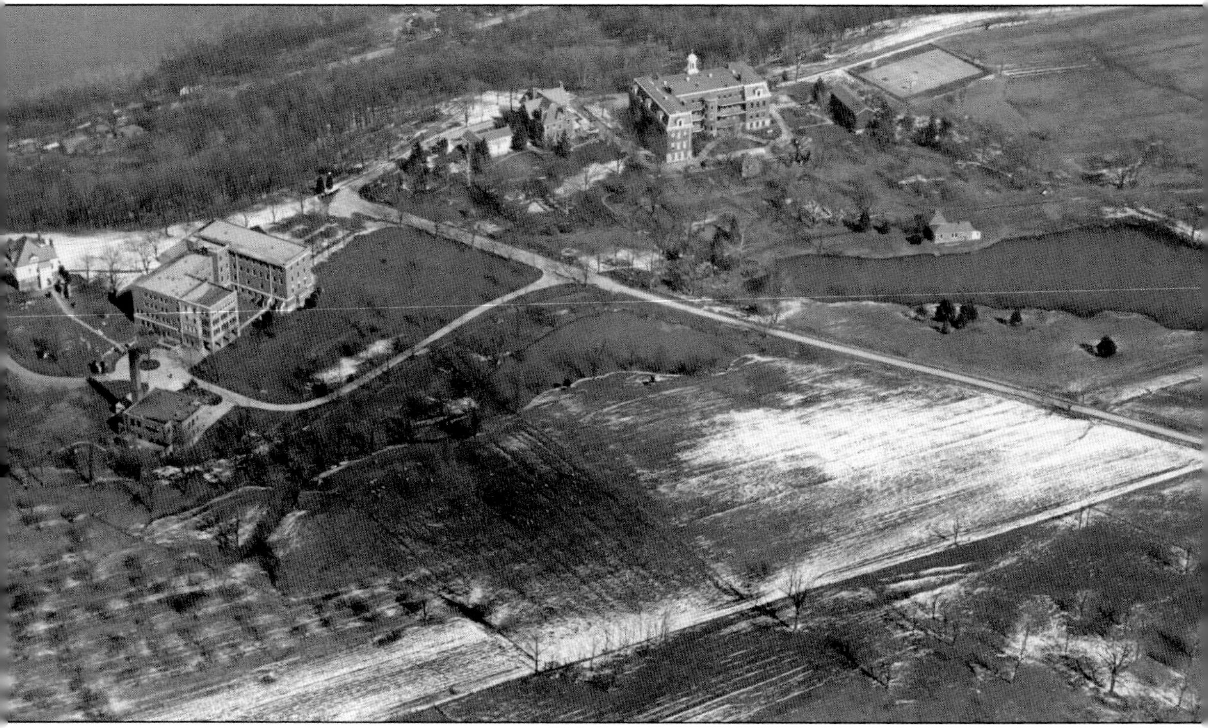

In this 1940s photograph, the property of St. Walburg Monastery can be seen. The Ohio River is visible in the upper left, and Amsterdam Road runs across the bottom. The buildings from left to right include the Lee House, monastery, white chaplin's house, the Collins House, the Academy Building, the Brown House, and tennis courts. The lakes and surrounding farmland are also visible. (Courtesy of the Benedictine Sisters of St. Walburg Monastery.)

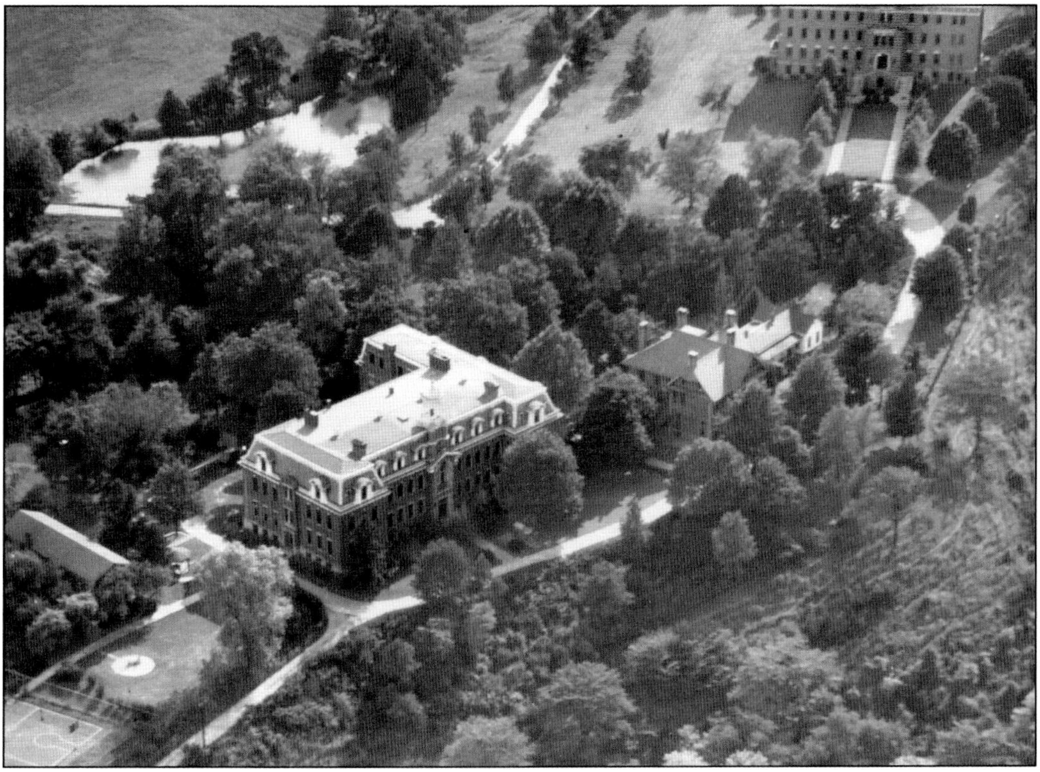

This early-1950s photograph shows the academy, monastery, and Collins Home. On the bottom left, near the tennis court, is the Brown House, which was purchased as a prefabricated building from Sears-Robuck Company and used for additional classrooms from 1921 to 1957. The wooded area surrounding the academy building would soon be the site of the $1 million high school building. (Courtesy of the Benedictine Sisters of St. Walburg Monastery.)

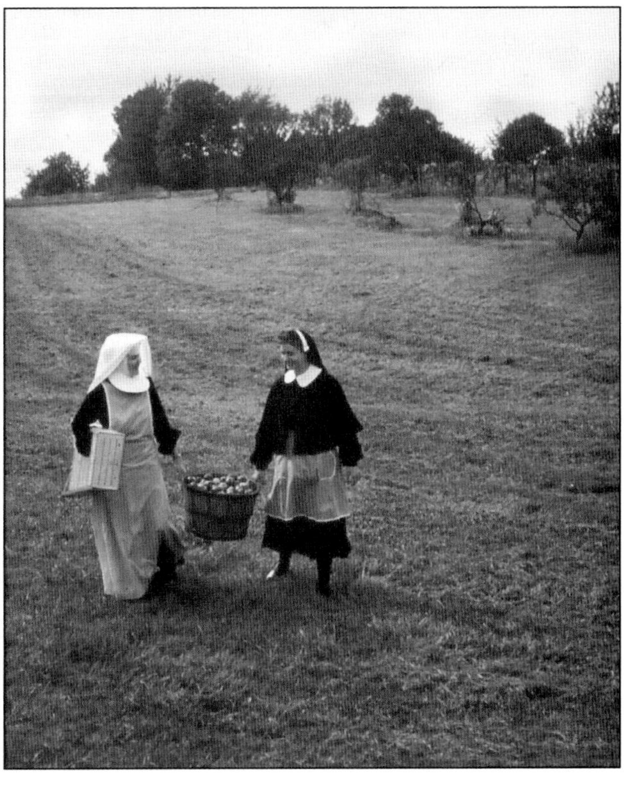

The grounds of St. Walburg Monastery were a working farm up until 1967. The sisters grew berries, apples, and all kinds of vegetables on the grounds surrounding the school and convent. The produce was raised for the use of the sisters. (Courtesy of the Benedictine Sisters of St. Walburg Monastery.)

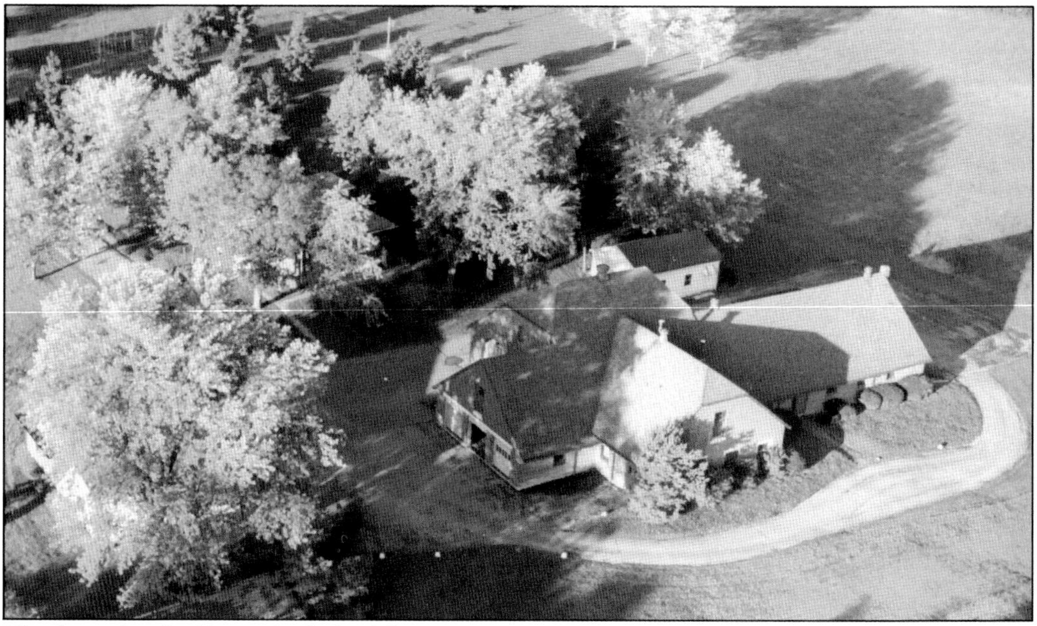

This barn that had been the hub of the sisters' farming operation was turned into a day camp and later a Montessori school. Prior to the 1960s, the barn housed animals and was also the site of the monastery's gas tanks. The farm was allowed to have gas tanks on site for use of the farming equipment, cars, and the bus known as the Wisdom Wagon. (Courtesy of the Benedictine Sisters of St. Walburg Monastery.)

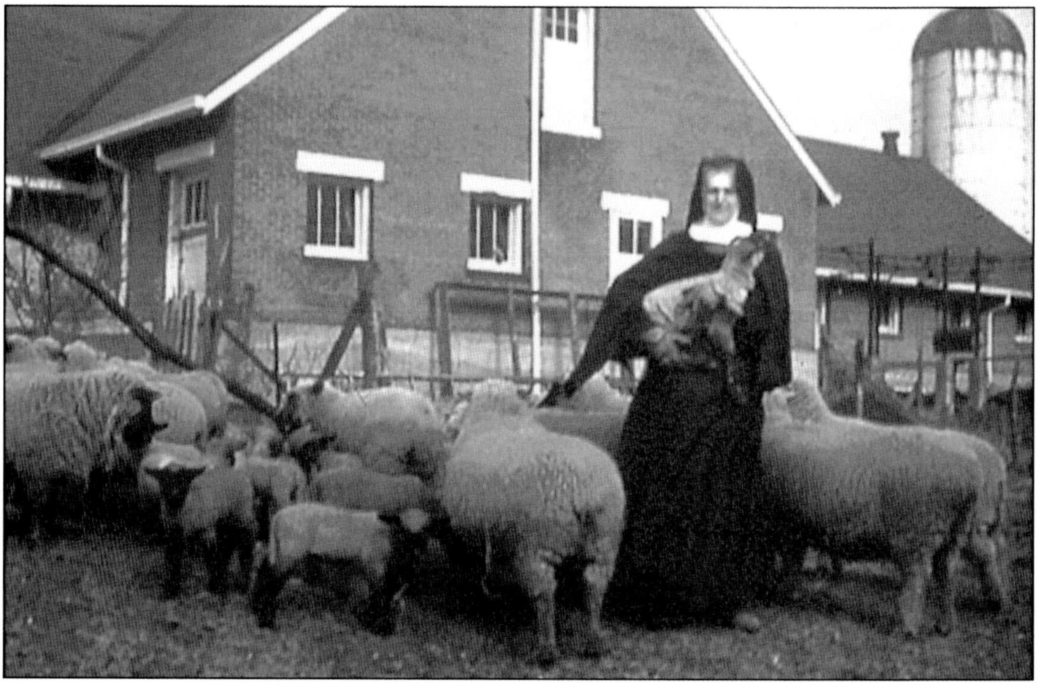

Prior to 1960, the sisters raised sheep, cows, pigs, and chickens in this barn that later was turned into a Montessori school. Sr. Bernard Gripsover, who was primarily in charge of the farm, is seen here with her sheep. (Courtesy of the Benedictine Sisters of St. Walburg Monastery.)

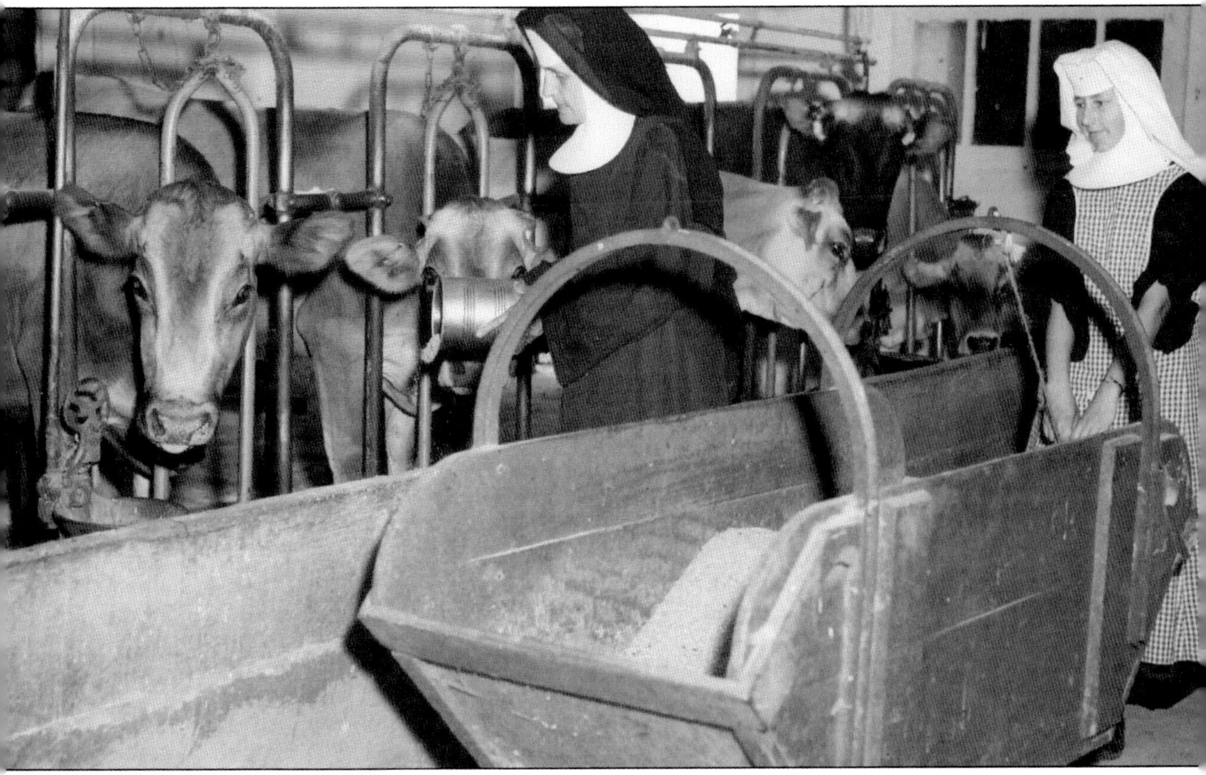

The sisters raised dairy cows for the monastery's milk and butter. Seen in this photograph from the early 1960s, Sr. Bernard Gripsover (left) and Sr. Betty Cahill feed the cows inside the barn that would eventually be the Villa Madonna Montessori School. Sr. Betty wears a white veil indicating that she is a novice, in the second stage of formation for membership in the community. The novice is someone who has been with the community for six months to a year; the taking of final vows would not happen for three more years. (Courtesy of the Benedictine Sisters of St. Walburg Monastery.)

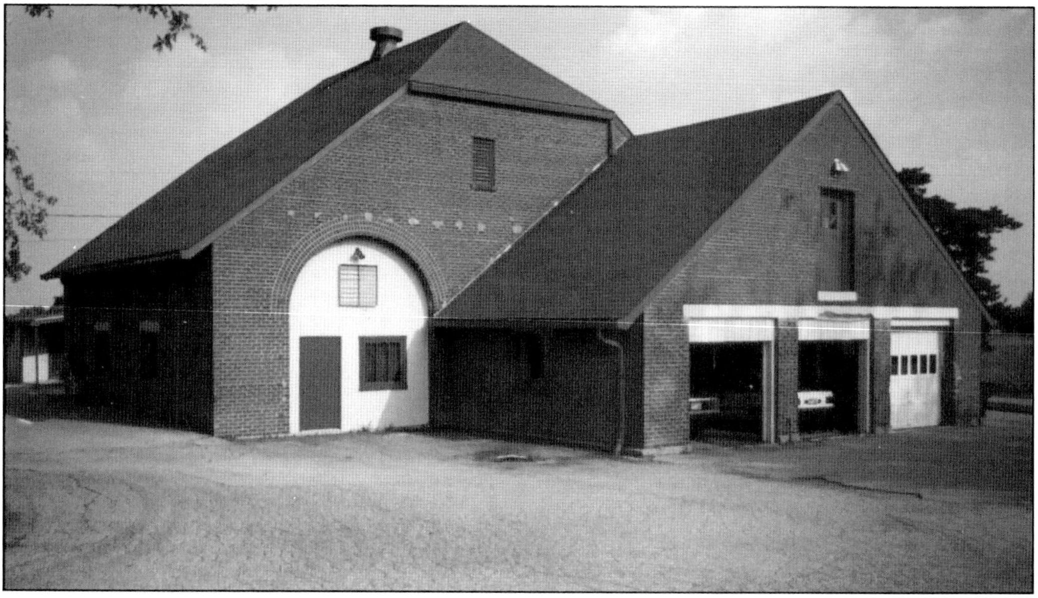

The sisters discontinued farming in 1967, and the barn and adjacent playground was used as a summer day camp for inner city children from Covington and Newport in the summers of 1968 to 1972. In 1972, the barn was turned into classrooms for the Villa Madonna Early Learning Center, which later changed its name to Villa Madonna Montessori. (Courtesy of the Benedictine Sisters of St. Walburg Monastery.)

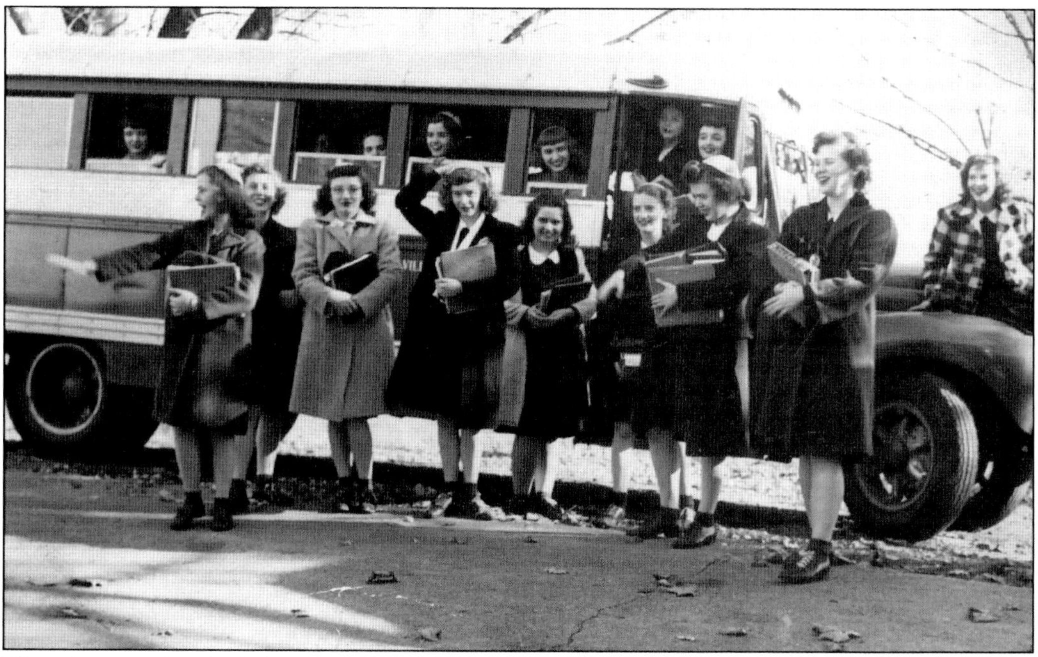

This photograph, which dates to the late 1940s or the early 1950s, shows students arriving at school on the Villa bus. The remote location of the school resulted in transportation issues. Two sisters were always aboard the bus to monitor the girls as they traveled between the school and the end of the streetcar line in Ft. Mitchell each morning and afternoon. (Courtesy of the Benedictine Sisters of St. Walburg Monastery.)

In 1955, the sisters received permission from Rome to borrow money in order to build a new high school building. For the first time in the history of Kenton County, a mortgage loan was taken out in the amount of $1 million. (Courtesy of the Benedictine Sisters of St. Walburg Monastery.)

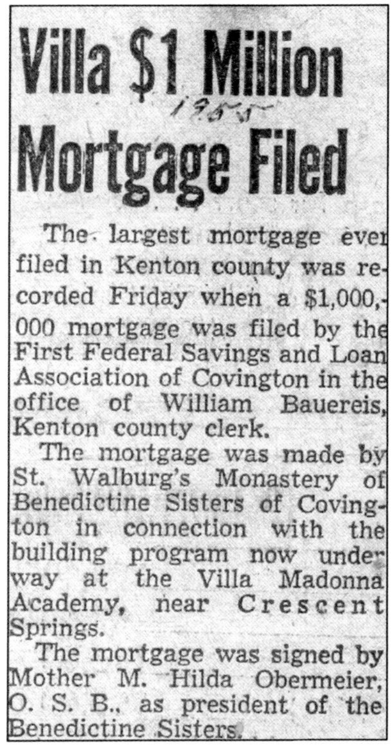

Villa $1 Million Mortgage Filed

The largest mortgage ever filed in Kenton county was recorded Friday when a $1,000,000 mortgage was filed by the First Federal Savings and Loan Association of Covington in the office of William Bauereis, Kenton county clerk.

The mortgage was made by St. Walburg's Monastery of Benedictine Sisters of Covington in connection with the building program now under way at the Villa Madonna Academy, near Crescent Springs.

The mortgage was signed by Mother M. Hilda Obermeier, O. S. B., as president of the Benedictine Sisters.

The mortgage was approved and ground was broken for the new high school building. Ground was broken in 1959 by Bishop William Theodore Mulloy (center) who served as bishop of Covington from 1945 until his death in 1959. Although most of the priests and students in the photograph are unidentified, the priest on the right is Fr. Leroy Smith. (Courtesy of the Benedictine Sisters of St. Walburg Monastery.)

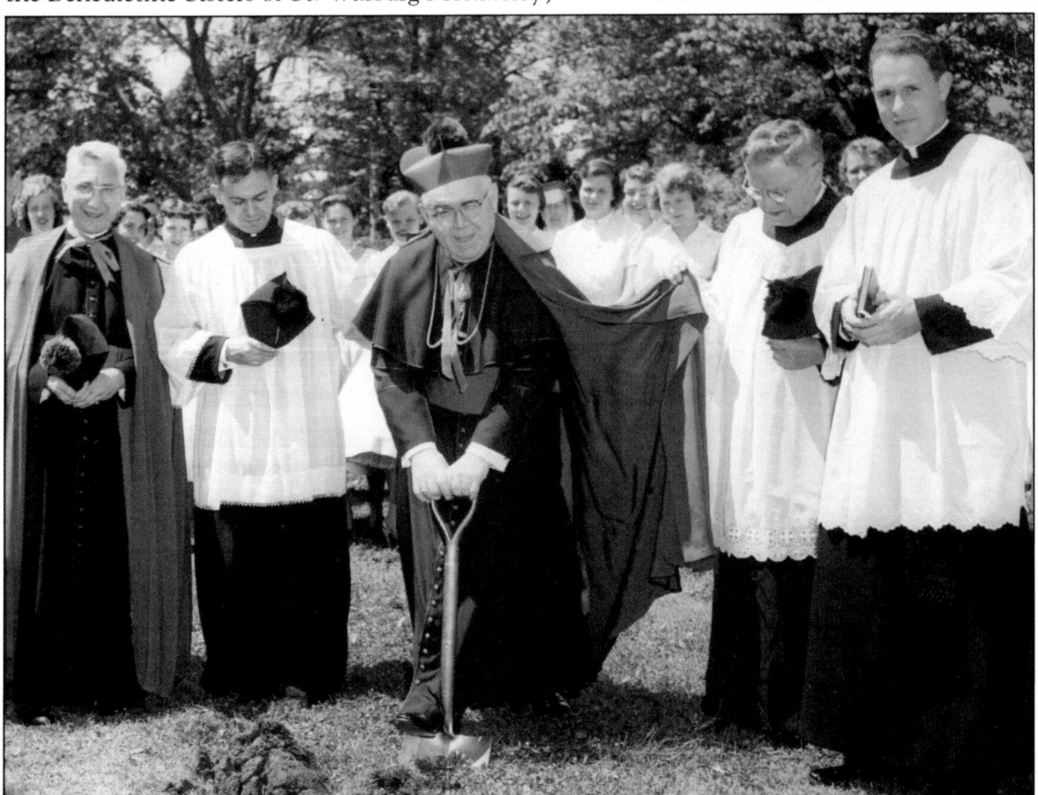

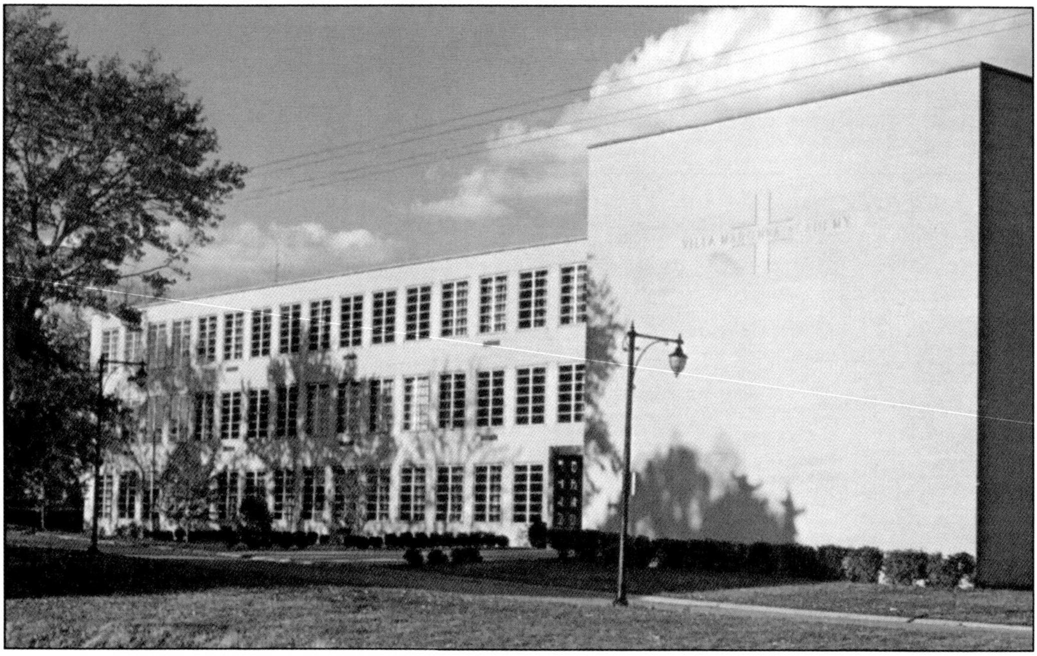

The long-awaited, new high school building opened in April 1958. In addition to the state-of-the-art science classrooms, the school also had an art room with a kiln, a gymnasium, a large cafeteria, and even a bowling alley. (Above courtesy of www.nkyviews.com; below courtesy of the Benedictine Sisters of St. Walburg Monastery.)

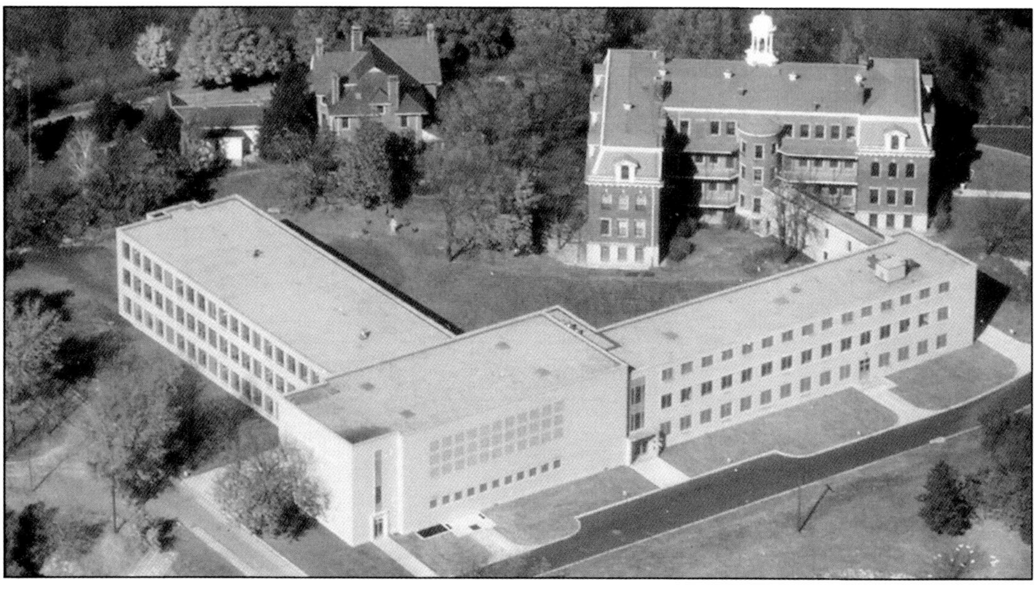

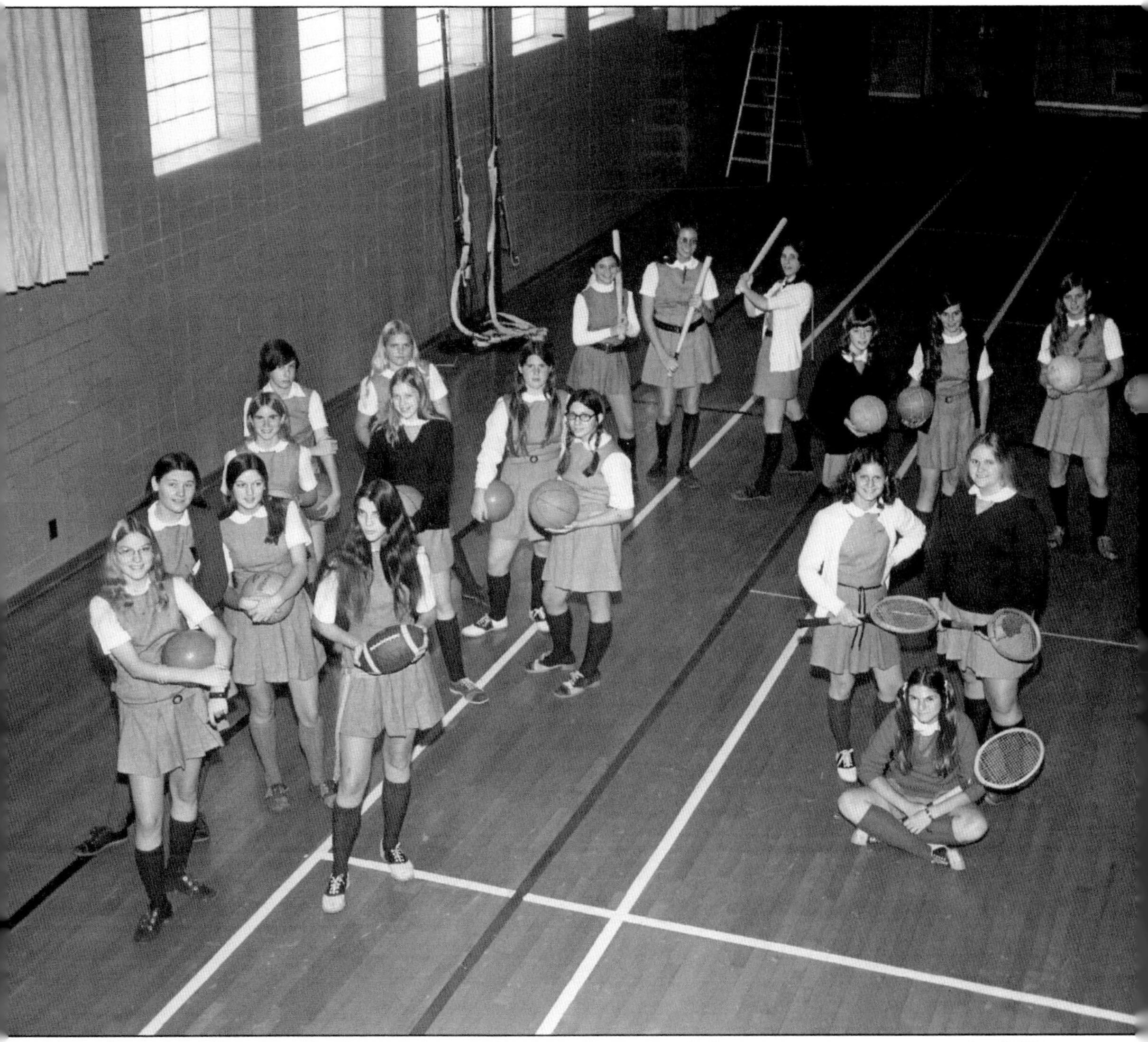

In this 1970s photograph, the girls are in the gym showing off their sporting equipment. In 1977, the elementary school became coeducational, and in 1985, the high school followed suit. The first male graduates were members of the class of 1990. (Courtesy of the Benedictine Sisters of St. Walburg Monastery.)

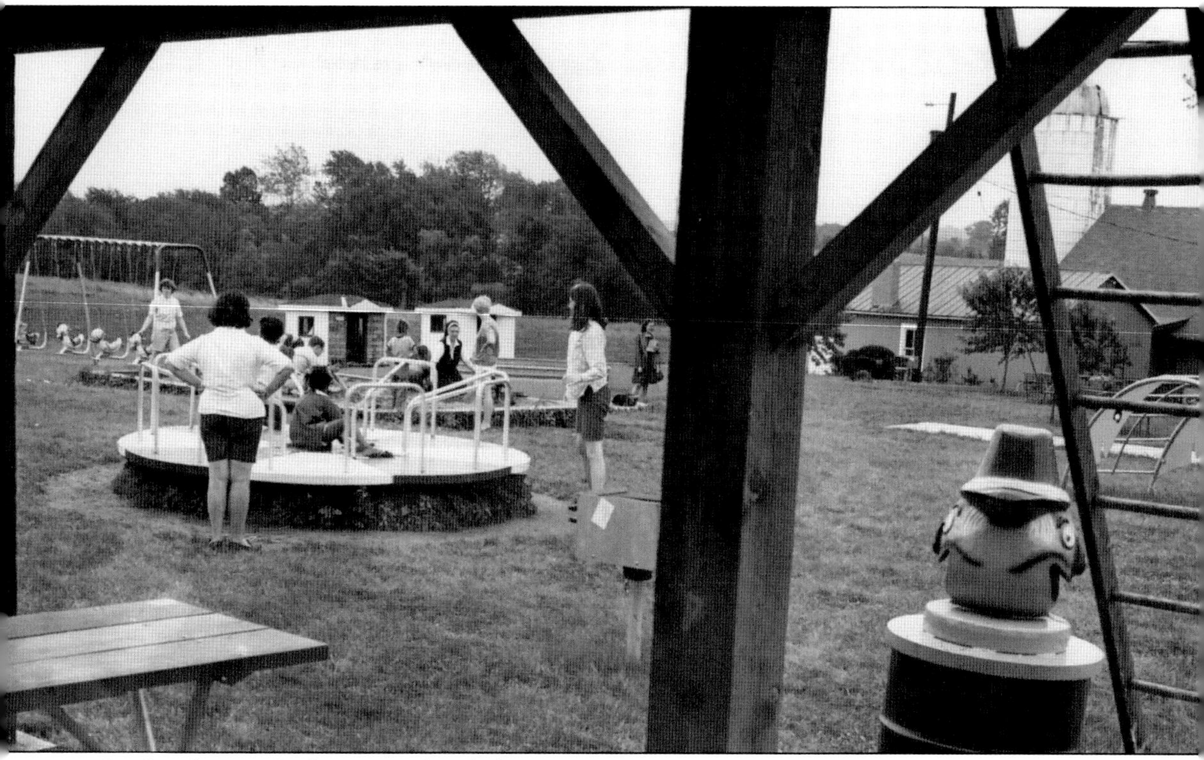

In October 1967, the sisters decided to convert their barn into a recreational center open to neighborhood children, as well as children from the inner city. In the summer of 1968, the sisters hosted the first day camp, which they called the Barn Program. Children from Covington and Newport were bussed out to the Villa grounds for a day of recreation. This program went on until 1977. The sisters also started renting out the grounds for family reunions and company picnics. In the early 1970s, this area was also used for the Villa Hills Civic Club's annual Easter egg hunt. (Courtesy of the Kenton County Library.)

In the early 1970s, a retired full-size red caboose was donated to the playground, a gift from the Kenton County Jaycees. It sat on a small strip of railroad track and was situated at the north end of the playground. The caboose was there for about 10 years and was a huge attraction for neighborhood kids, as well as students of the Montessori program. After several years the caboose fell into disrepair, and the sisters, with the blessing of the Jaycees, sold it. In these mid-1970s photographs, the Cooney children, who lived on nearby Mary Street, play in the caboose and pose for photographs. (Courtesy of Barb Lohre Cooney.)

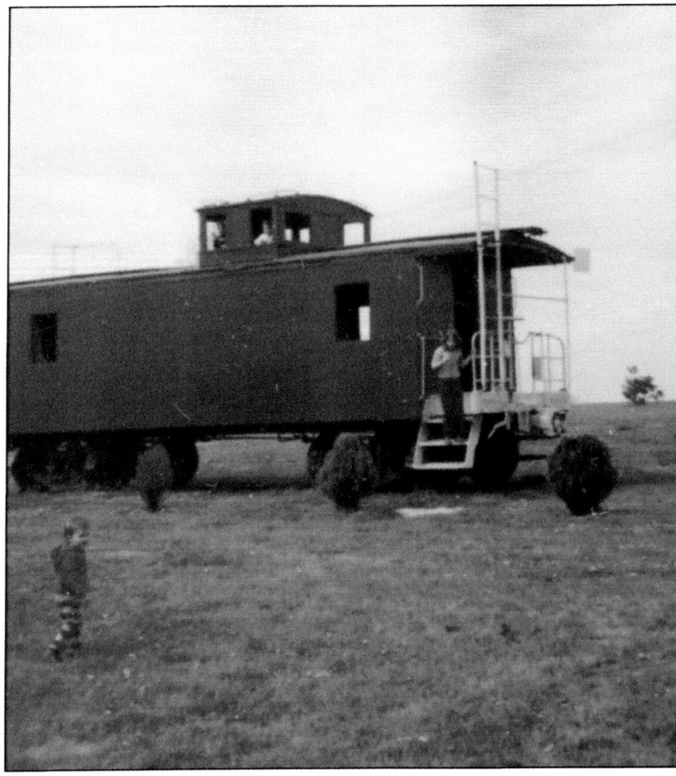

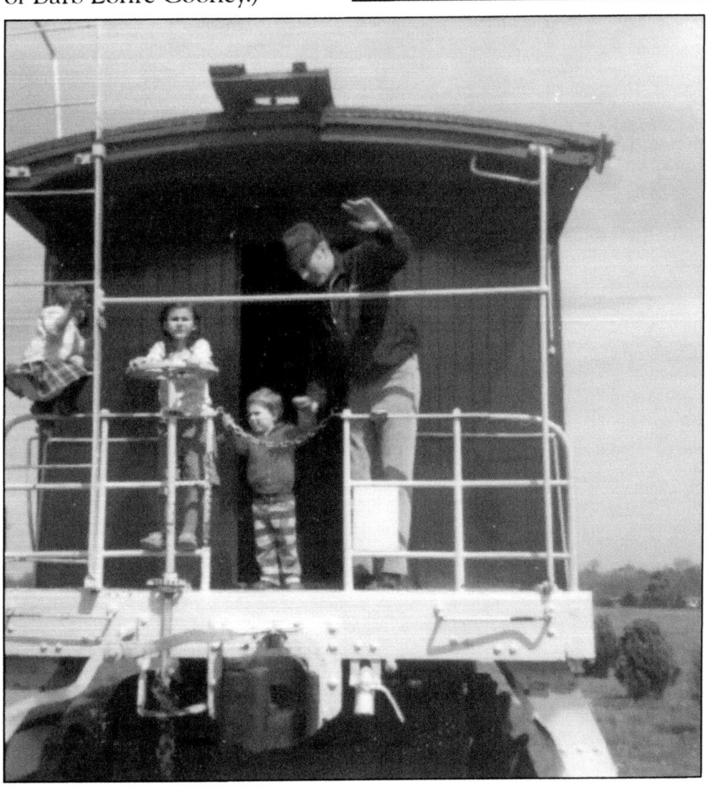

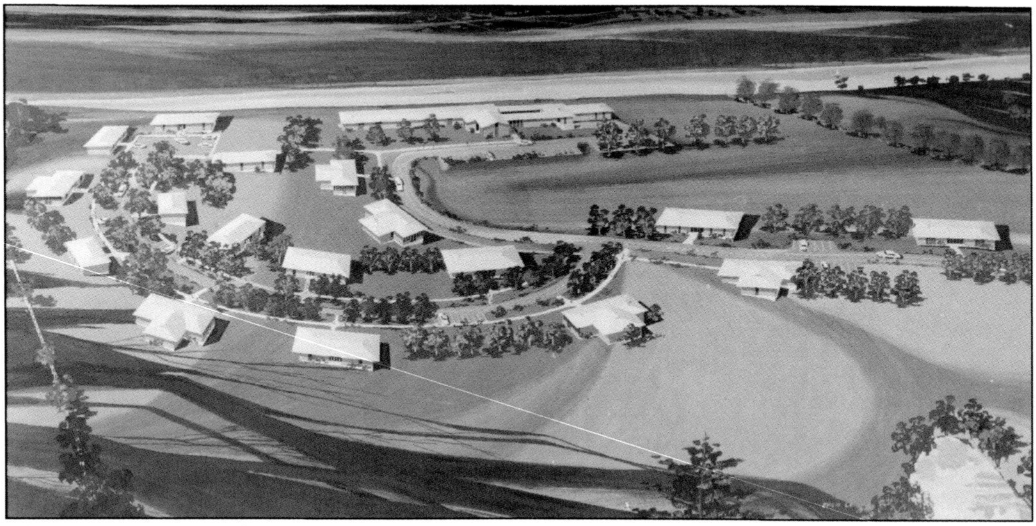

This is an artist's rendering of the proposed Madonna Manor Nursing Home. The idea for the home developed as the sisters looked for ways to care for their own aging families, as well as some of their grounds workers. Madonna Manor was the third nursing home in Northern Kentucky, following St. Charles Nursing Home in Fort Wright and Garrett Convalescent Home in Covington. (Courtesy of Madonna Manor Nursing Home.)

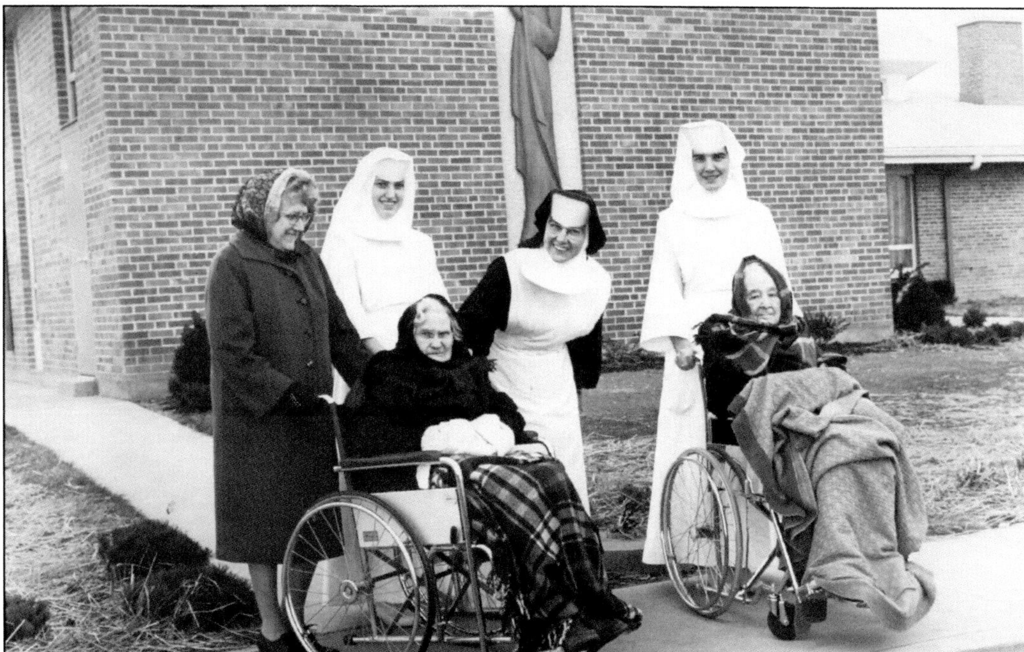

The Sisters of St. Walburg established Madonna Manor Nursing Home in 1964, by building three cottages for senior citizens. The original plan was to house seniors who were self sufficient, but the sisters quickly realized there was need for more nursing care. Just a year later the nursing building, complete with kitchen, chapel, and 20 beds, was completed on the property. The building cost about $344,000. Seen here are, from left to right, (first row) Lillian Seiler and Mary Rutterer; (second row) Thelma Maloney (Mrs. Seiler's daughter); Sister Stephan, OSB; Sister Martina, OSB; and Sr. Peter Marie, OSB. (Courtesy of Madonna Manor Nursing Home.)

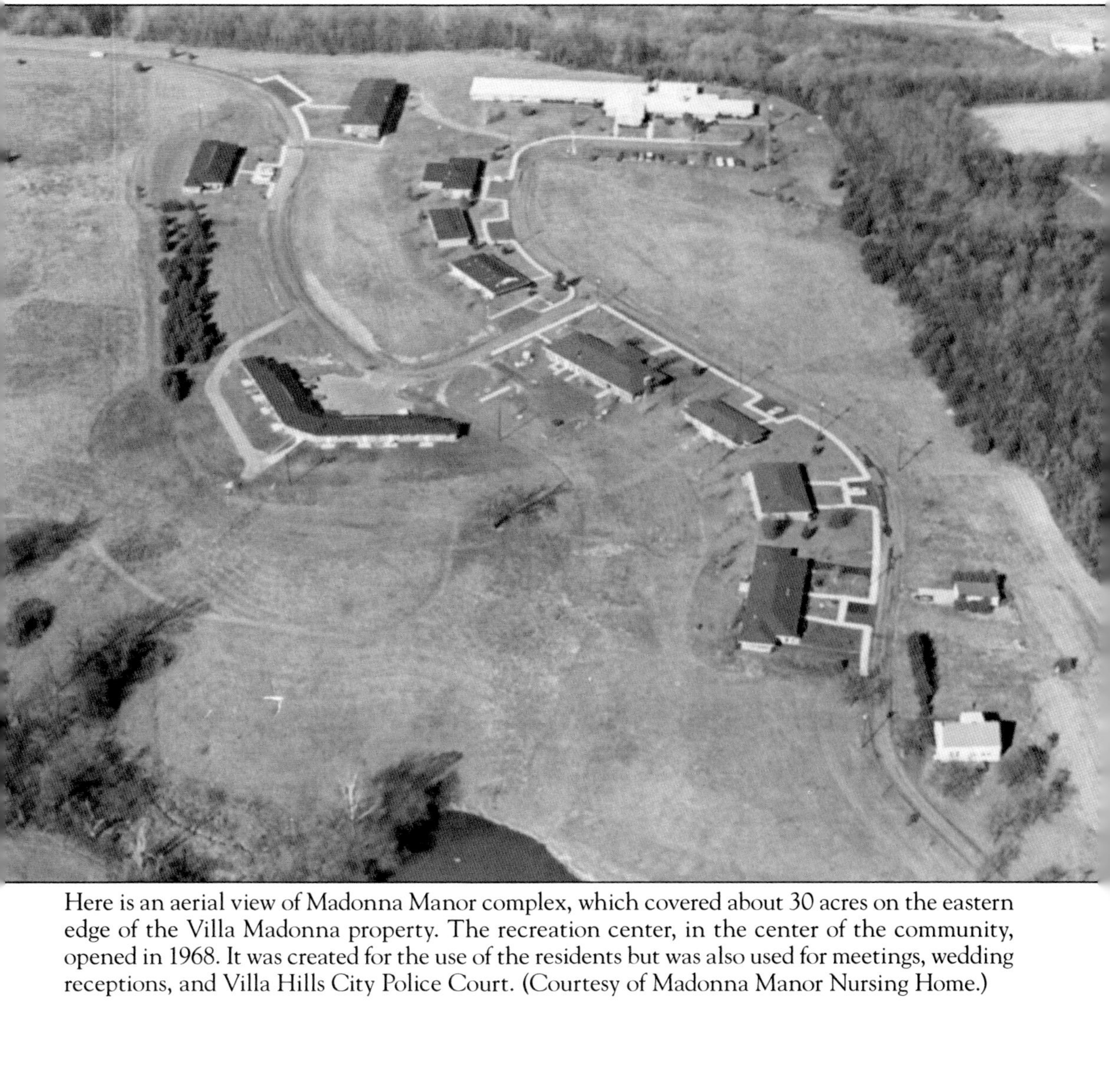

Here is an aerial view of Madonna Manor complex, which covered about 30 acres on the eastern edge of the Villa Madonna property. The recreation center, in the center of the community, opened in 1968. It was created for the use of the residents but was also used for meetings, wedding receptions, and Villa Hills City Police Court. (Courtesy of Madonna Manor Nursing Home.)

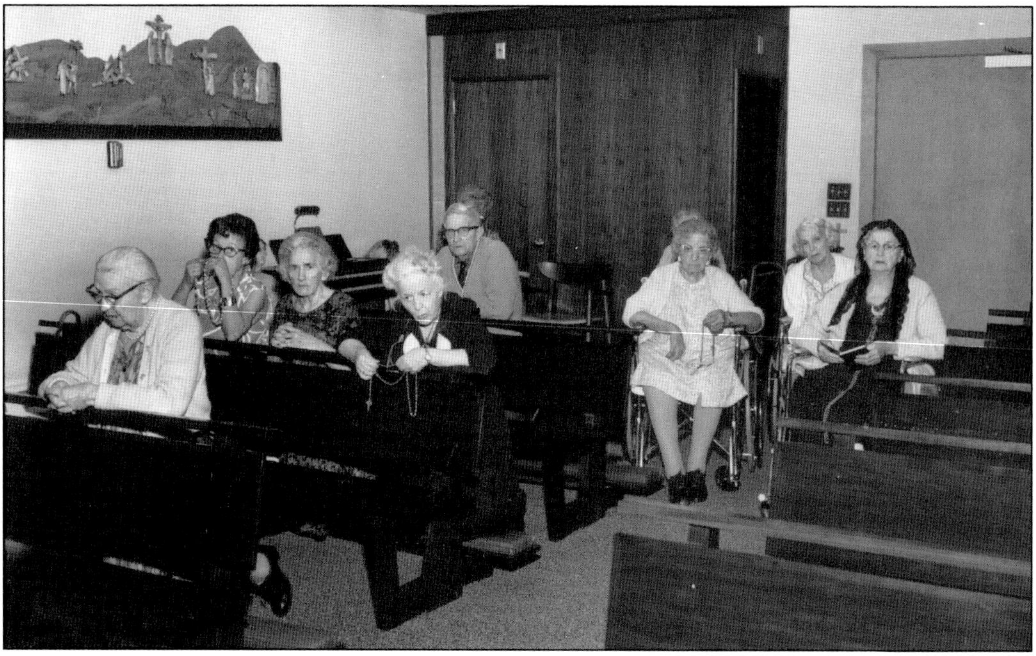

This early-1970s photograph shows the inside of the chapel at Madonna Manor Nursing Home. By 1975, the number of residents of the nursing home had grown to 88 from the 12 who originally came to live there in the mid-1960s. The grounds also included 48 apartments, originally having only three. (Courtesy of Madonna Manor Nursing Home.)

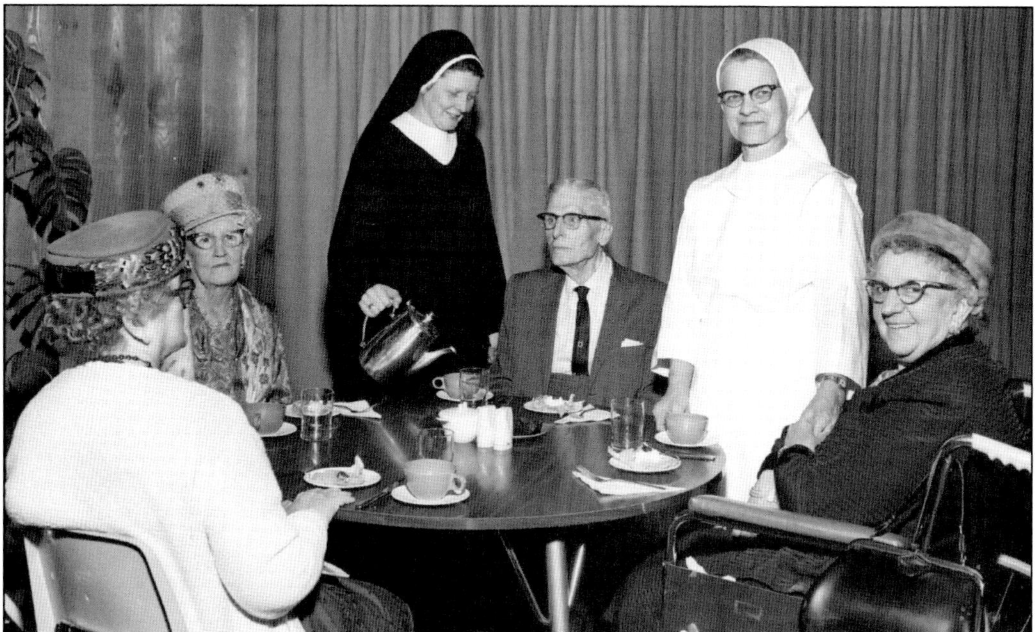

The residents of Madonna Manor enjoyed interacting with each other, as well as the sisters. This early-1970s photograph shows, from left to right, Mrs. Ollie Brennan, Mrs. and Mr. Frank Hauser, Mrs. John Bender, Sister Charles (pouring), and Sister Joseph (white) enjoying dinner at Madonna Manor. (Courtesy of Kenton County Public Library.)

Three

Laying the Streets and Creating the Subdivisions

Up until the mid-1950s, the area that is now called Villa Hills was made up of the patchwork quilt of farms and the land belonging to the Sisters of St. Walburg. There were no businesses and just a few roads. All that began to change with the development of the Boh farm, which spanned the area that is now Kenridge and Sunglow Drives. As houses began to be built and young families moved in, the residents started talking about forming a city. This chapter shows photographs of streets being created, homes being built, and sometimes land that was about to be forever changed from a farm to a subdivision. Also included are real documents that illustrate Villa Hills's humble beginnings. Announcements about incorporation meetings, the first *Voice of Villa Hills* newspaper, and even House Bill 410, which made Villa Hills a sixth-class city, are all included. These documents, although they are not photographs, tell the story too. Be sure to look closely at the photographs, looking beyond what appears to be the subject. It is sometimes the landscape or a home in the background that will show where the photograph was taken, or what is on that location currently.

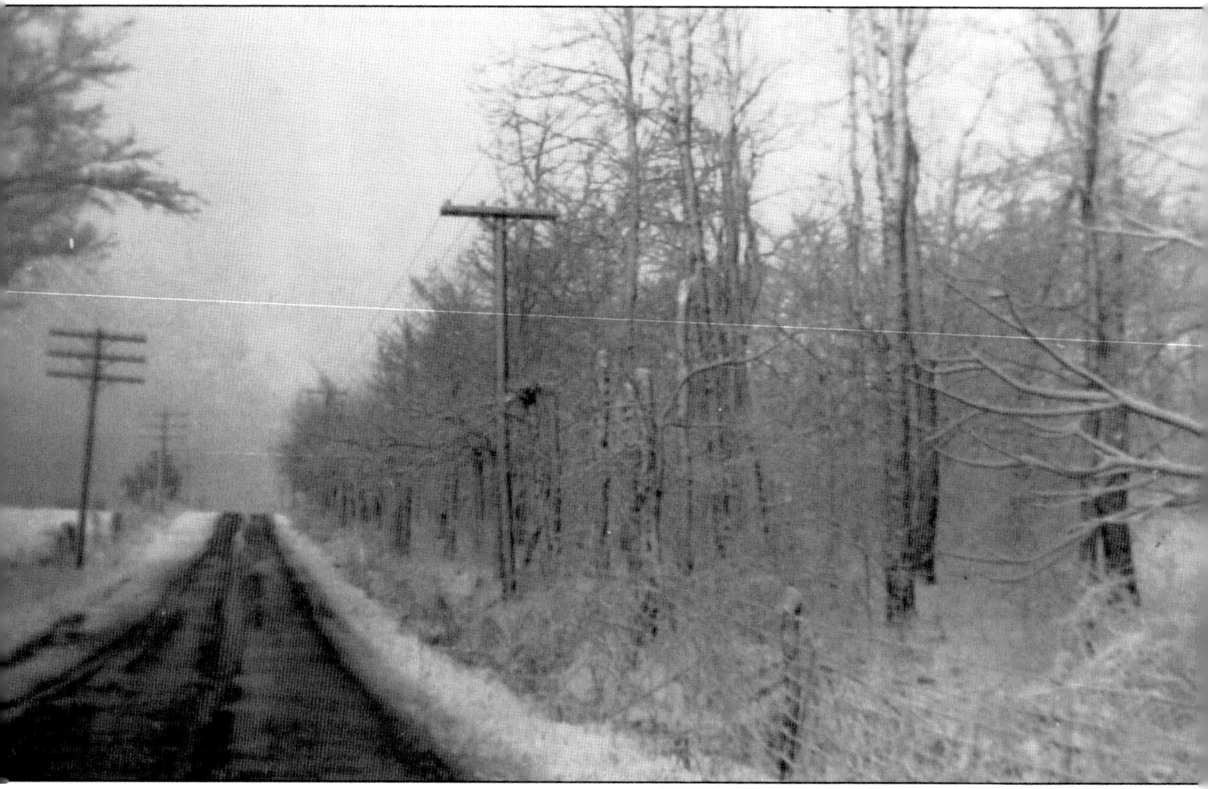

This 1939 photograph was taken in the middle of a snowy Collins Road. The photographer was standing in the area of what is now Cecilia Drive looking north toward Amsterdam Road. Collins Road was originally very narrow and made up of a series of small hills, which was hard on cars but fun for kids on bikes. The road was built by and named for the Collins family who resided on 86 acres on Amsterdam Road, which became Villa Madonna in 1903. (Courtesy of Julie Kremer.)

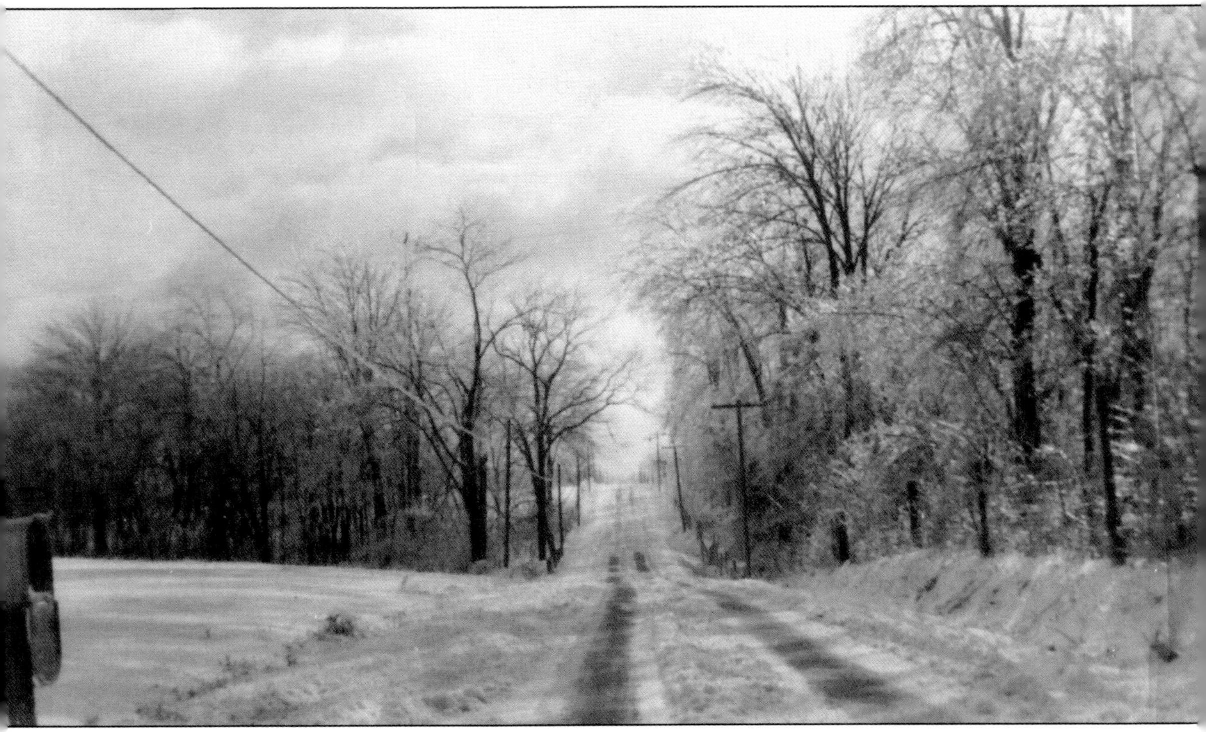

Looking south on Collins Road toward Crescent Springs, this photograph was taken near what is now the intersection of Ann Street and Collins Road. The mailbox on the left belonged to the Felice family, who lived at 902 Collins Road. This photograph was taken in January 1951. The photographer had no trouble standing in the middle of Collins Road, as just a few cars passed each day. (Courtesy of the Felice family.)

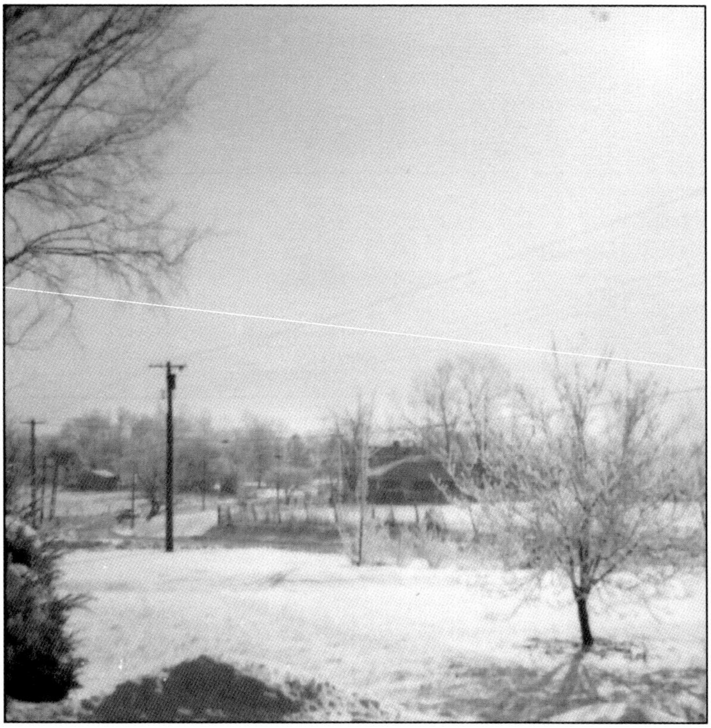

This photograph from the winter of 1964 was taken from the Lohre home at 2518 Buttermilk Pike, looking toward the intersection of Western Reserve and Buttermilk Pike. (Courtesy of Barb Lohre Cooney.)

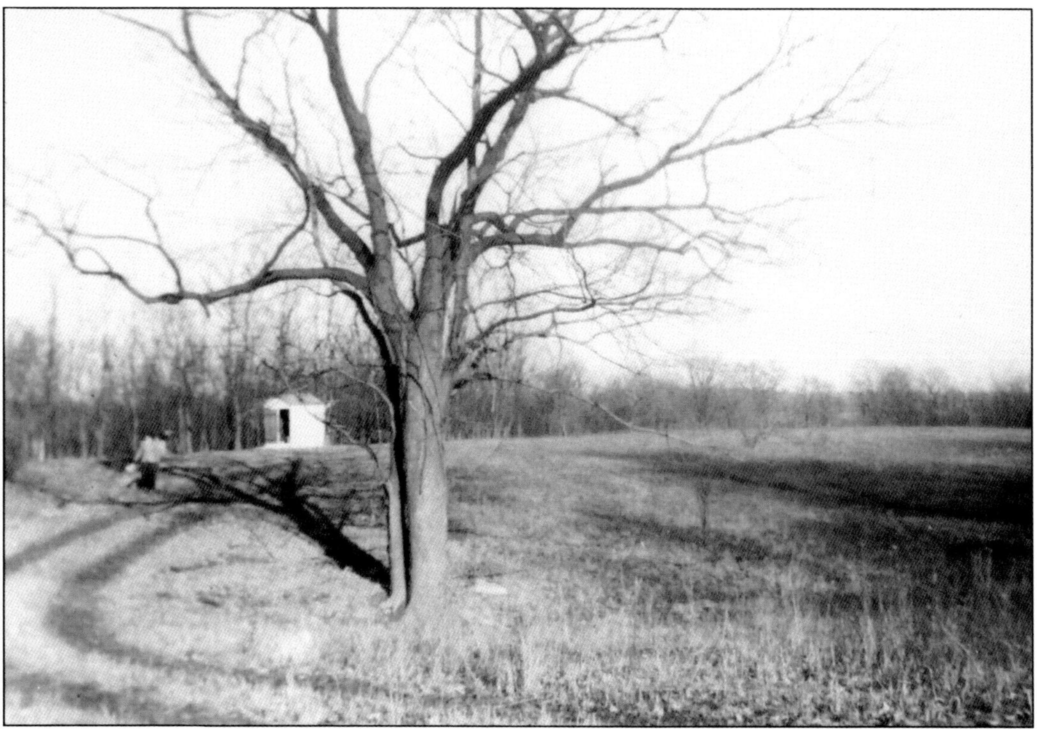

The Felice family owned this lot at 902 Collins Road and planned to build a home there. The lot, shown here in 1946, sits across the street from what is now the intersection of Collins Road and Ann Street. (Courtesy of the Felice family.)

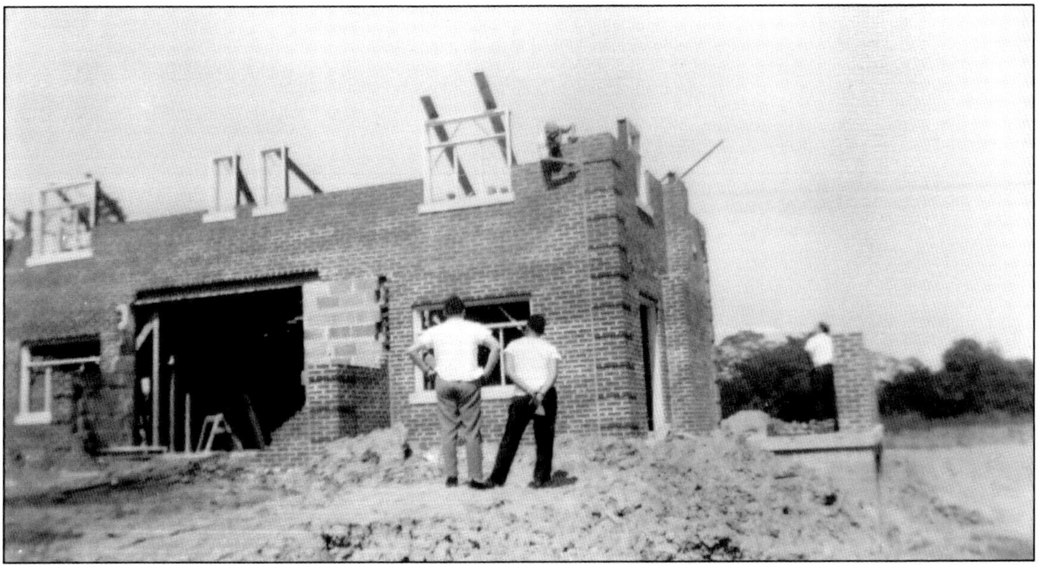

August Felice purchased a 60-acre farm along Collins and Amsterdam Roads in the late 1800s. His grandson Louis kept 10 acres at the south end of the property to build his home at 902 Collins Road. (Courtesy of the Felice family.)

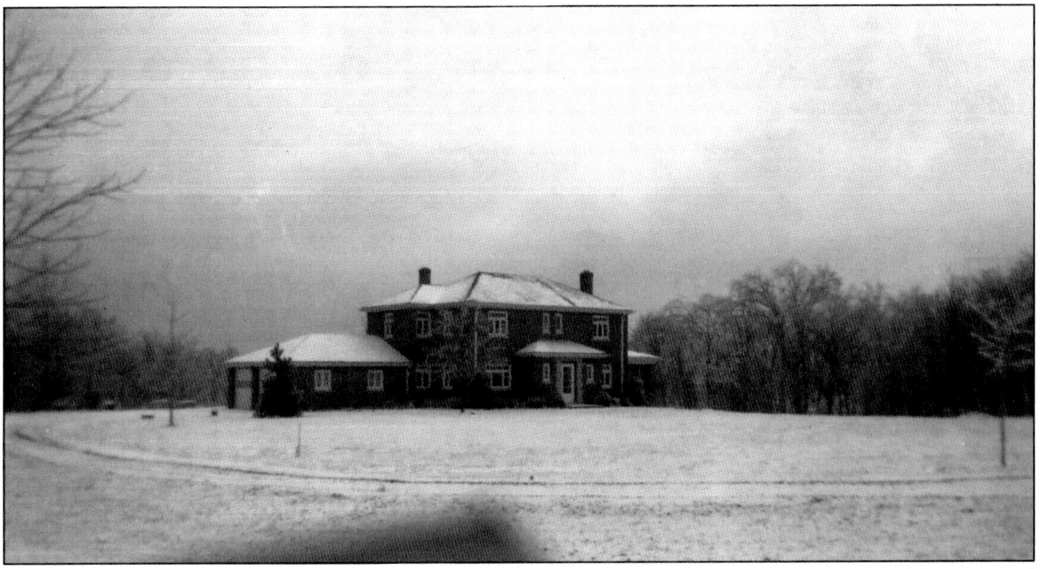

The home of Louis Felice was completed in the late 1940s. It sits on the last 10 acres of the original Felice property. The Felice family did not farm this land but did raise chickens and ducks so that they could have fresh eggs. (Courtesy of the Felice family.)

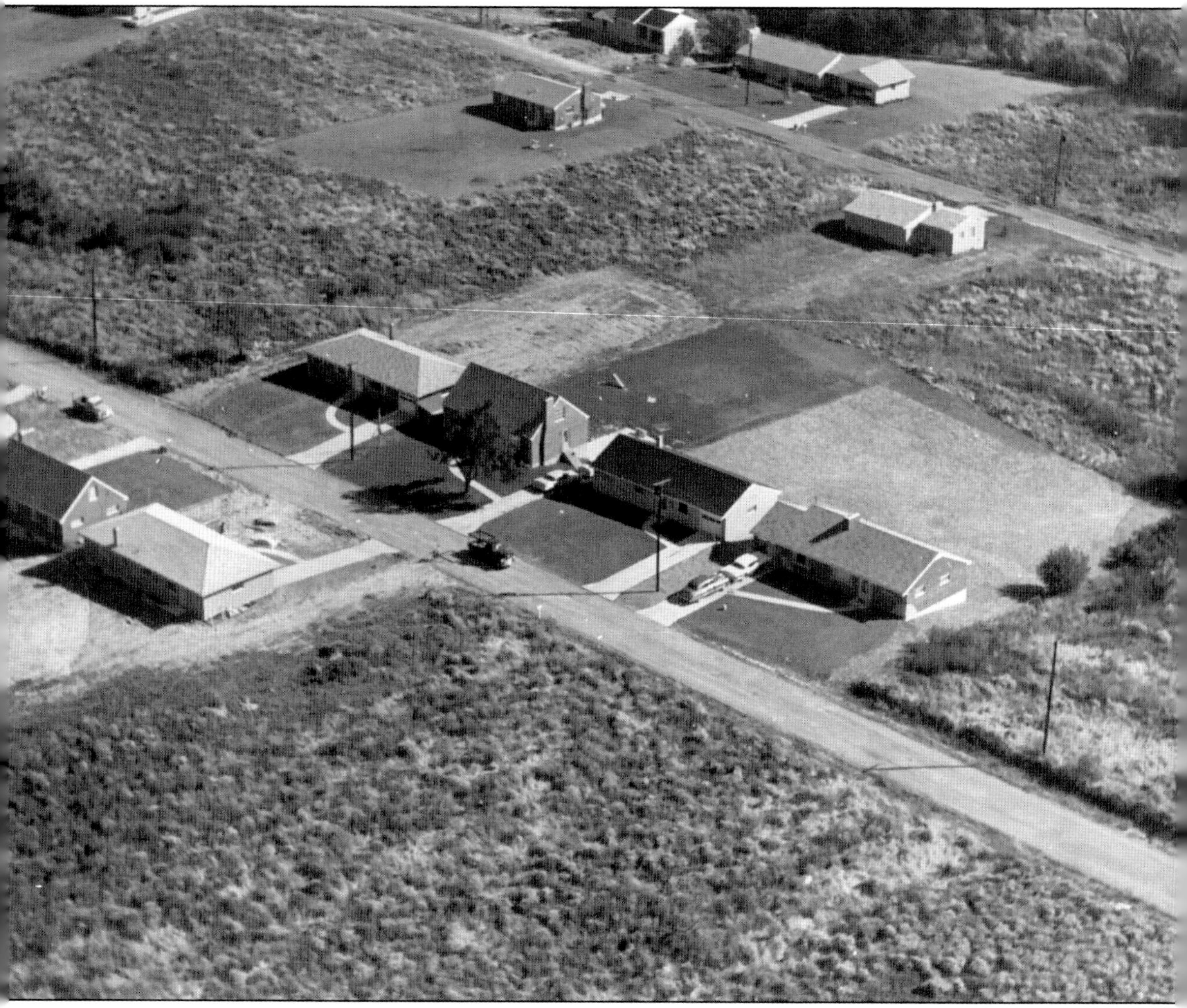

This aerial photograph, taken October 4, 1958, shows Kenridge (bottom) and Sunglow Drives, near Buttermilk Pike. The streets were originally the site of the Boh farm. This original neighborhood was referred to as Madonna Acres. Most of the homes on Kenridge Drive were built by Bill Krumpelman and were sold for under $20,000. (Courtesy of the William Schulte family.)

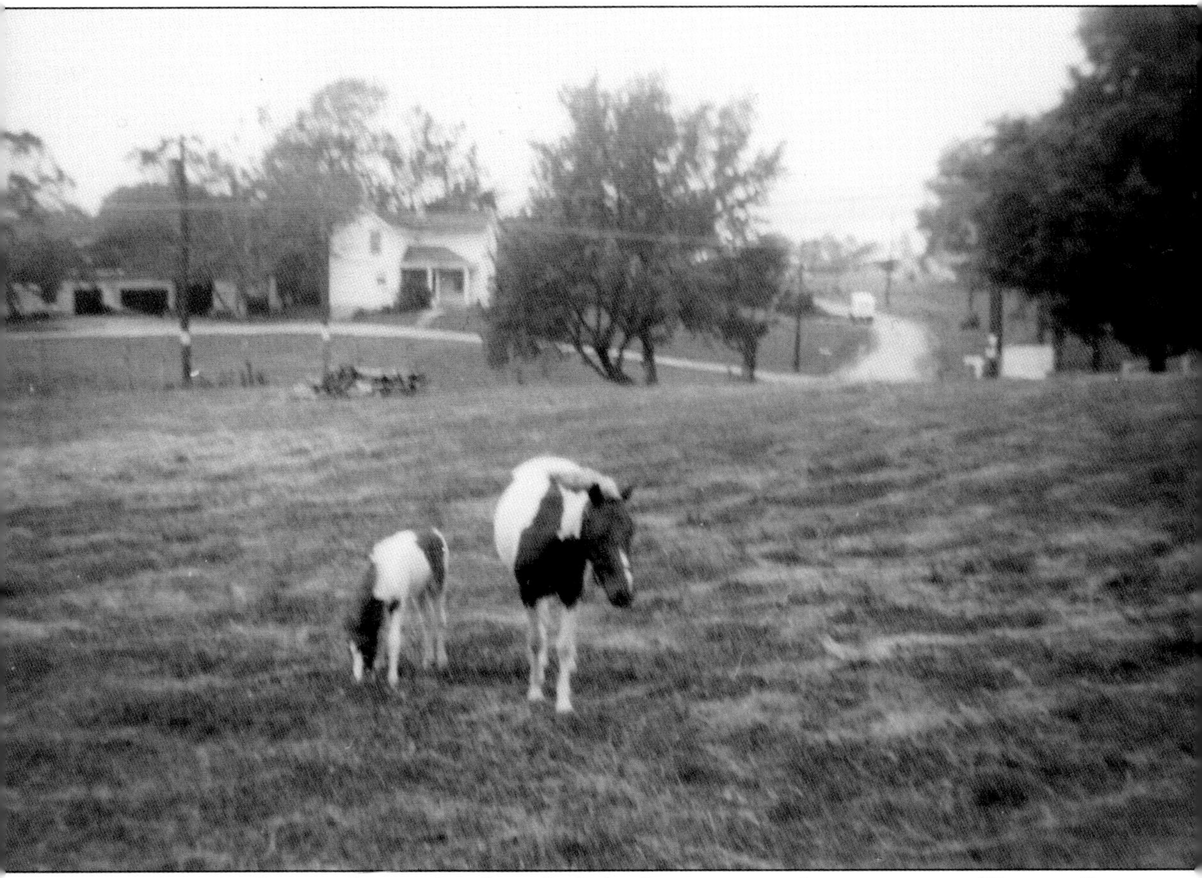

This early-1960s photograph was taken from the Eubanks property at the intersection of Buttermilk Pike, Western Reserve, and Collins Road. The camera is looking into the entrance of Villa Hills. In the distance, a milk truck can be seen traveling up the hill into Villa Hills. So many dairies in the area had to travel the bumpy old road, it was reported that when the milk reached its destination, it had been shaken so much that it had transformed to buttermilk, which is how the street got its name. (Courtesy of Gayle Niewahner Starks.)

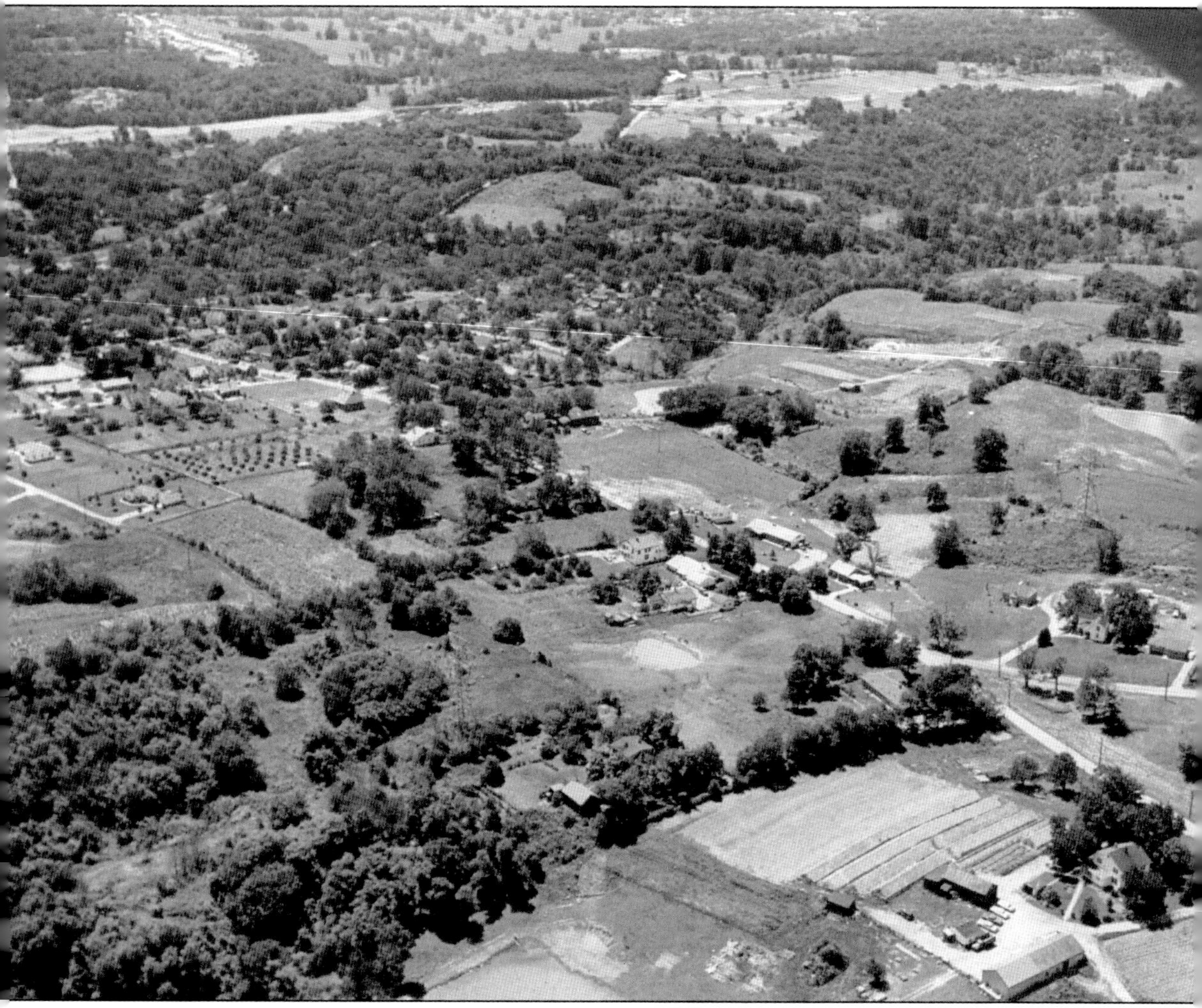

This aerial photograph from 1960 is looking toward Villa Hills and Crescent Springs. At lower right, Collins Road runs to the right of the farm and intersects with Buttermilk Pike on the right. Collins Road then turns into Western Reserve. Present-day Buttermilk Pike, which now bisects Crescent Springs, was not built yet. Also in this photograph, the dead-end street on the left is Overlook Drive in Crescent Springs. Running from left to right across the top is Interstate 75, which was under construction. (Courtesy of Gayle Niewahner Starks.)

In early 1962, residents were afraid of annexation by Crescent Springs or Covington. So the board of directors called a special meeting of officers and directors to decide what the small community was going to do. The four options were the following: "annexation to Crescent Springs, annexation to Covington, incorporation of our area, or stay as we are." (Courtesy of Randy Nolting.)

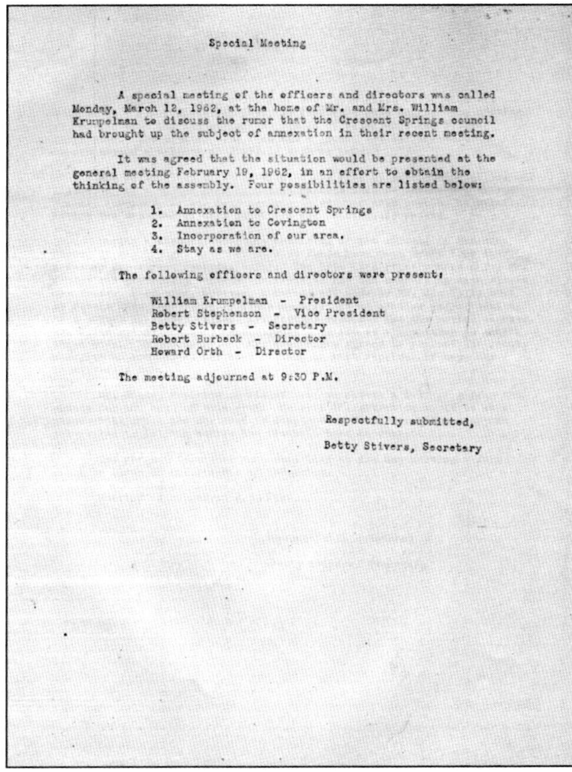

Special Meeting

A special meeting of the officers and directors was called Monday, March 12, 1962, at the home of Mr. and Mrs. William Krumpelman to discuss the rumor that the Crescent Springs council had brought up the subject of annexation in their recent meeting.

It was agreed that the situation would be presented at the general meeting February 19, 1962, in an effort to obtain the thinking of the assembly. Four possibilities are listed below:

1. Annexation to Crescent Springs
2. Annexation to Covington
3. Incorporation of our area.
4. Stay as we are.

The following officers and directors were present:

William Krumpelman - President
Robert Stephenson - Vice President
Betty Stivers - Secretary
Robert Burbeck - Director
Howard Orth - Director

The meeting adjourned at 9:30 P.M.

Respectfully submitted,

Betty Stivers, Secretary

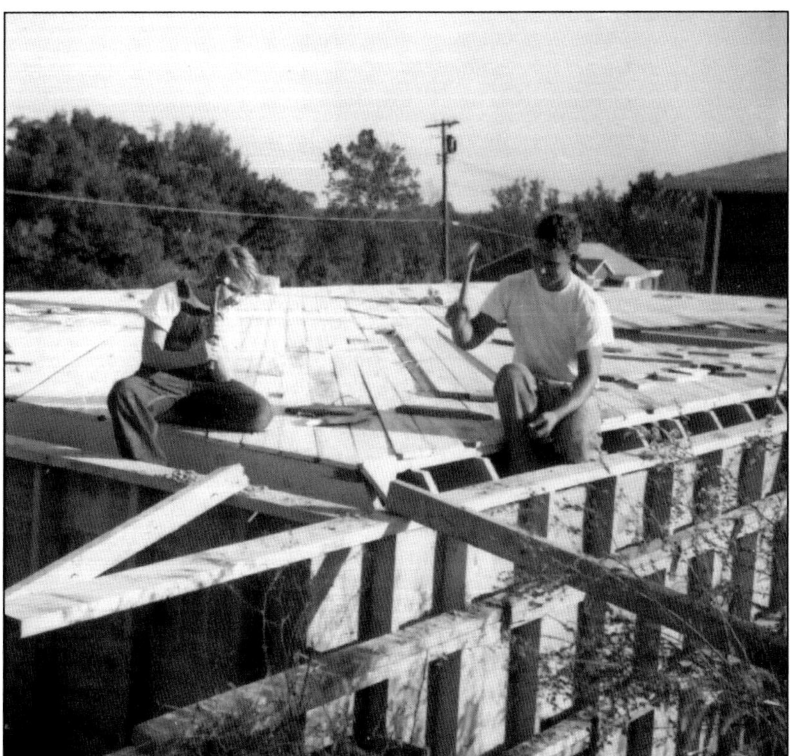

From left to right, Tim and Joe Spille are pictured building their new home at 931 Sunglow Drive. The house, which sits near the corner of Sunglow Drive and Amsterdam Road, was completed in 1956. After he had built his own house, Joe Spille went on to build many others in Villa Hills. (Courtesy of Mr. and Mrs. Joseph Spille.)

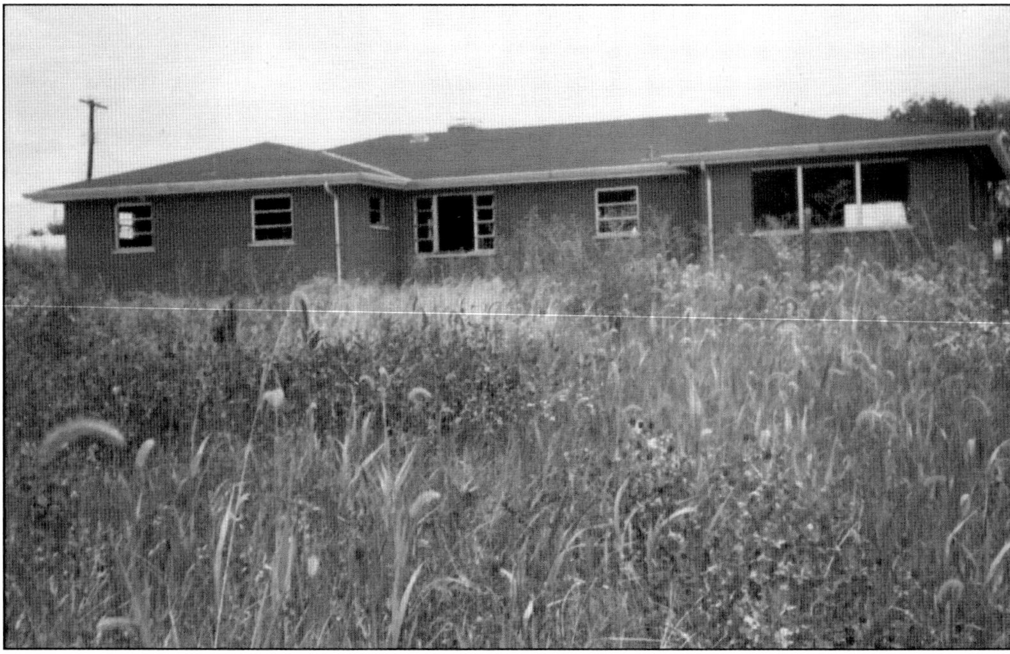

Construction was well underway on the Joseph Foltz home at 904 Sunglow Drive in this 1957 photograph. This house was built by Joe Sanders. (Courtesy of Joseph Foltz.)

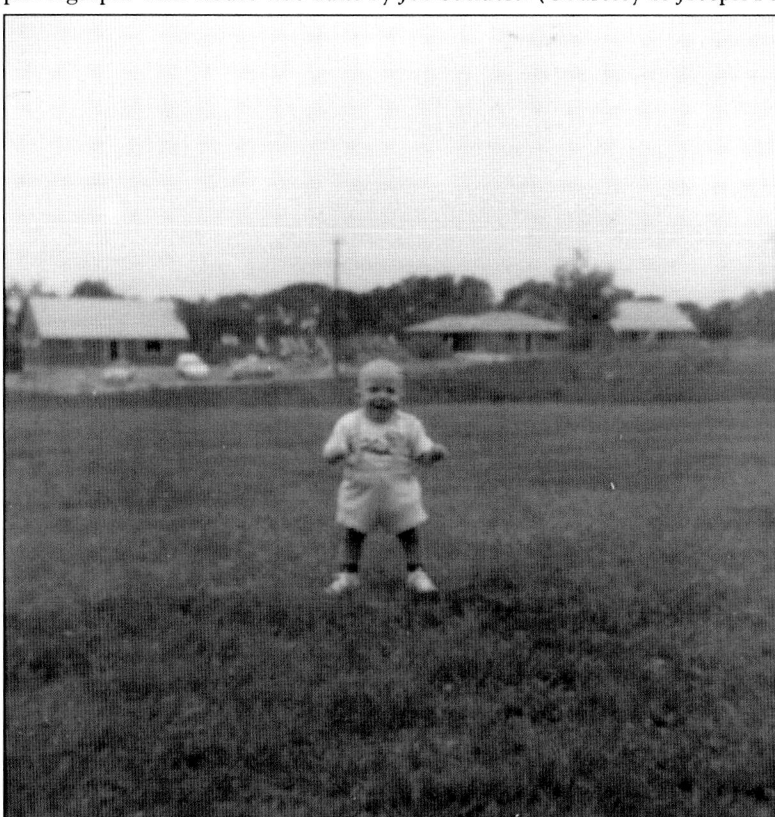

In this 1958 photograph, tiny Gerry Foltz was standing in the backyard of the Foltz home at 904 Sunglow Drive. In the background, houses built on the western side of Kenridge Drive can be seen. (Courtesy of Joseph Foltz.)

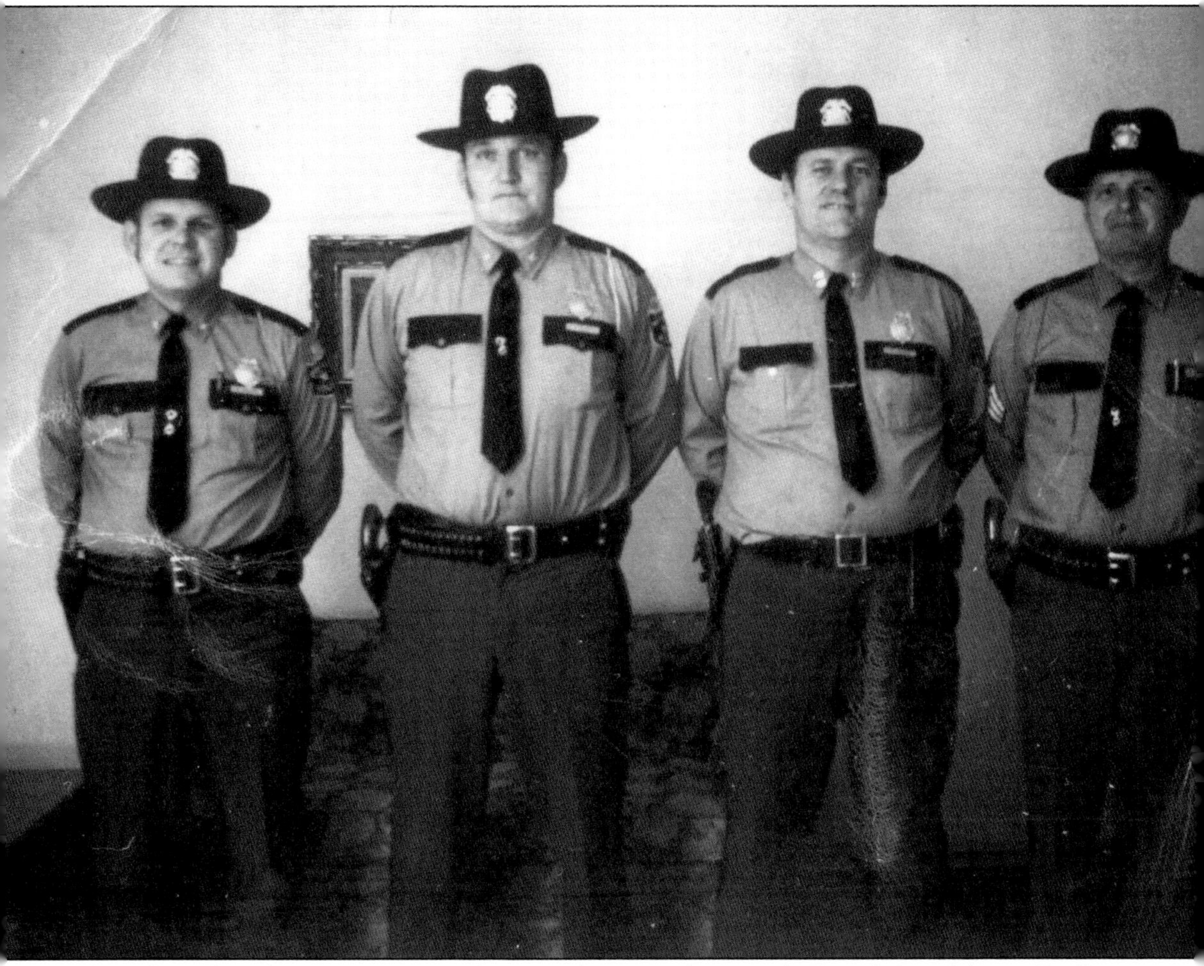

The Villa Hills Police Department is shown in this 1973 photograph. From left to right are Estille Burdette, Bob Huesman, Harry Long, and Ron Bising. The police department started out with one marshal and one deputy, who both used their own cars for patrol duty. (Courtesy Bob and Pat Huesman.)

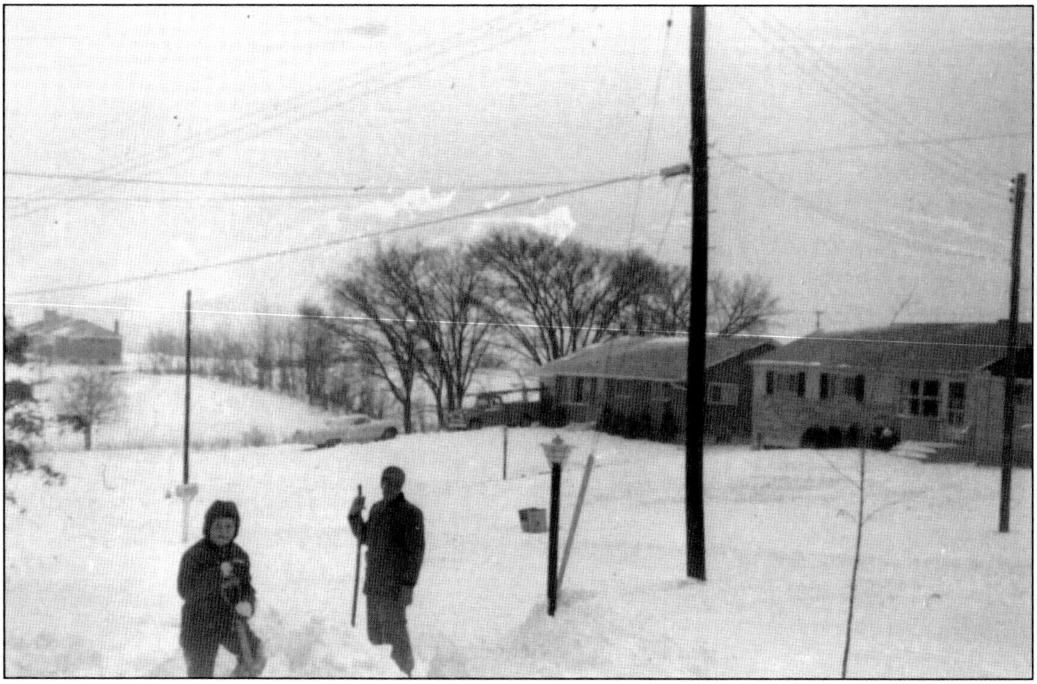

From left to right, Tim and Joe Spille shovel out their drive after a big snowfall in the early 1960s. It is a good thing they had shovels, because the young City of Villa Hills did not have much snowplow equipment until 1968. Prior to that, neighbors typically shoveled the street in front of their home, or resident Joe Franzen, who had a tractor and snowplow, would drive through the streets plowing what he could. (Courtesy of Mr. and Mrs. Joseph Spille.)

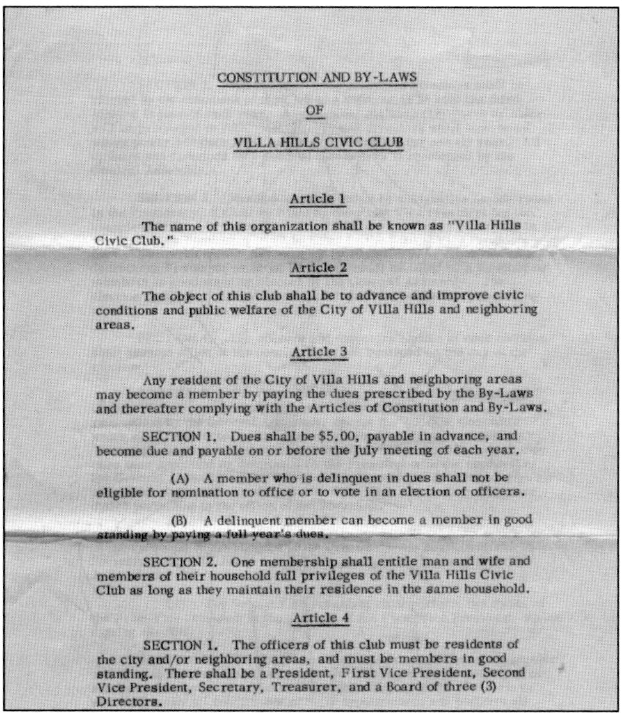

CONSTITUTION AND BY-LAWS

OF

VILLA HILLS CIVIC CLUB

Article 1

The name of this organization shall be known as "Villa Hills Civic Club."

Article 2

The object of this club shall be to advance and improve civic conditions and public welfare of the City of Villa Hills and neighboring areas.

Article 3

Any resident of the City of Villa Hills and neighboring areas may become a member by paying the dues prescribed by the By-Laws and thereafter complying with the Articles of Constitution and By-Laws.

SECTION 1. Dues shall be $5.00, payable in advance, and become due and payable on or before the July meeting of each year.

(A) A member who is delinquent in dues shall not be eligible for nomination to office or to vote in an election of officers.

(B) A delinquent member can become a member in good standing by paying a full year's dues.

SECTION 2. One membership shall entitle man and wife and members of their household full privileges of the Villa Hills Civic Club as long as they maintain their residence in the same household.

Article 4

SECTION 1. The officers of this club must be residents of the city and/or neighboring areas, and must be members in good standing. There shall be a President, First Vice President, Second Vice President, Secretary, Treasurer, and a Board of three (3) Directors.

The Villa Hills Civic Club was established in 1961, with 38 residents attending the first meeting, which was held at the home of William Krumpelman. Seen here are the bylaws of the Villa Hills Civic Club. The initial goal of the group was to repair streets, erect street signs, and create a playground for children. (Courtesy of Randy Nolting.)

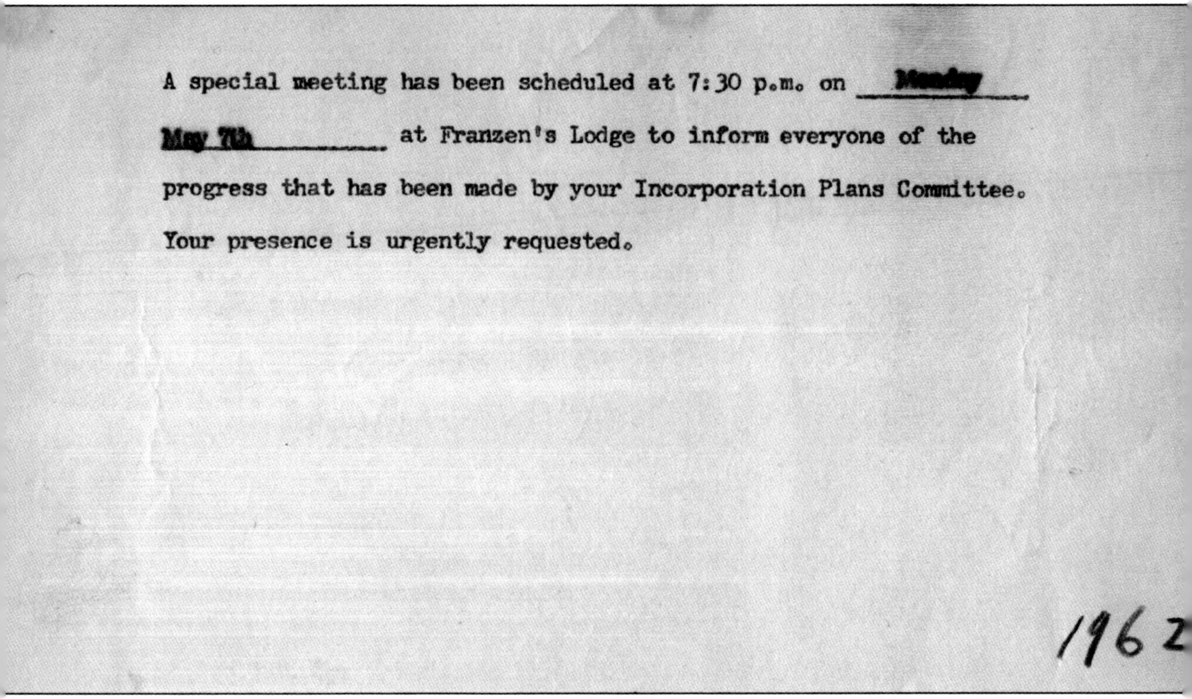

A special meeting has been scheduled at 7:30 p.m. on Monday May 7th at Franzen's Lodge to inform everyone of the progress that has been made by your Incorporation Plans Committee. Your presence is urgently requested.

1962

By May 1962, residents had created an Incorporation Plans Committee to pursue the goal of incorporating as a city. This notice was sent out to all residents, inviting them to come hear the progress. On June 7, 1962, Villa Hills became a sixth-class city. (Courtesy of Randy Nolting.)

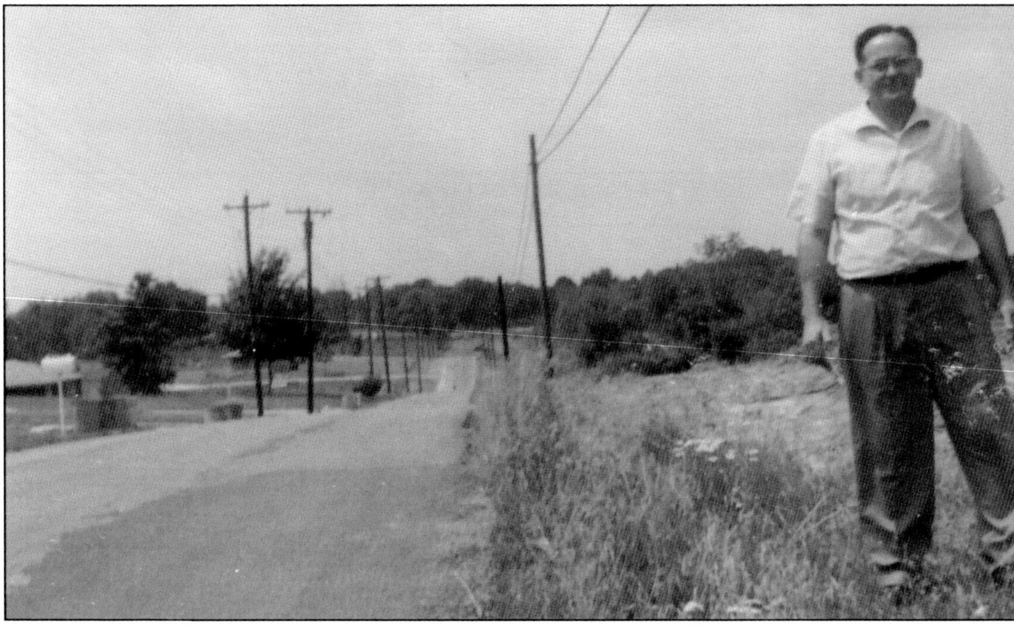

In 1964, the bumpy Collins Road was about to be flattened out, widened, and straightened. Louis P. Felice stands in front of his home on Collins Road, near the intersection of Ann Street. The photograph above is looking toward Amsterdam Road. In the photograph below, Felice is standing next to his driveway, and the camera is facing south on Collins Road toward Crescent Springs. Notice that there were very few homes on Collins Road in 1964. (Courtesy of the Felice family.)

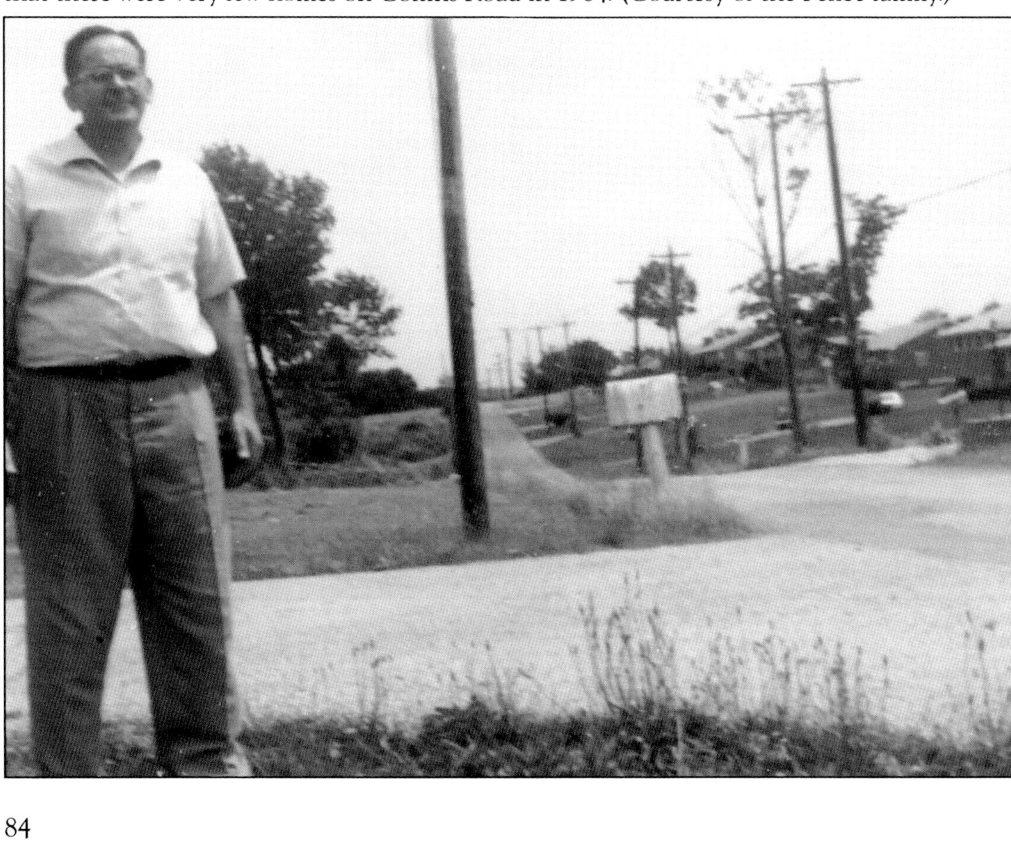

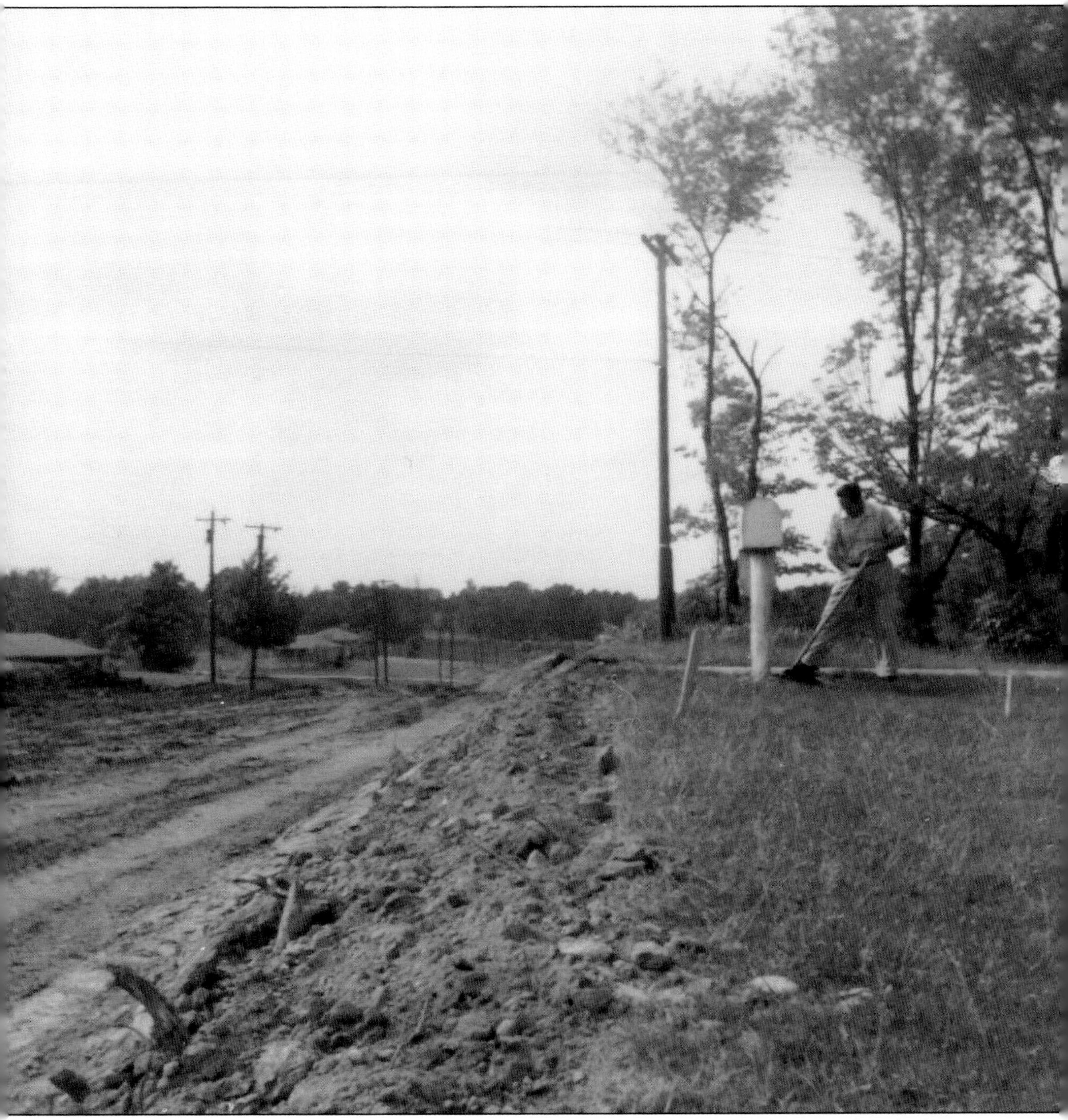

Construction of the new Collins Road was well underway in this 1965 photograph, which was taken near the intersection of Ann Street. Louis Felice is shown moving his mailbox at 902 Collins Road. This photograph is looking north toward Amsterdam Road. (Courtesy of the Felice family.)

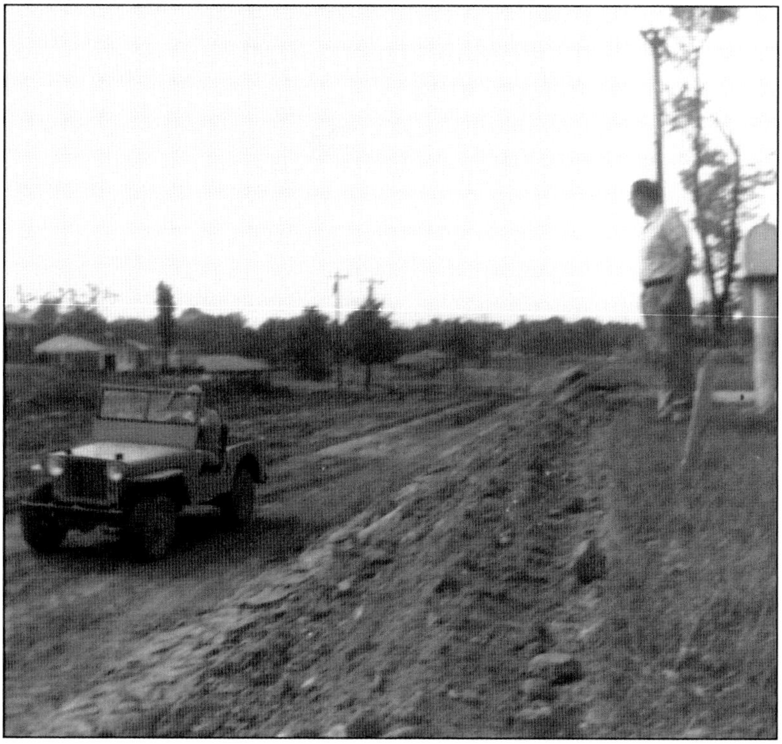

In 1965, Louis Felice stands near his mailbox at 902 Collins Road as someone in a Jeep drives by. Collins Road was named for the Collins Family, who resided on what is now the property of Villa Madonna Academy. Everyone called the road Collin's road, and it stuck. (Courtesy of the Felice family.)

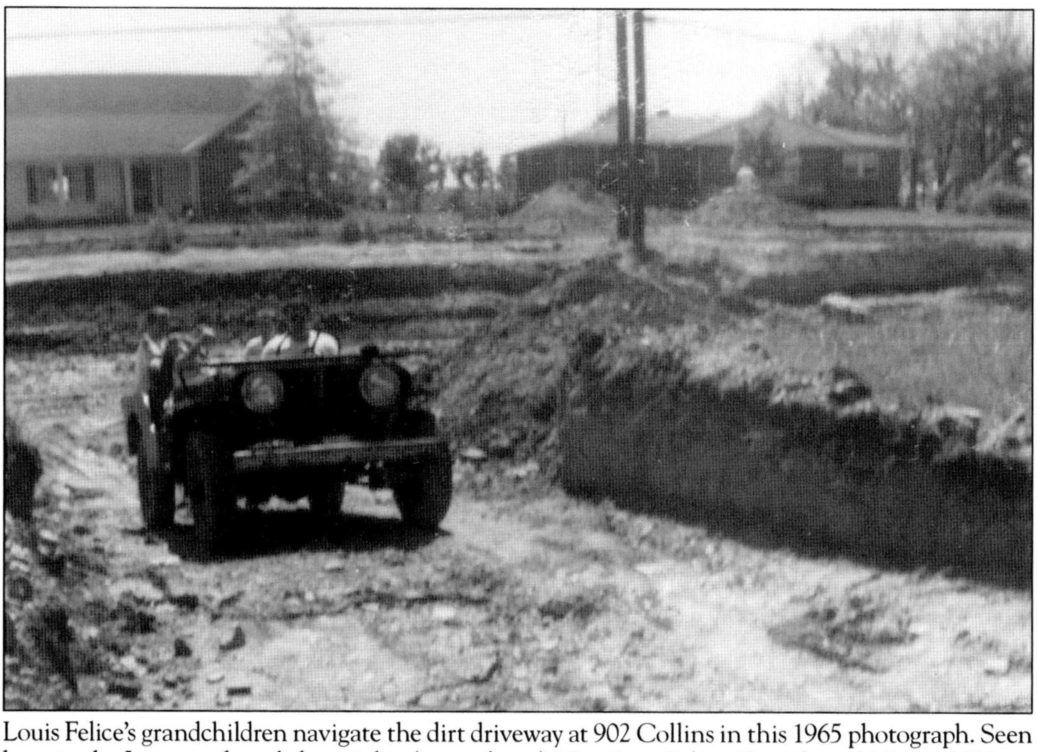

Louis Felice's grandchildren navigate the dirt driveway at 902 Collins in this 1965 photograph. Seen here in the Jeep are, from left to right, (second row) Mary Lou Felice Crouch and Michael Felice; (first row) Susan Felice Gasdorf Wood and Louis Felice Jr. (Courtesy of the Felice family.)

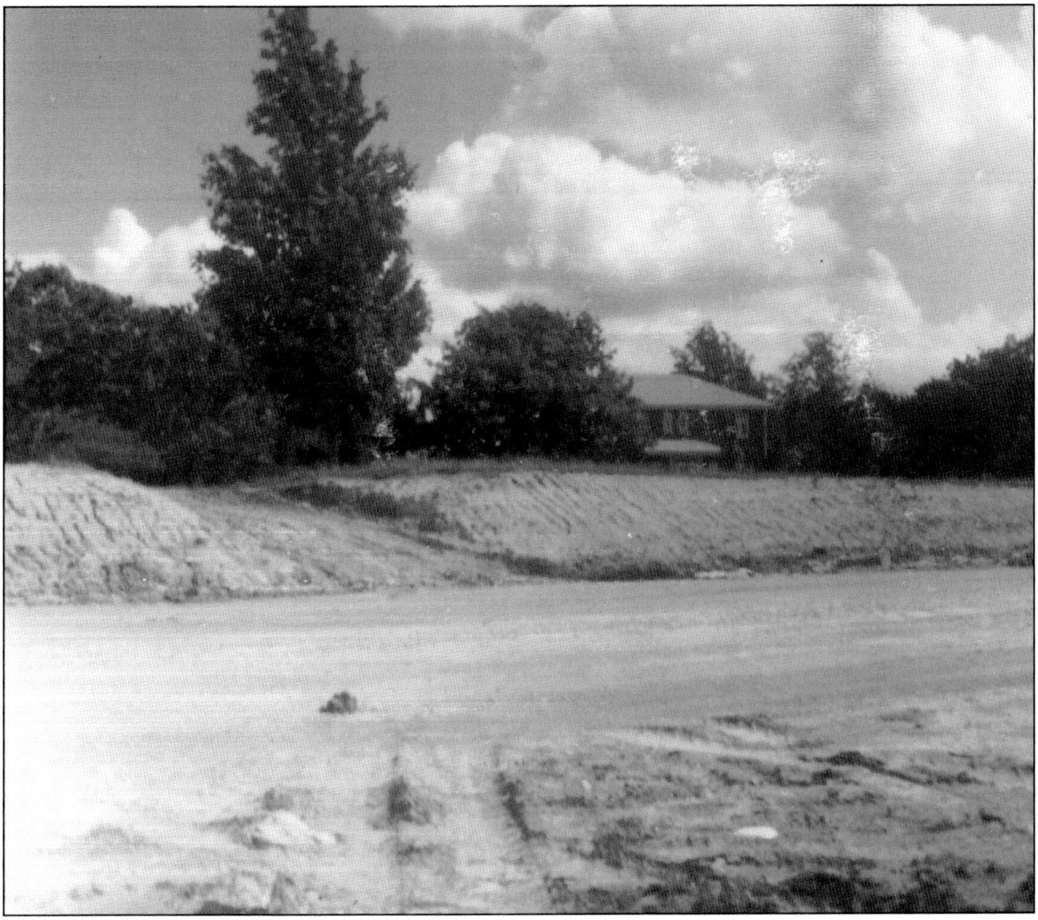

As the construction of a new Collins Road progressed, residents along the road were faced with huge piles of dirt in their front yards. In this 1965 photograph, taken from the intersection of Ann Street and Collins Road, the Felice home at 902 Collins appears to be buried behind the dirt mountains. (Courtesy of the Felice family.)

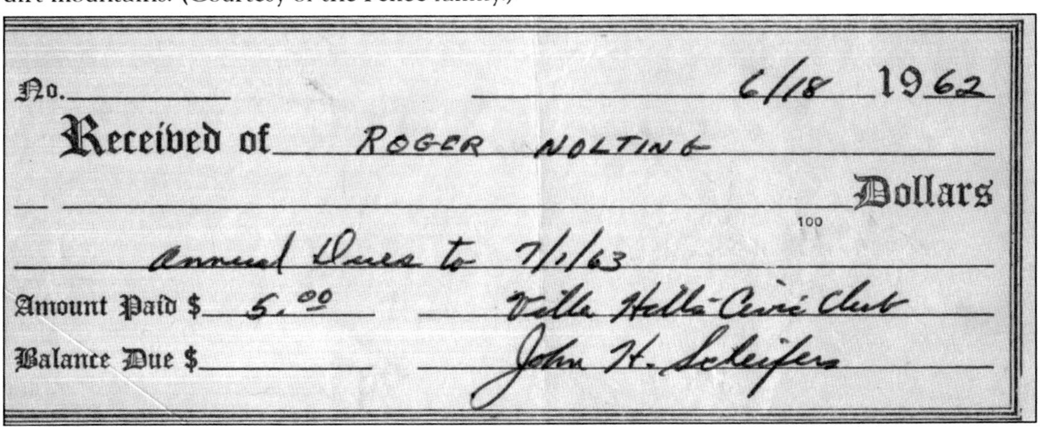

No. ______ 6/18 1962

Received of ROGER NOLTING

______ Dollars
100

Annual Dues to 7/1/63

Amount Paid $ 5.00 Villa Hills Civic Club

Balance Due $ ______ John H. Schleifers

As stated in the bylaws, a family membership to the Villa Hills Civic Club was $5. This receipt belonged to Roger Nolting, who had paid his annual dues in 1962. Nolting, who lived on Frank Street, was very active in the city and the Civic Club. (Courtesy of Randy Nolting.)

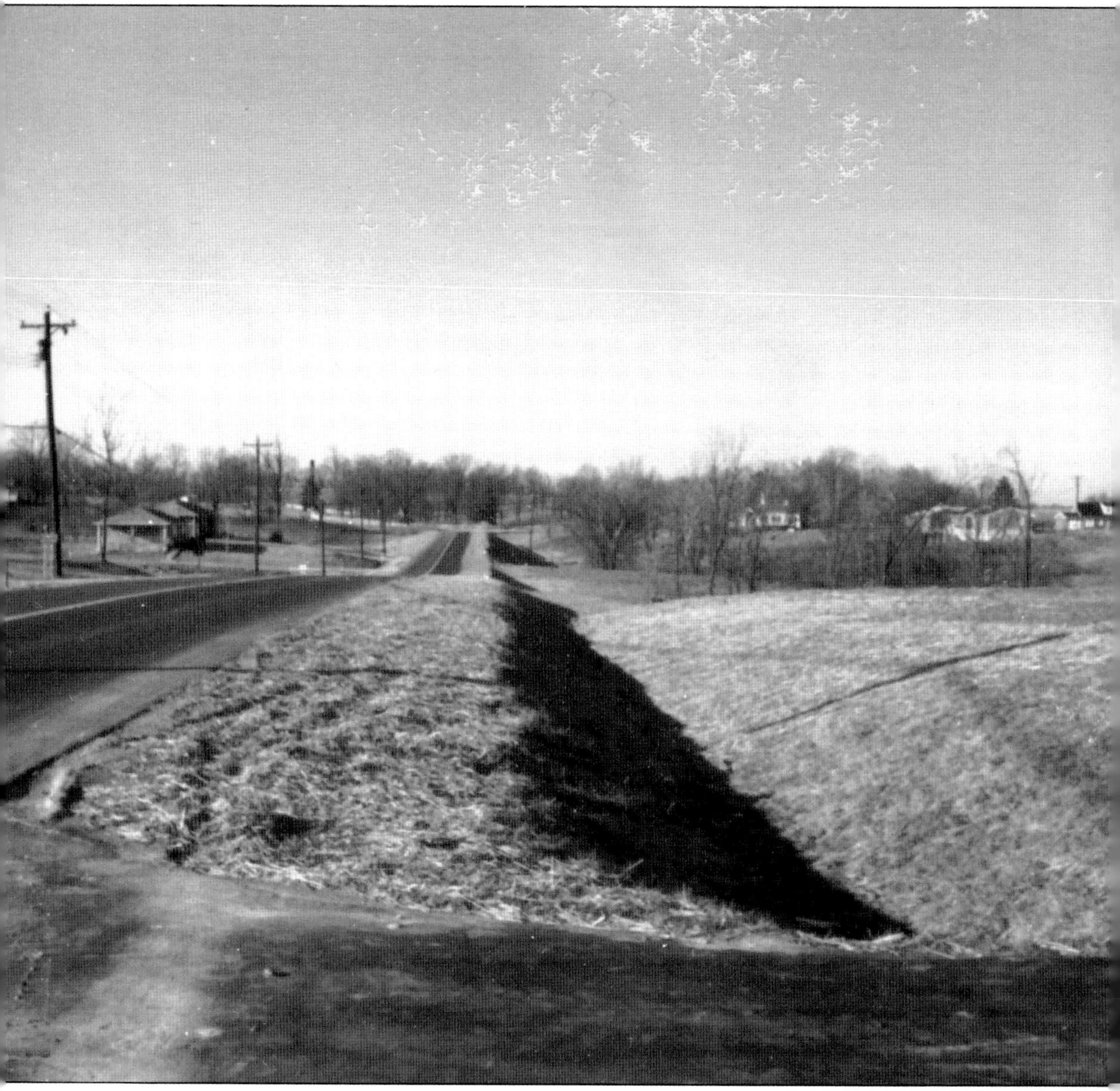

The new straighter, wider, and flatter Collins Road was finally completed around 1965. In this photograph, which is looking north, the location where Collins Road dead-ends into Amsterdam can be seen. To the right are the beginnings of the Villa Heights neighborhood along Villa Drive. (Courtesy of the Felice family.)

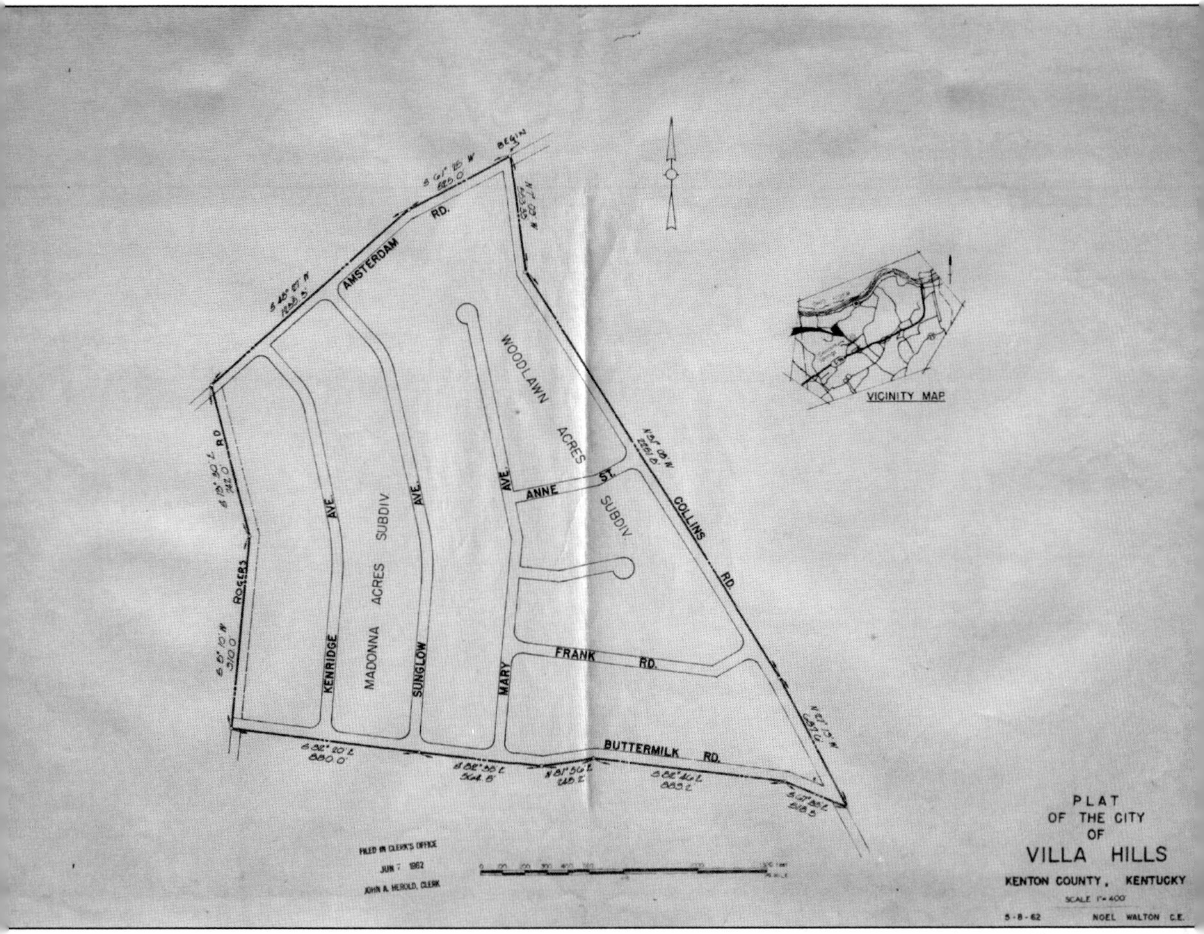

Here is the official plat of the City of Villa Hills as filed in the Kenton County clerk's office in June 1962. The new city was made up of the Madonna Acres and Woodlawn Acres subdivisions. The city was bounded by Amsterdam, Collins, Rogers, and Buttermilk Roads. The Boh farm originally covered the approximate area of Rogers Road, Kenridge Drive, and Sunglow Drive. The Schreck-Lowry farm originally covered what are now Mary, Frank, and Ann Streets and Rardin Court. (Courtesy of Randy Nolting.)

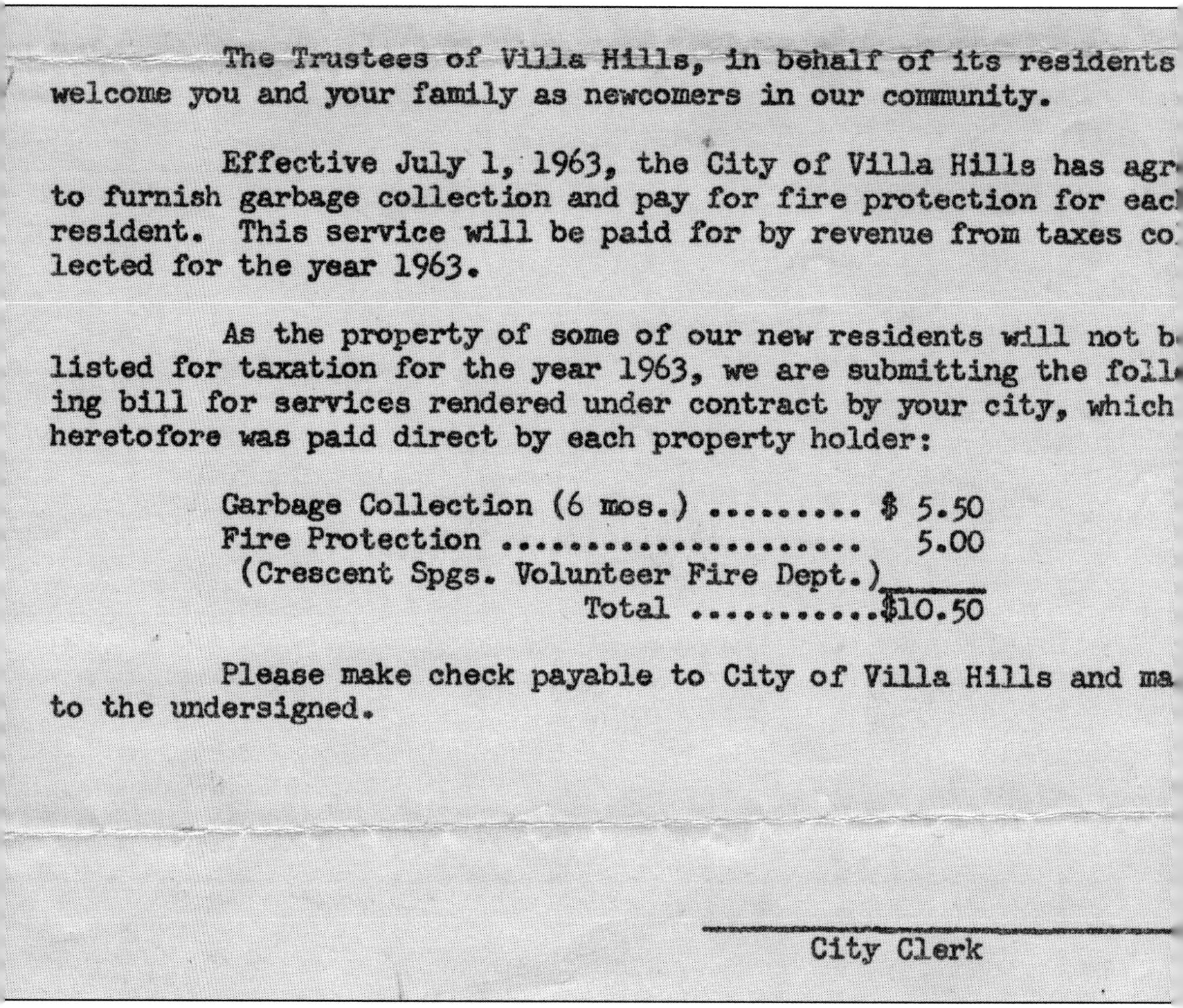

The Trustees of Villa Hills, in behalf of its residents welcome you and your family as newcomers in our community.

Effective July 1, 1963, the City of Villa Hills has agr to furnish garbage collection and pay for fire protection for eac resident. This service will be paid for by revenue from taxes co lected for the year 1963.

As the property of some of our new residents will not b listed for taxation for the year 1963, we are submitting the foll ing bill for services rendered under contract by your city, which heretofore was paid direct by each property holder:

Garbage Collection (6 mos.) .... $ 5.50
Fire Protection 5.00
(Crescent Spgs. Volunteer Fire Dept.)
Total $10.50

Please make check payable to City of Villa Hills and ma to the undersigned.

City Clerk

In July 1963, the City of Villa Hills began charging residents for weekly garbage collection and fire protection. Garbage collection was $11 per year. Fire protection was provided by the Crescent Springs Volunteer Fire Department, of which many Villa Hills residents were members. (Courtesy of Randy Nolting.)

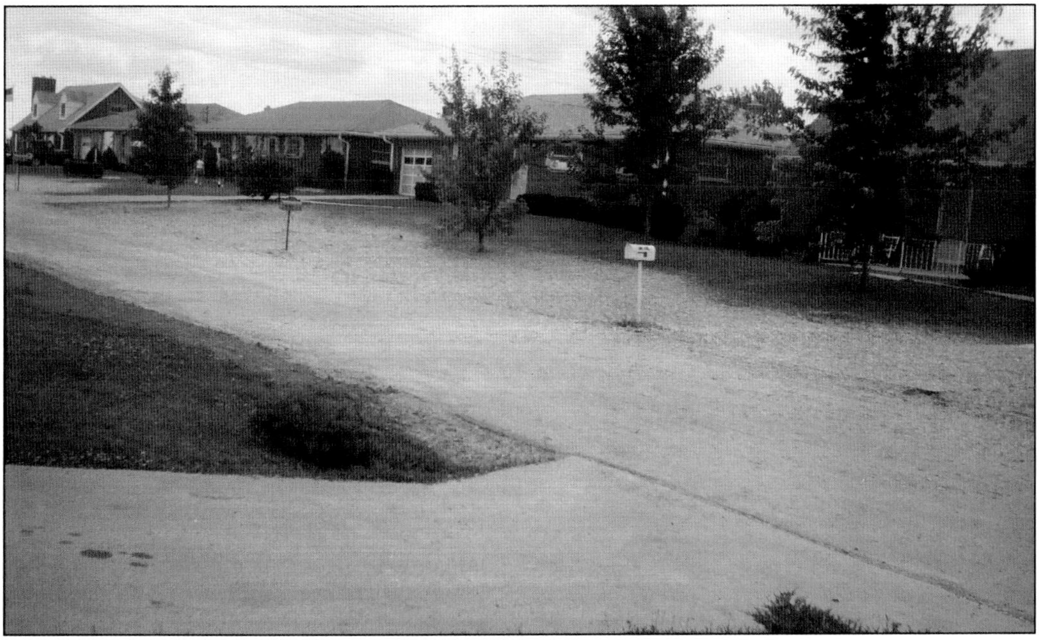

In the early years of development, residents used septic tanks for sanitation needs. City planners recognized that underground sanitary sewers were the key to development and growth. With the help of Kenton County Sanitation District, plans were drawn up, a bonding company was retained, and O'Dell Construction Company was selected to complete the project. The sewers were installed in 1966 and 1967, and 290 homes originally tapped into the system. These 1967 photographs show the grass along Kenridge Drive being reseeded after the sewer pipes had been installed. The above photograph is facing toward Buttermilk Pike. The below photograph is looking toward the direction of Amsterdam Road. (Courtesy of Paul and Peg Kohl.)

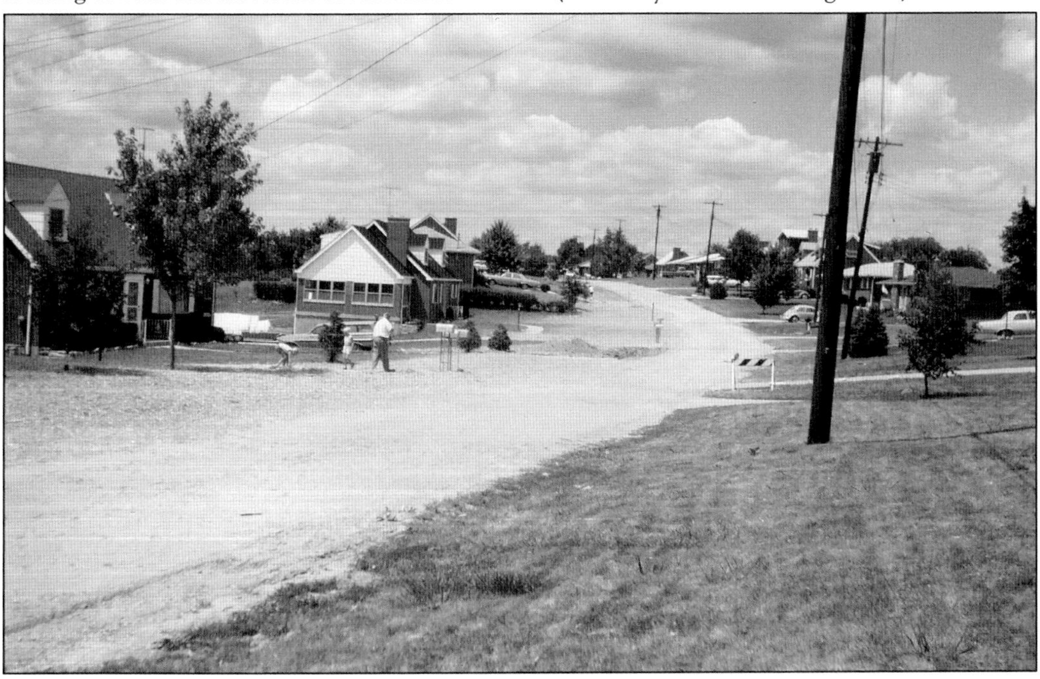

July 1966.

To: The Citizens of Villa Hills

The City of Villa Hills has entered into a contract with the Odell Construction Company for a sanitary sewer collector system. Construction will begin very soon.

Undoubtedly some problems and inconveniences will be encountered. We ask your patience and cooperation during this construction period. Please, for their own safety and welfare, keep your children away from construction sites.

Any legitimate or just complaint will be handled by Mr. Art Brummer, a member of the Board of Trustees.

Thanking you in advance for your full cooperation,

The Board of Trustees
City of Villa Hills

The long-awaited sewer system construction project was about to begin in July 1966. This letter was sent out to residents informing them of the process. This was a lengthy project, and many residents remember that on Halloween of that year trick-or-treat was held during daylight hours, so no children would fall in the trenches dug for the sewer installation. (Courtesy of Randy Nolting.)

CITY OF VILLA HILLS
DISBURSEMENTS
FOR THE YEAR ENDED DECEMBER 31, 1964

Advertising		$ 419.36
Trash Collection		2,196.00
Legal Fees		750.00
Clerk's Fees		420.00
Supplies		69.95
Insurance		25.97
Inspector's Fees		103.37
Engineer's Fees (Contracted June 2, 1962)		206.50
Fire Protection		1,020.00
Rental on Hall (7 Mos.)		35.00
Traveling Expense to Atlanta, Ga.		175.00
Equipment		30.90
Street Repair		480.00
Police Patrol Supplies		138.26
Miscellaneous		285.17
		$ 6,355.48
Cash Balance, December 31, 1964		
Community Bank	$ 833.40	
Crescent Springs Bldg.	5,678.56	
		6,511.96
TOTAL		$12,867.44

Even a small city has expenses, and according to this list, the City of Villa Hills spent $6,255.48 in 1964. According to the meeting no. 28 minutes, R. Loomis, city engineer, and J. G. Osborn, city attorney, had to go to Atlanta (shown here as "Traveling Expense to Atlanta") to present the application for a loan from the Housing and Home Finance Agency to pay for the city's sewer system. (Courtesy of Randy Nolting.)

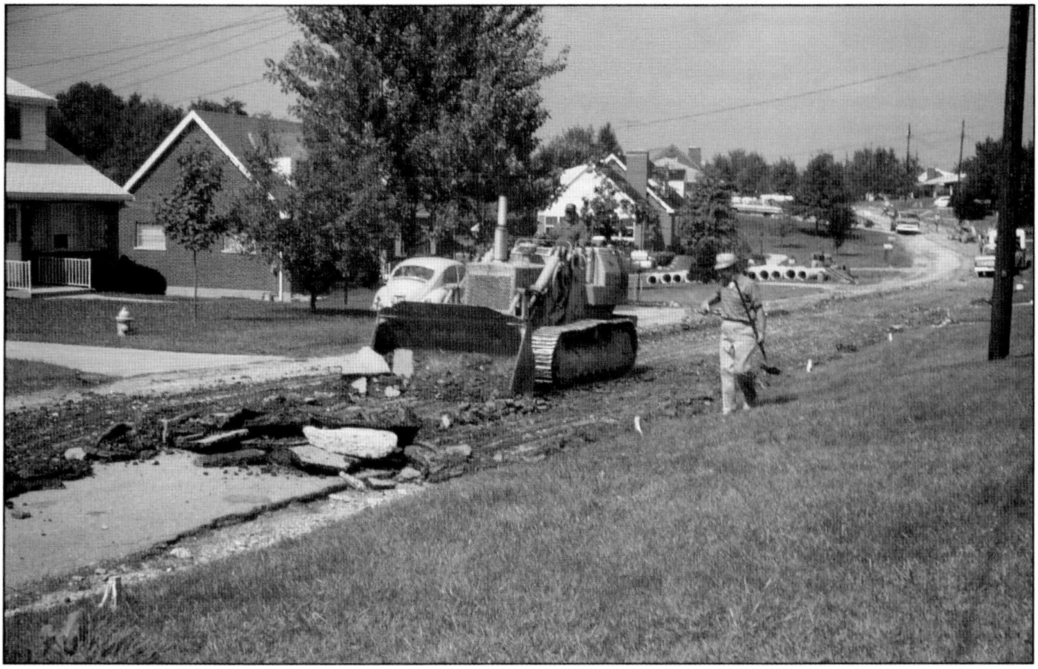

Around 1971, concrete streets were poured to replace the pothole-filled, black top and gravel streets that had originally been laid. Kenridge Drive, Sunglow Drive, Mary Street, Frank Street, and Rardin Court were all repaved. Both of these photographs were taken on Kenridge Drive, looking north toward Amsterdam Road. Although the demolition of the old streets and the construction of the new was a headache for residents, they were a welcomed addition when they were completed, giving the neighborhood a more modern look. (Courtesy of Paul and Peg Kohl.)

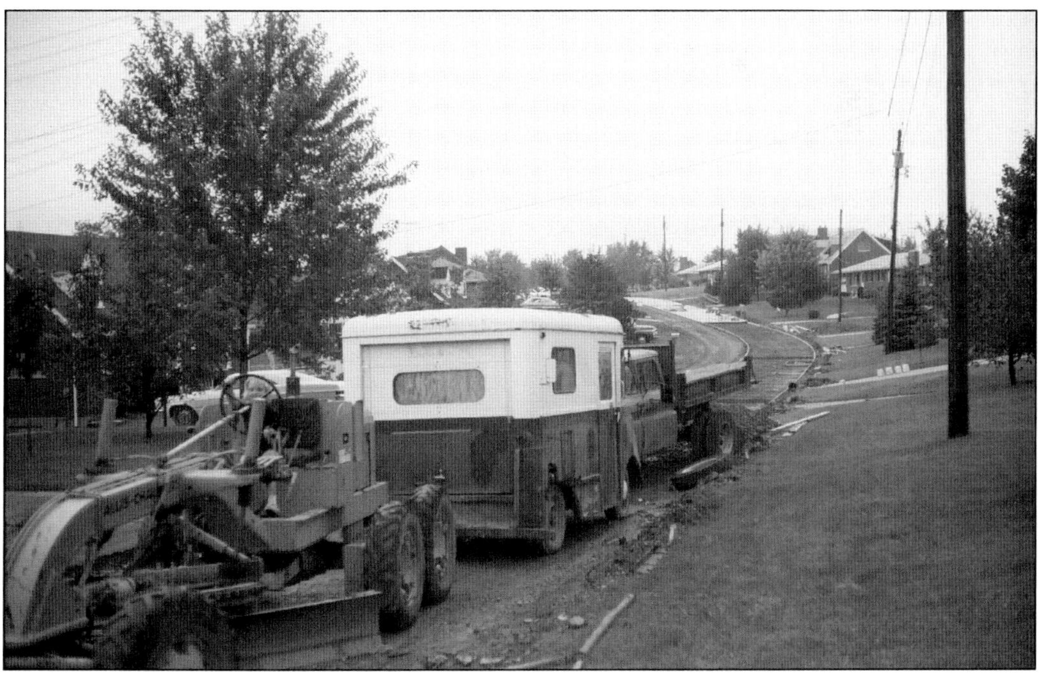

November 11,1964

CITY MARSHALL AND DEPUTY EQUIPMENT

PERSONAL

2 Smith & Wesson 38 Police Special	@ $48.80 ea.	$97.60
2 Belt Sets (Belt, Holster, Cartridge Case, and Handcuff case)	@ $14.00 ea.	$28.00
2 pr. Handcuffs	@ $ 8.00 ea.	$16.00
2 Billy Clubs	@ $ 2.25 ea.	$ 4.50
2 Slap Jacks	@ $ 2.25 ea.	$ 4.50
2 Uniforms (Cap, Jacket, Shirt and Trousers.)	@ $60.00 ea.	$120.00
2 Cap Insigias	@ $ 3.50 ea.	$ 7.00
2 Jacket Badges	@ $ 4.00 ea.	$ 8.00
2 5 cell flashlights	@ $3.00 ea.	$ 6.00
$1,000 bond (Deputy Marshall Bond)		$ 10.00

CAR EQUIPMENT

1 Used Speedometer Clock	$ 25.00
1 Warning Light	$ 25.00
1 Siren	$ 80.00
Installation of S iren and Speedometer Clock	$ 7.00
Car Liability Insurance for Police Work	?
S tationary Supplies (10 books traffic tickets of 50 each, Minimum order)	$ 16.50
100 Cash Bonds	$ 6.00
100 Bench Warrants	$ 6.00
	$357.10

The early Villa Hills Police Department was made up of a city marshal, Gerald Tebelman, and a deputy, Ron Bising. This 1964 assessment of equipment shows they had two guns and two sets of handcuffs, but only one siren and one warning light. The officers shared those, as they used their own cars for patrol duty. (Courtesy of Randy Nolting.)

Taken near the entrance to the city, this 1966 photograph shows the creation of the new Buttermilk Pike, which connected Villa Hills and Crescent Springs. Prior to this road, traffic through Crescent Springs traveled along Western Reserve. The home in the photograph belonged to the Dryer family and is currently the site of the Kenton County Veterans Memorial and Crescent Springs Park. (Courtesy of Lois Hall.)

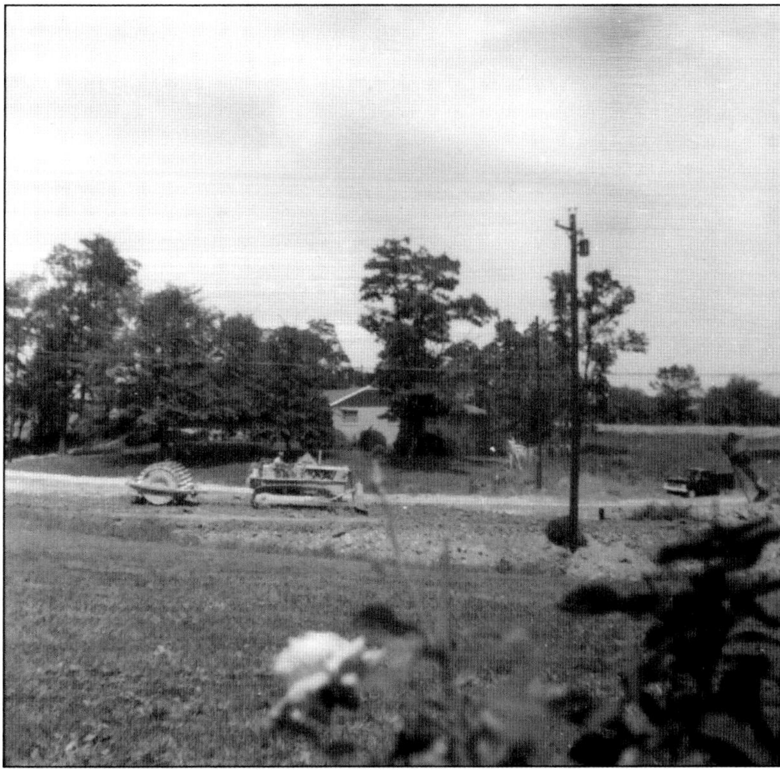

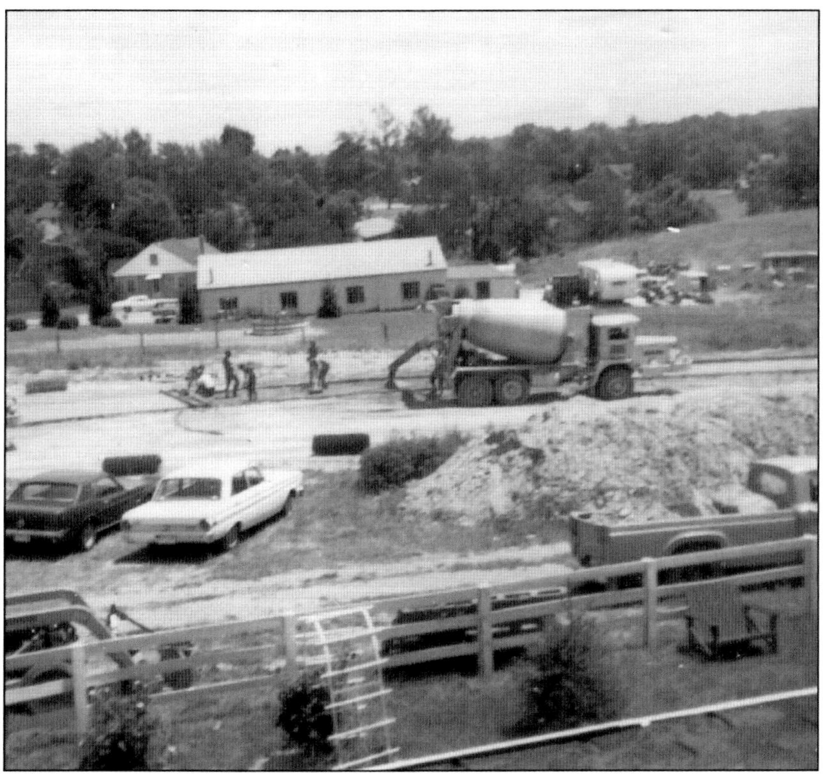

In the late 1960s, construction began on the Buttermilk Meadows subdivision. This photograph shows the building of Meadow Wood Drive near Buttermilk Pike. Crescent Springs can be seen in the background. (Courtesy of the Grout family.)

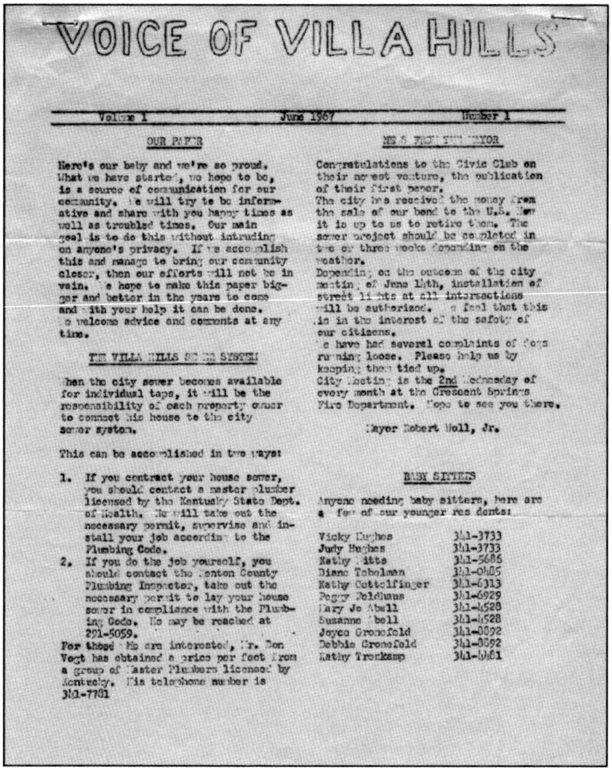

VOICE OF VILLA HILLS

Volume 1 | June 1967 | Number 1

OUR PAPER

Here's our baby and we're so proud. What we have started, we hope to be, is a source of communication for our community. We will try to be informative and share with you happy times as well as troubled times. Our main goal is to do this without intruding on anyone's privacy. If we accomplish this and manage to bring our community closer, then our efforts will not be in vain. We hope to make this paper bigger and better in the years to come and with your help it can be done. We welcome advice and comments at any time.

THE VILLA HILLS SEWER SYSTEM

When the city sewer becomes available for individual taps, it will be the responsibility of each property owner to connect his house to the city sewer system.

This can be accomplished in two ways:

1. If you contract your house sewer, you should contact a master plumber licensed by the Kentucky State Dept. of Health. He will take out the necessary permit, supervise and install your job according to the Plumbing Code.
2. If you do the job yourself, you should contact the Kenton County Plumbing Inspector, take out the necessary permit to lay your house sewer in compliance with the Plumbing Code. He may be reached at 291-5059.

For those who are interested, Mr. Don Vogt has obtained a price per foot from a group of Master Plumbers licensed by Kentucky. His telephone number is 341-7781

NEWS FROM THE MAYOR

Congratulations to the Civic Club on their newest venture, the publication of their first paper.
The city has received the money from the sale of our bond to the U.S. Now it is up to us to retire them. The sewer project should be completed in two or three weeks depending on the weather.
Depending on the outcome of the city meeting of June 14th, installation of street lights at all intersections will be authorized. We feel that this is in the interest of the safety of our citizens.
We have had several complaints of dogs running loose. Please help us by keeping them tied up.
City Meeting is the 2nd Wednesday of every month at the Crescent Springs Fire Department. Hope to see you there.

Mayor Robert Noll, Jr.

BABY SITTERS

Anyone needing baby sitters, here are a few of our younger residents:

Vicky Hughes	341-3733
Judy Hughes	341-3733
Kathy Pitts	341-5686
Diane Tebelman	341-0485
Kathy Gettelfinger	341-6313
Peggy Feldhaus	341-6929
Mary Jo Abell	341-4528
Suzanne Abell	341-4528
Joyce Gronefeld	341-8892
Debbie Gronefeld	341-8892
Kathy Tronkamp	341-4481

The very first issue of the *Voice of Villa Hills* was published in June 1967. The first coeditors were Velma Abell and Jo Ann Vogt. The paper has always been published by residents submitting news and volunteers compiling it and distributing the finished newspaper. The *Voice* regularly includes Villa Hills Council and Civic Club news, as well as lists of residents who could babysit or do yard work. Early editions featured news broken down by each street, which usually included highlights of residents' vacations. (Courtesy of Randy Nolting.)

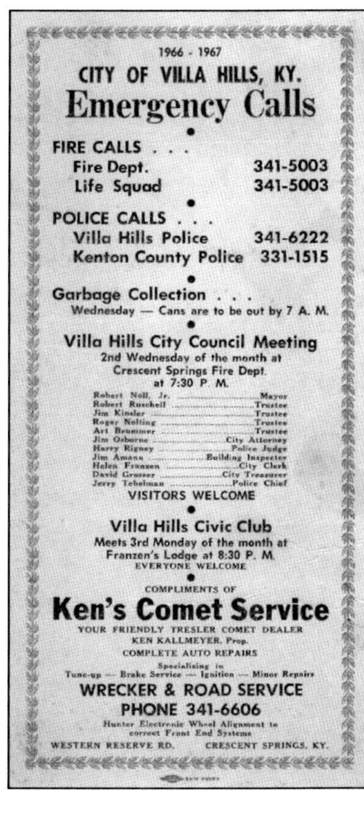

1966 - 1967
CITY OF VILLA HILLS, KY.
Emergency Calls

FIRE CALLS . . .
Fire Dept. 341-5003
Life Squad 341-5003

POLICE CALLS . . .
Villa Hills Police 341-6222
Kenton County Police 331-1515

Garbage Collection . . .
Wednesday — Cans are to be out by 7 A. M.

Villa Hills City Council Meeting
2nd Wednesday of the month at
Crescent Springs Fire Dept.
at 7:30 P. M.

Robert Noll, Jr.	Mayor
Robert Ruschell	Trustee
Jim Kinsler	Trustee
Roger Nolting	Trustee
Art Brummer	Trustee
Jim Osborne	City Attorney
Harry Rigney	Police Judge
Jim Amann	Building Inspector
Helen Franzen	City Clerk
David Grosser	City Treasurer
Jerry Tebelman	Police Chief

VISITORS WELCOME

Villa Hills Civic Club
Meets 3rd Monday of the month at
Franzen's Lodge at 8:30 P. M.
EVERYONE WELCOME

COMPLIMENTS OF
Ken's Comet Service
YOUR FRIENDLY TRESLER COMET DEALER
KEN KALLMEYER, Prop.
COMPLETE AUTO REPAIRS
Specializing in
Tune-up — Brake Service — Ignition — Minor Repairs
WRECKER & ROAD SERVICE
PHONE 341-6606
Hunter Electronic Wheel Alignment to correct Front End Systems
WESTERN RESERVE RD. CRESCENT SPRINGS, KY.

This 1966–1967 handy reference of Villa Hills information was supplied to customers of Kens Comet Gas and Service station, which was located on the corner of Western Reserve and Anderson Road in Crescent Springs. It hung on the wall next to many phones in Villa Hills. (Courtesy of Randy Nolting.)

House Bill 410 was the official bill of the Kentucky House of Representatives that changed Villa Hills from a sixth-class city to a fifth-class city. Along with this change in classification came more changes. The city, which had been conducting city council meetings at the Crescent Springs Fire Department, was required by law to meet within the city limits. Meetings were moved to Madonna Manor Nursing Home. The next change was that the current chairman of the board be promoted to the title of mayor. Tom Braun, who was chairman in 1968, became Villa Hills's first mayor. (Courtesy of Randy Nolting.)

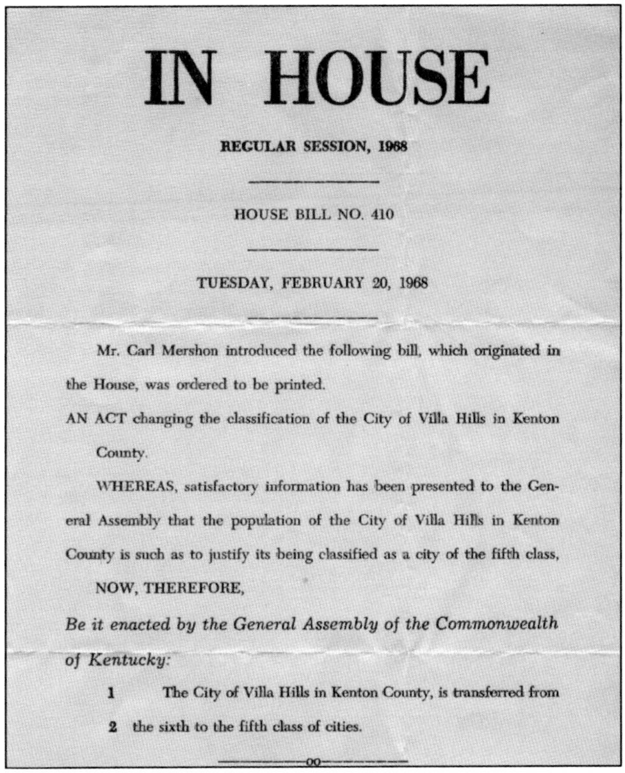

IN HOUSE

REGULAR SESSION, 1968

HOUSE BILL NO. 410

TUESDAY, FEBRUARY 20, 1968

Mr. Carl Mershon introduced the following bill, which originated in the House, was ordered to be printed.

AN ACT changing the classification of the City of Villa Hills in Kenton County.

WHEREAS, satisfactory information has been presented to the General Assembly that the population of the City of Villa Hills in Kenton County is such as to justify its being classified as a city of the fifth class,

NOW, THEREFORE,

Be it enacted by the General Assembly of the Commonwealth of Kentucky:

The City of Villa Hills in Kenton County, is transferred from the sixth to the fifth class of cities.

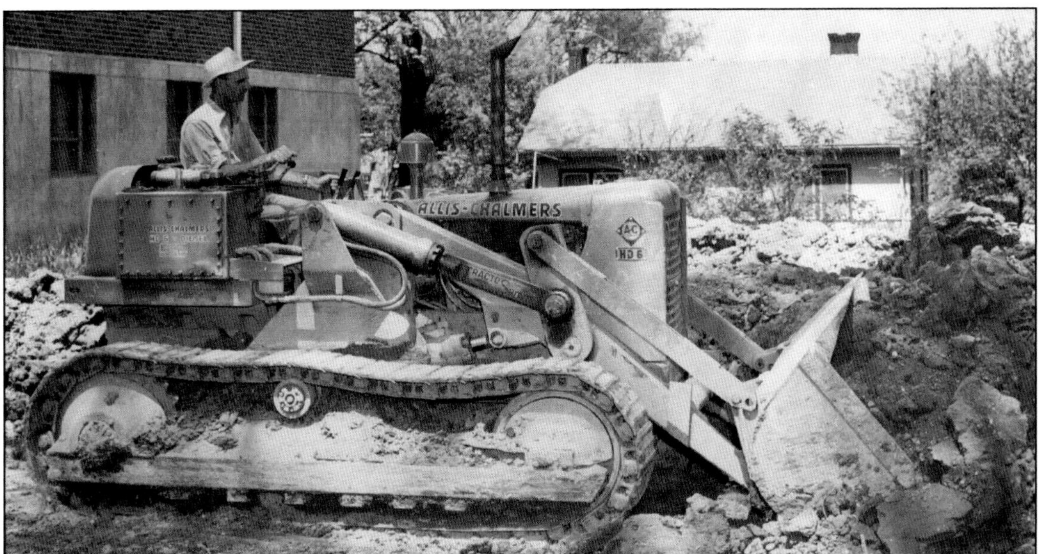

Arthur Kremer, who grew up on the Kremer farm on Collins Road, started an excavating company in 1947, just a few years after returning from World War II. This photograph, probably from the 1950s, shows Art in his familiar place aboard his bulldozer. Kremer Excavating started out digging ponds but grew to digging foundations at the start of the post-war housing boom. Kremer dug foundations for an estimated 50 to 75 percent of the homes in Villa Hills. Although he retired in 1985, the company is still run by his son Ken, who has been digging Villa Hills's foundations since then. (Courtesy of Ken Kremer.)

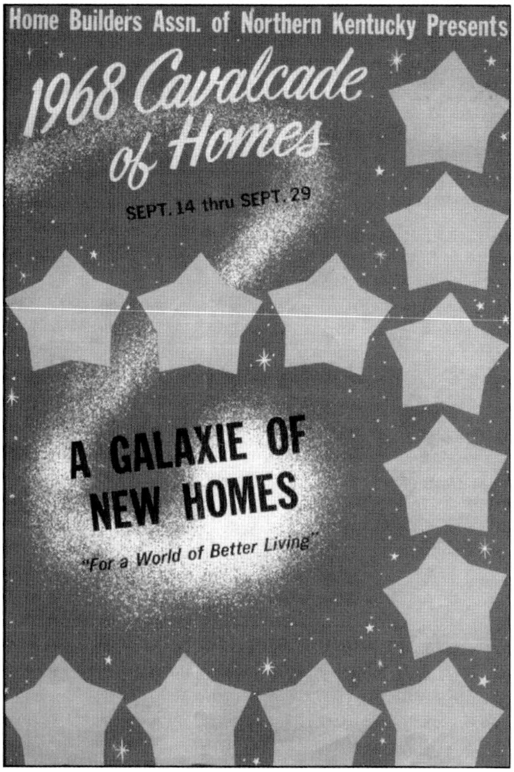

In the fall of 1968, Villa Hills welcomed the Home Builder's Association and the Cavalcade of Homes to the Buttermilk Meadows subdivision. Cavalcade featured 11 homes in Northern Kentucky. At left is a program from the event. The sketch below shows the Scholarship Home, which was designed by an 18-year-old student at Boone County High School. This home was the winner of the Design a Home Contest, sponsored by Northern Kentucky Home Builders Association and built by Joe Spille. The three-bedroom, two-bath home, which was built on Meadowview Drive, boasts an AM/FM intercom system and a paneled family room. (Courtesy of Tom Braun and Loraine Braun.)

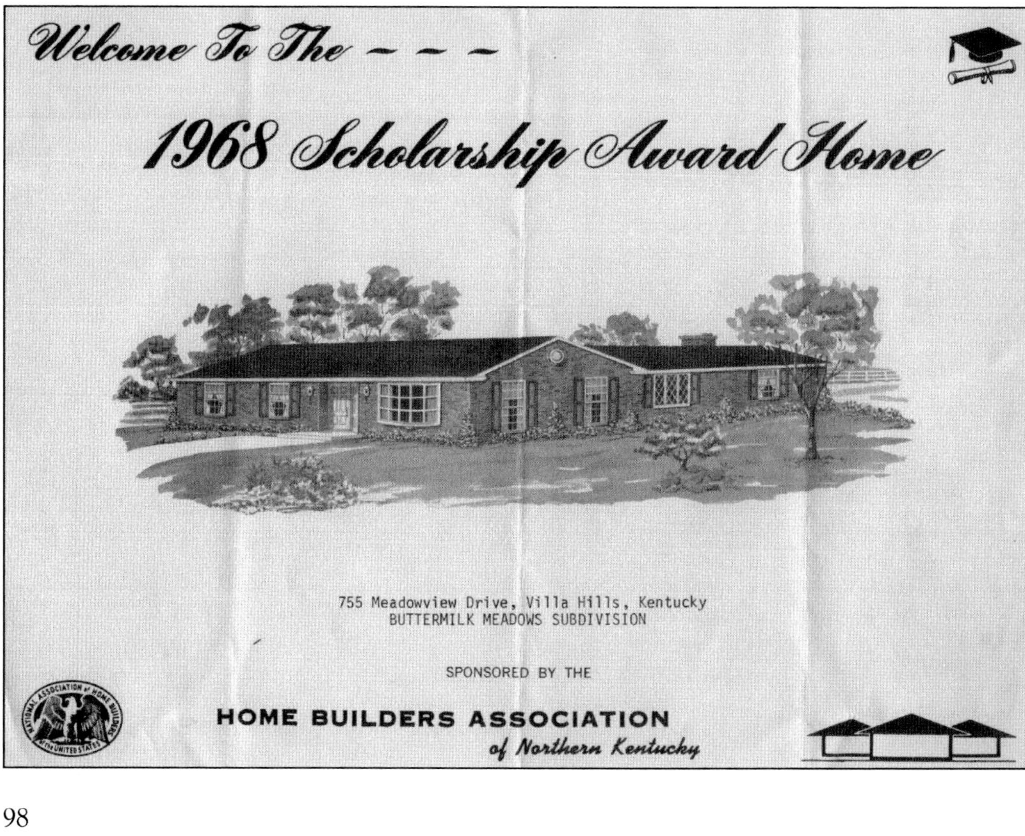

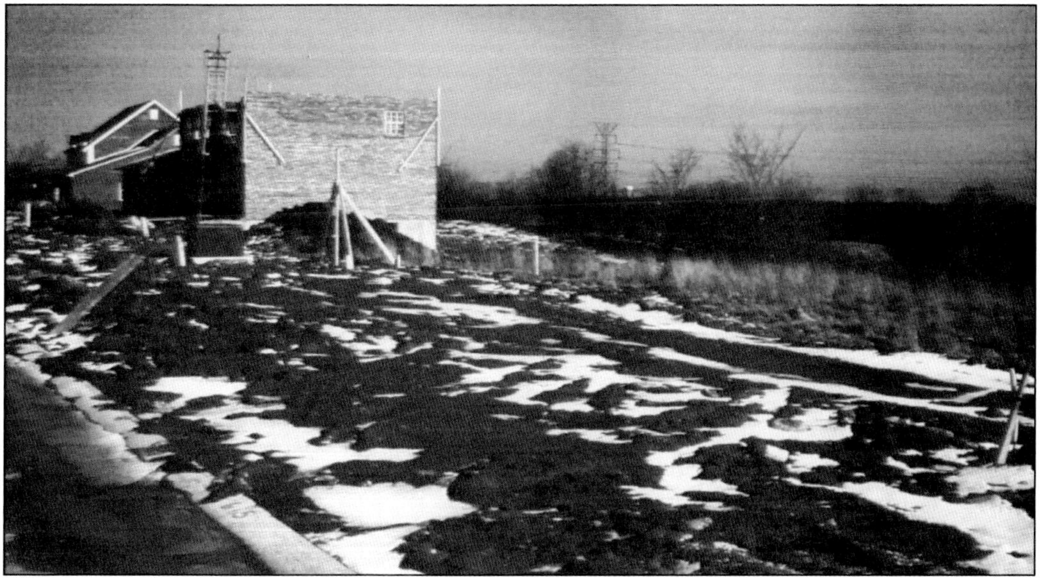

In the early 1970s, the farm once belonging to Pete Kremer on Collins Road was sold for development. The neighborhood, which was called Vista Villa Estates, is comprised of Cecilia Drive and Orchid Lane. The name Cecilia comes from Pete Kremer's daughter, Cecilia Kordenbrock, who was the owner of the land at that time. Almost every home in the neighborhood was built by Krumpelman Builders. These photographs show early Cecilia Drive. In the photograph above, the farthest house, which is located at 2461 Cecilia Drive, was the first house in the neighborhood, followed by the house that does not yet have a roof, located at 2465 Cecilia Drive. In the background is the Frank Kremer farm, which is known as Kremer Lane today. The mid-1970s photograph below shows Cecilia Drive progressing. The farthest home in the photograph stands near the intersection of Cecilia Drive and Orchid Lane. (Courtesy of Paul and Peg Kohl.)

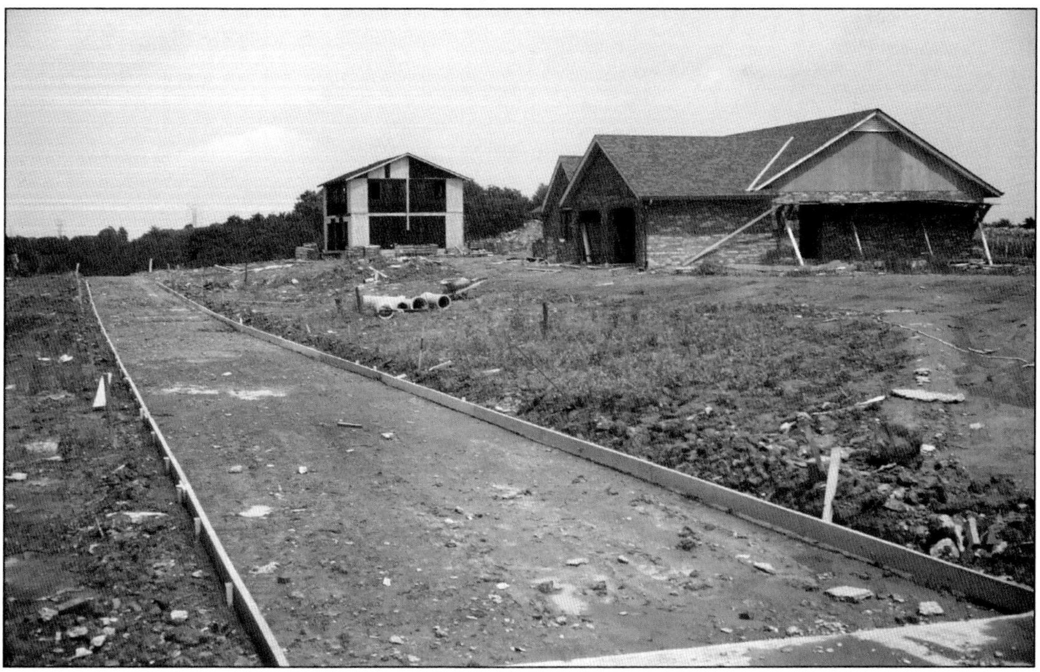

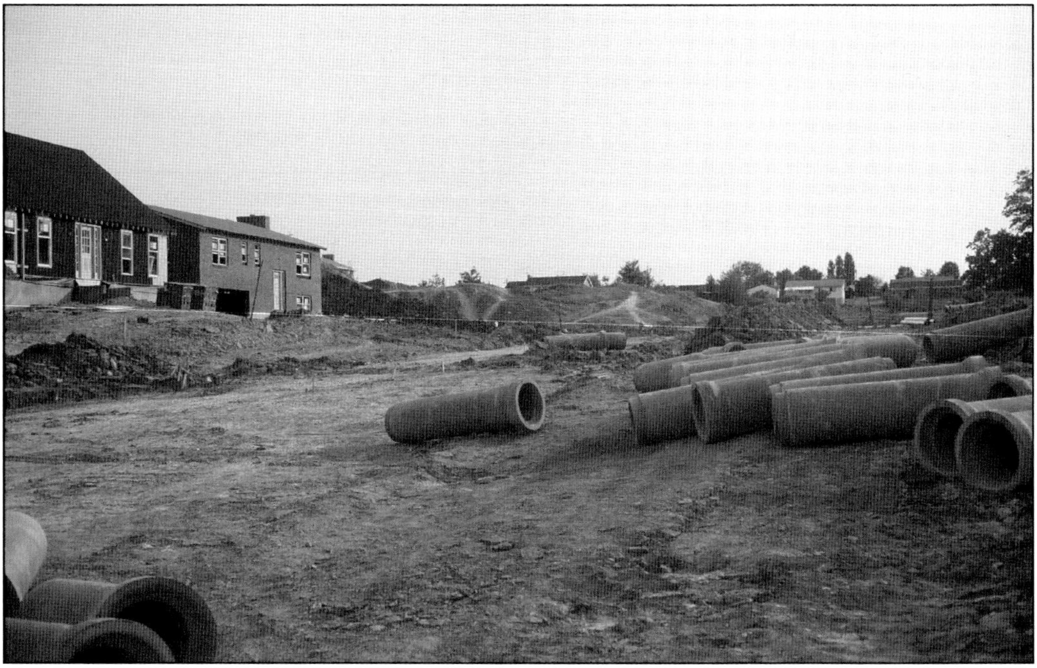

Although the concrete had not yet been poured, these photographs are of early Orchid Lane, taken in the late 1970s. The photograph above shows two houses under construction, looking toward Collins Road. The photograph below shows the same house, but now the camera is facing the opposite direction. Located just beyond the woods are the Toebben farm, which is straight ahead, and the Maegley farm, which is on the left. (Courtesy of Paul and Peg Kohl.)

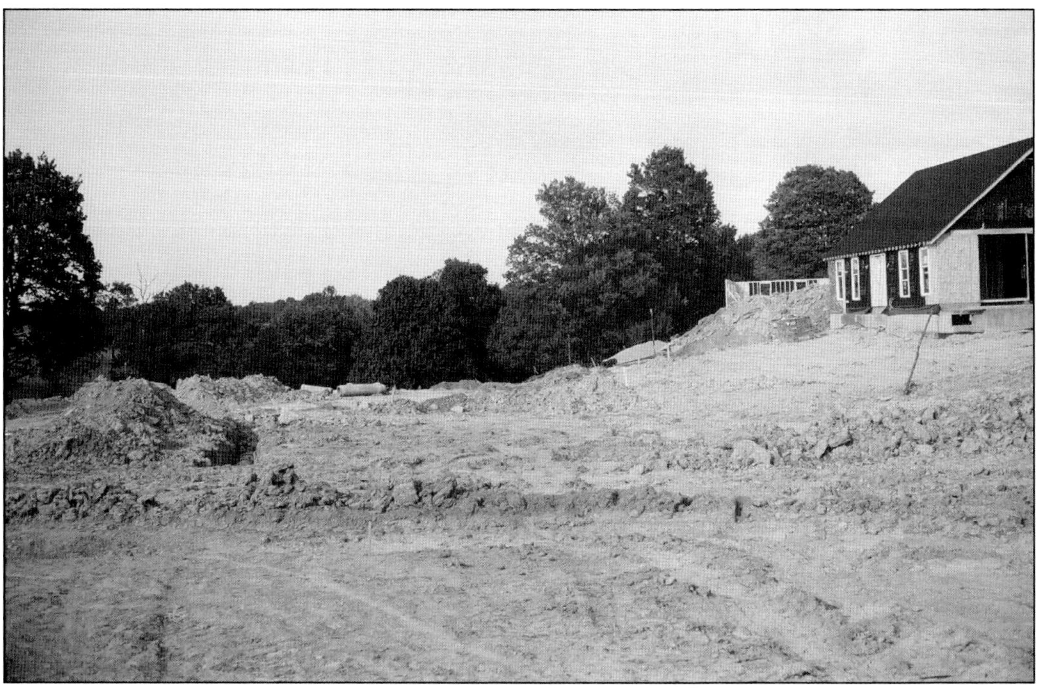

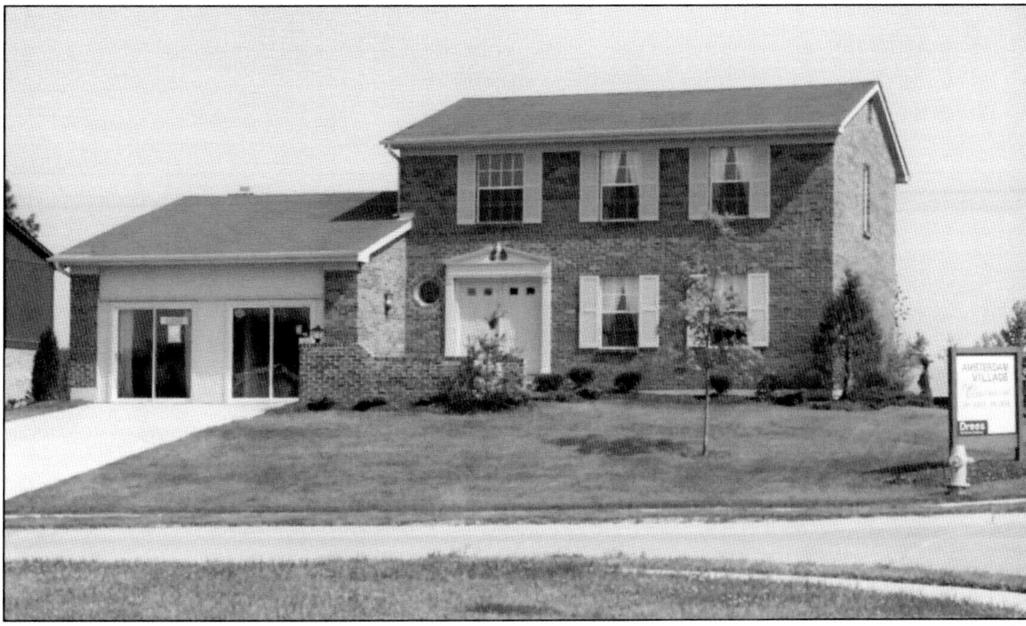

The sale of the 204-acre Summe farm to the Drees Company in the late 1960s resulted in the largest subdivision in Northern Kentucky. The first homes in the Amsterdam Village subdivision were built in 1969. The land included the area west of Rogers Road and south of Amsterdam Road. In this 1979 photograph, one of the Drees model homes was on display at the corner of Valley Trails and Wesley Drive. (Courtesy of the Drees Company.)

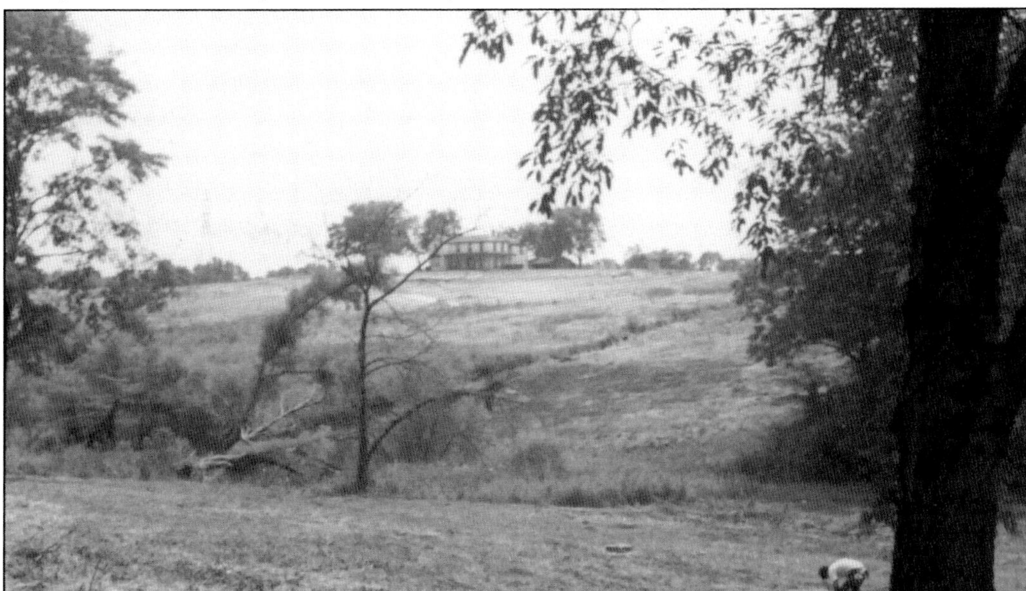

The Steenken farmhouse stood high on a hill along what is now Rogers Road in Villa Hills. The Steenken family members were dairy farmers. In this 1973 photograph, which was taken near the Villa Hills Civic Club, an unidentified person is searching for arrowheads. The remnants of Native American culture were commonly found in the area of Amsterdam Village and Thirs farms. (Courtesy of the Villa Hills Historical Society.)

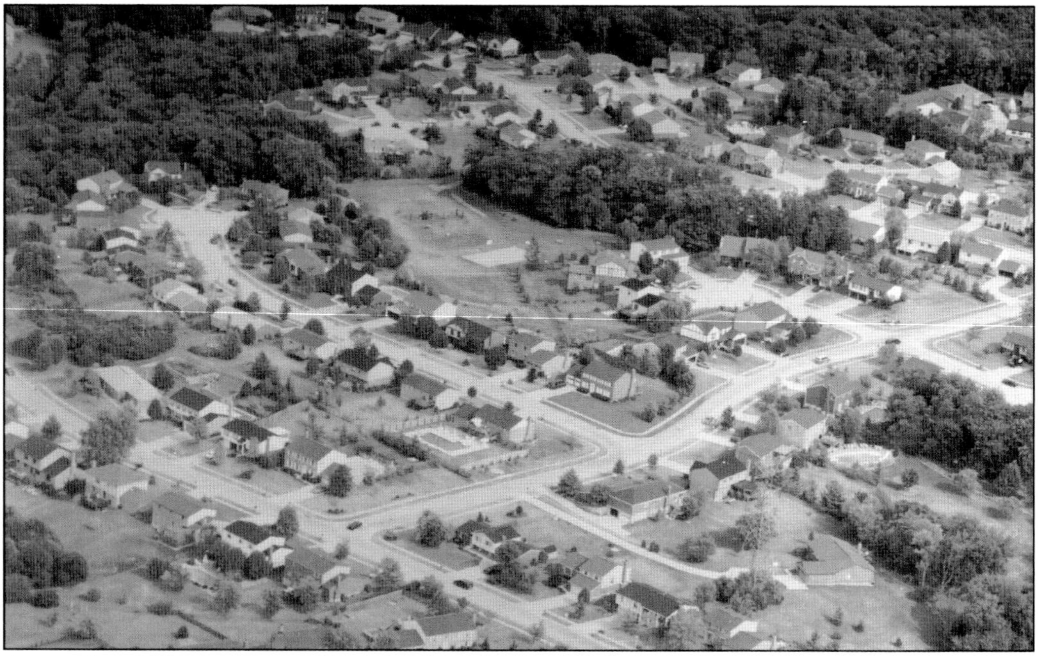

Amsterdam Village continued to grow into the 1980s. This aerial photograph shows what locals still call "New" Rogers Road on the left as it intersects Sierra Drive and Pineview Drive, which run along the bottom. In the middle is Harry Rigney Park. The surrounding wooded area is Crescent Springs. (Courtesy of Sue Marshall.)

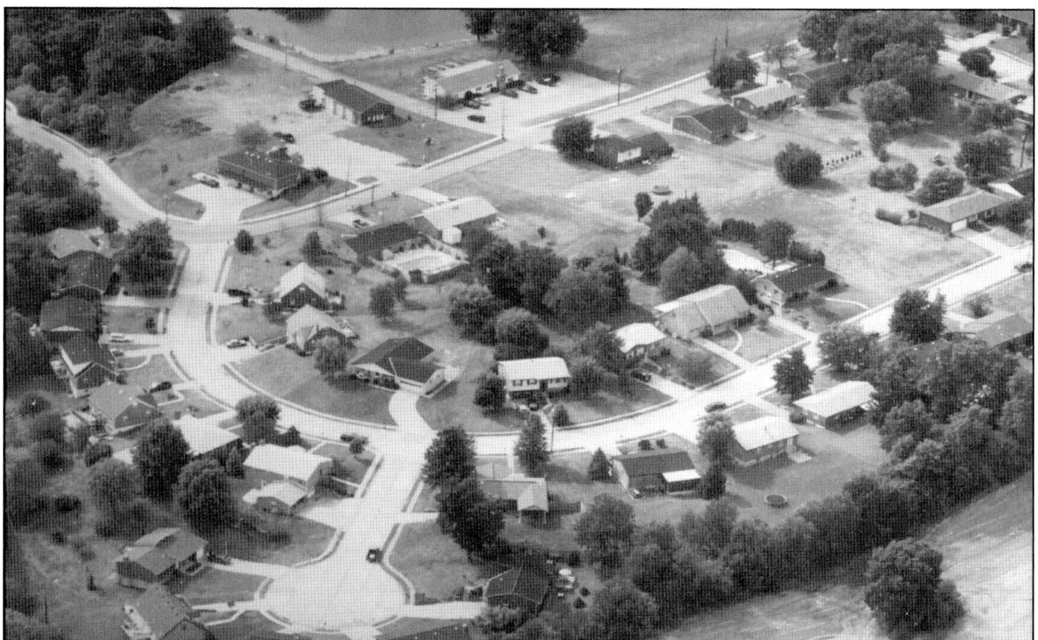

In 1968, ground was broken on Park Villa Estates, which is made up of Lake Shore Drive and Villa Marie Lane. This aerial shot shows the neighborhood, which is on the east side of Rogers Road. The Villa Hills Civic Club and Villa Hills city buildings can also be seen. (Courtesy of the Thomas Molony family.)

In the mid-1970s, the Drees Company began building the subdivision known as Prospect Point off of Amsterdam Road on the northwestern tip of Villa Hills, overlooking the Ohio River. The area was made up of condominiums and apartments and was the first condo community in Northern Kentucky. In this photograph, the silo from the original farmland has been transformed into the apartment rental office. The photograph below shows an aerial view of a portion of Prospect Point. Home to 365 condominiums, the community offers a pool, clubhouse, tennis courts, walking trails, and breathtaking views of the Ohio River. (Courtesy of the Drees Company.)

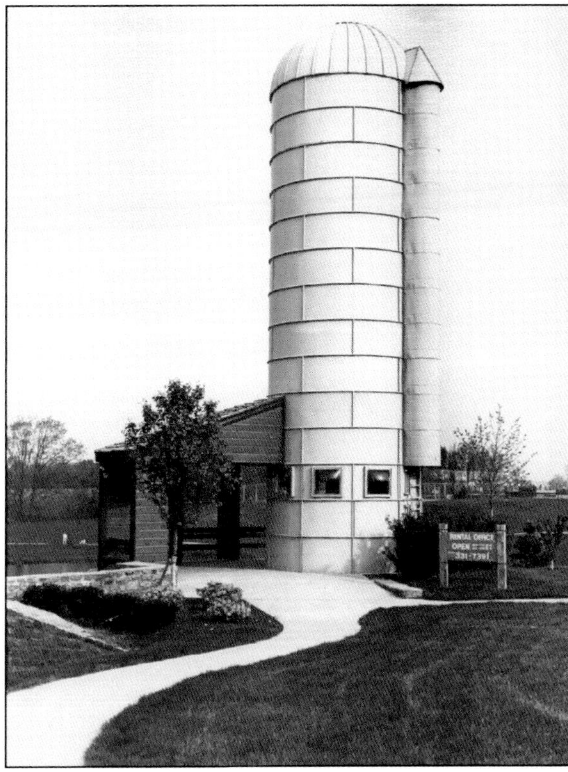

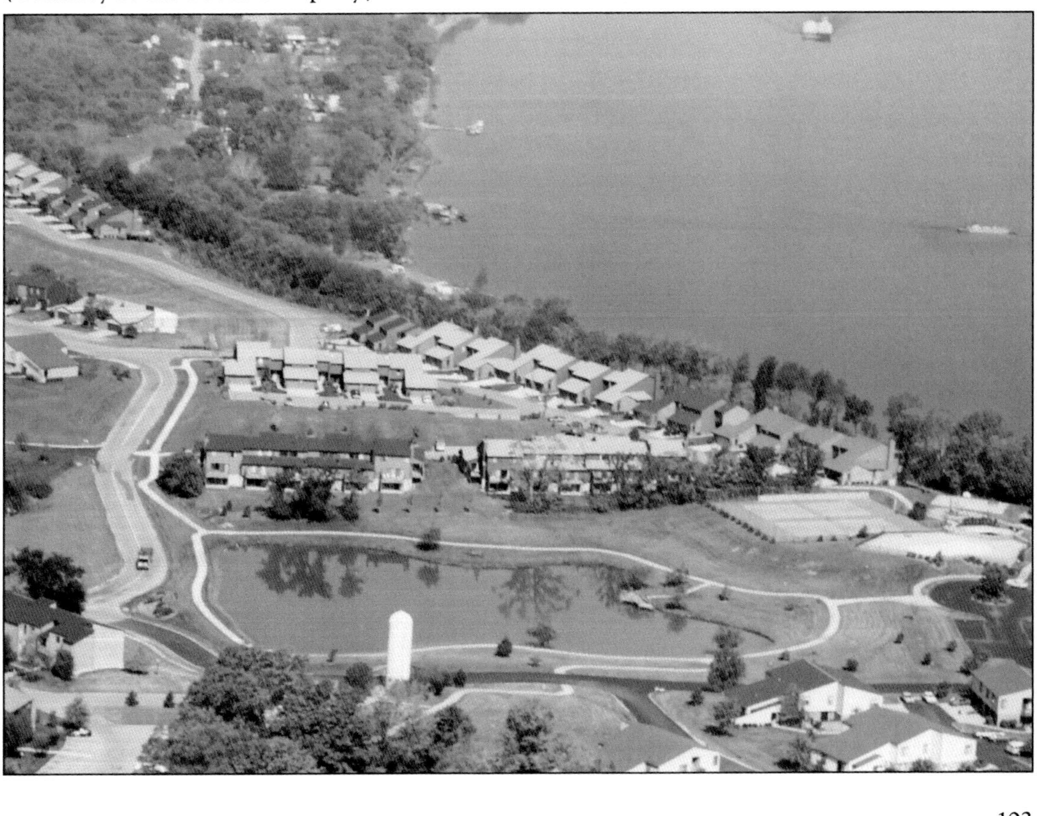

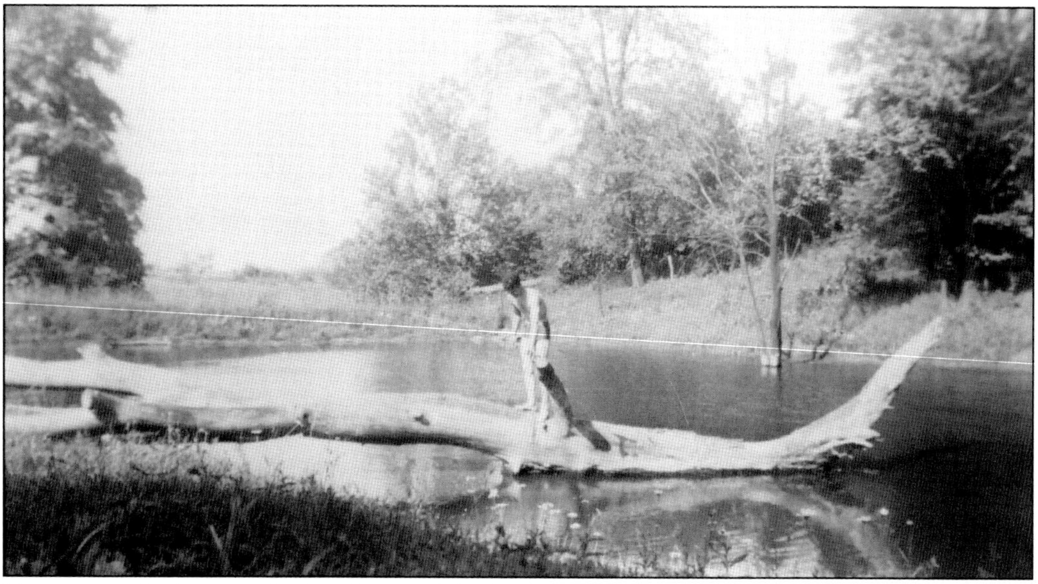

This pond, which was tucked in the woods behind the Felice home at 902 Collins Road, was used in the early years for fishing and ice-skating. It eventually filled with silt from nearby construction and was only a few feet deep. Its remote location made it a favorite hangout for kids from the surrounding streets, until Margherite Felice, who owned the land and quickly reminded the kids they were on private property, met them. Known to friends as Marge, she could be intimidating to trespassers even though she only stood 4 feet, 11 inches tall. (Courtesy of the Felice family.)

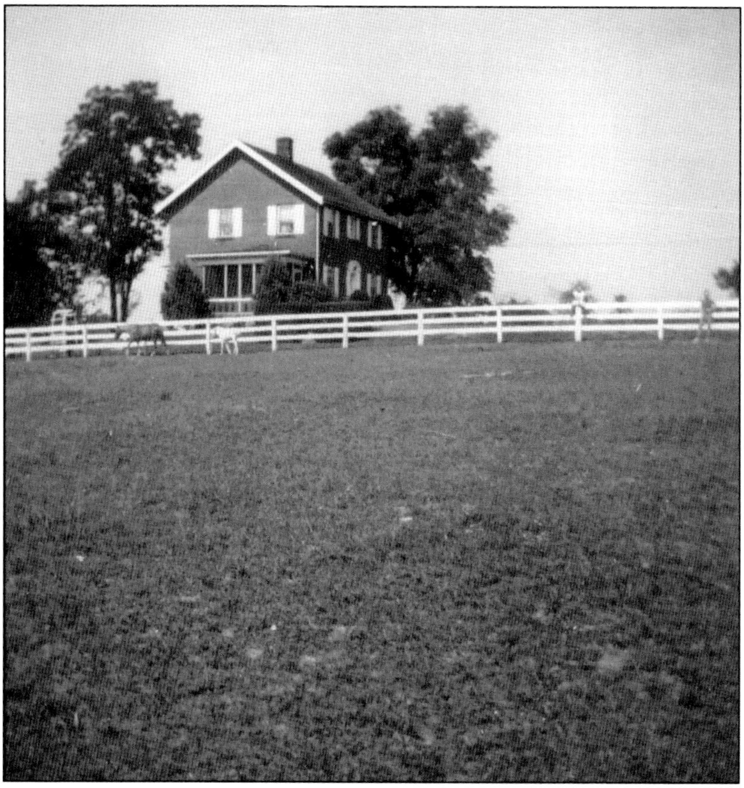

This is a view from the Rich Eubank farm on Buttermilk Pike, looking at the side of the Grout home at 2519 Buttermilk Pike. The Grouts, who had 12 children, purchased this home in 1963 for about $18,000. (Courtesy of the Grout family.)

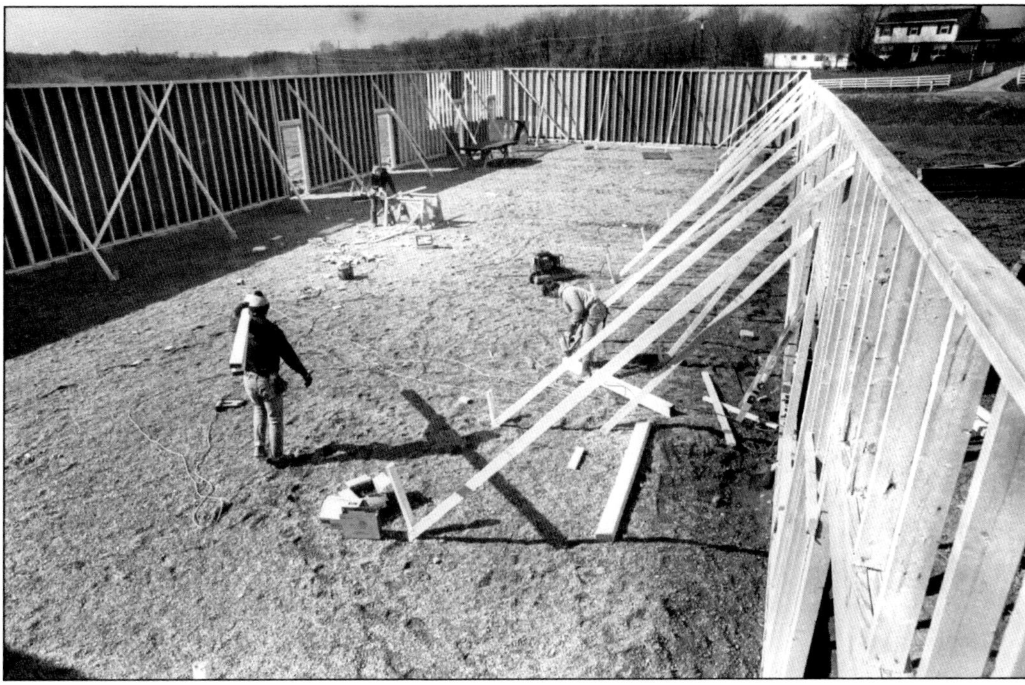

The early 1980s brought retail business to Villa Hills with the opening of the Convenient Food Mart at the corner of Amsterdam Road and Valley Trails Drive. The mini-shopping plaza also had a branch of People's Liberty Bank and a Liquor Loft store. In the photograph above, the shopping center is still under construction. (Above, courtesy of the Kenton County Public Library; below, courtesy of Lida Smith McClure.)

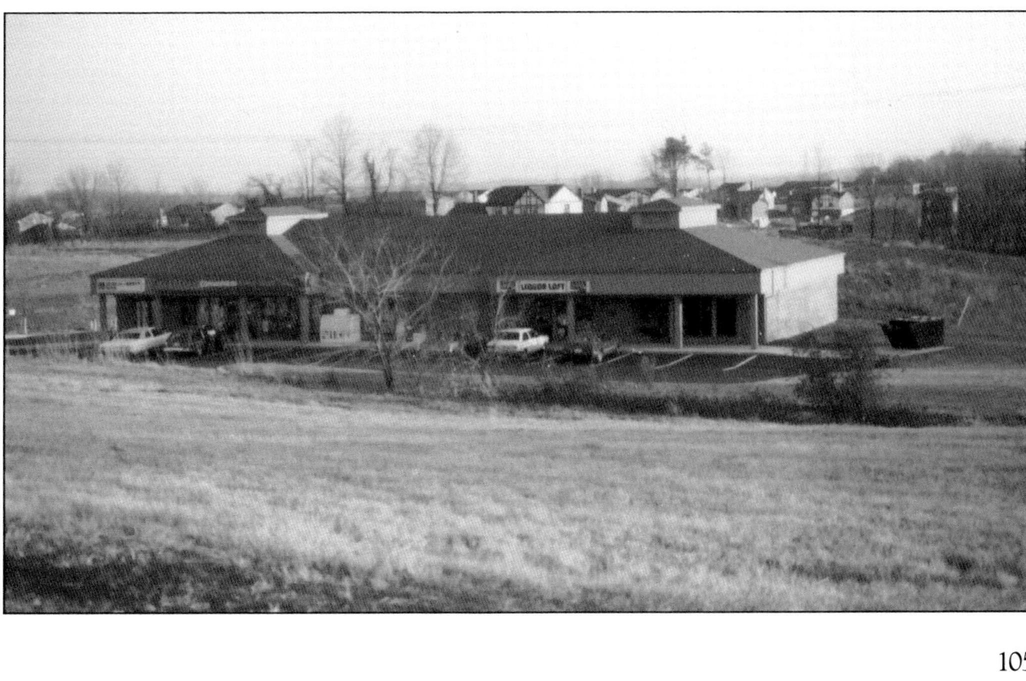

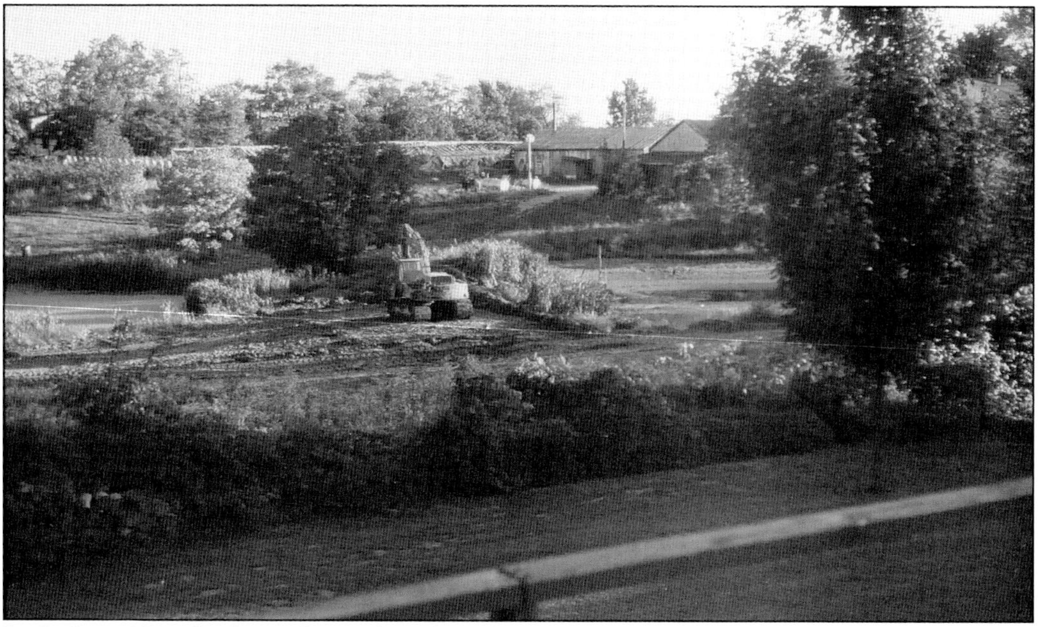

In the late 1970s, the descendants of Frank and Julie Kremer decided to sell most of the family farm at 818 Collins Road. The fields, which raised tomatoes, corn, and many vegetables, would become Kremer Lane. In the photograph above, taken from Cecilia Drive, the greenhouses of the farm were being disassembled, and a bulldozer had been brought in to drain the "little lake" (as it was called) into the "big lake" on the left. Both lakes had been used for fishing, swimming, and ice-skating by the Kremer family and neighbors since Frank Kremer Sr. bought the property in 1913. The photograph below, also taken from Cecilia Drive, shows that one lane of Kremer Lane had been poured, covering up the former "little lake" of Kremer's farm. (Courtesy of Paul and Peg Kohl.)

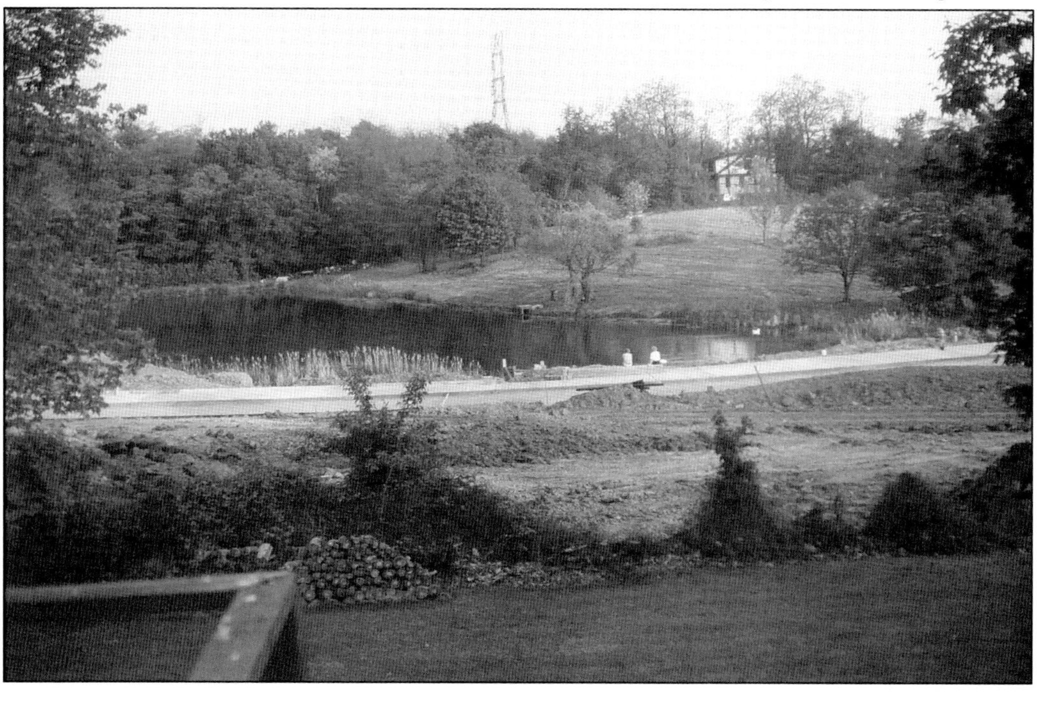

Four

The People and Sights of Villa Hills

A residential city like Villa Hills does not have historic businesses or landmarks that can be included as a chapter on their own. Having already covered farms, Villa Madonna, and subdivisions, what is left are the sights and the fine people of Villa Hills. Spanning the years of the early 1960s through the early 1980s, the following chapter highlights sights that were, and still are, familiar to residents.

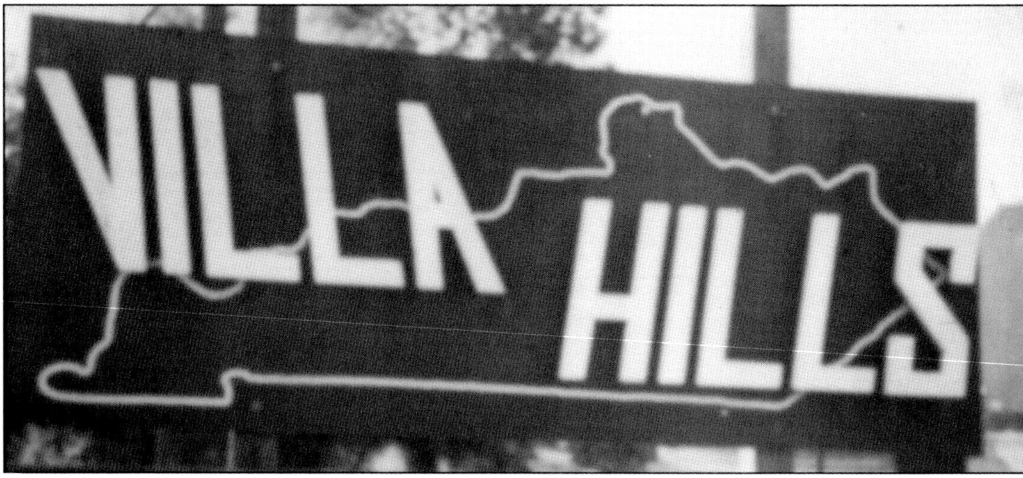

The first Villa Hills sign sat between Collins Road and Buttermilk Pike and welcomed everyone to the city. This sign was a gift from Roger Nolting, who was very active in both the Civic Club and the city's development. He built the sign himself in his basement on Frank Street and erected it in 1966. (Courtesy of Virginia Felthaus.)

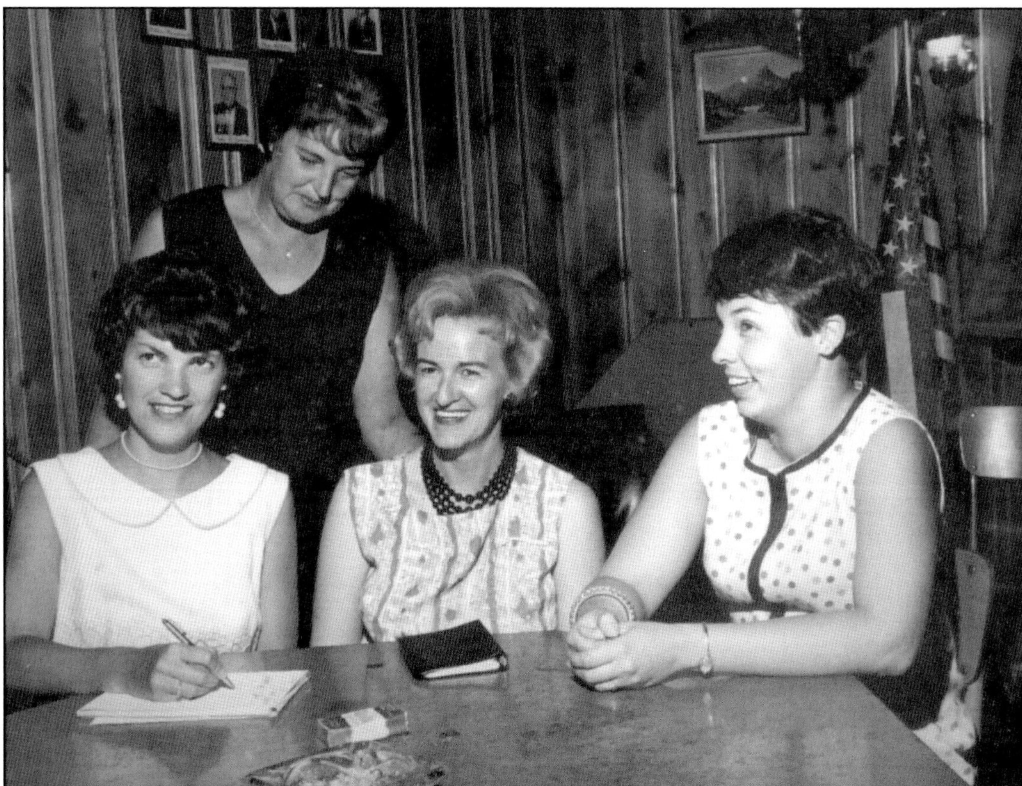

This early-1960s photograph shows an early meeting of the Villa Hills Women's Club. Standing is Ginny Mitts, and those sitting are, from left to right, Jackie Bising, Lois Bruns (Hall), and Ann Stewart. The photograph was taken inside the Civic Club. The group raised money to support the club by holding dances. They used the money for things like the children's annual Easter egg hunt and Christmas party. (Courtesy of Lois Hall.)

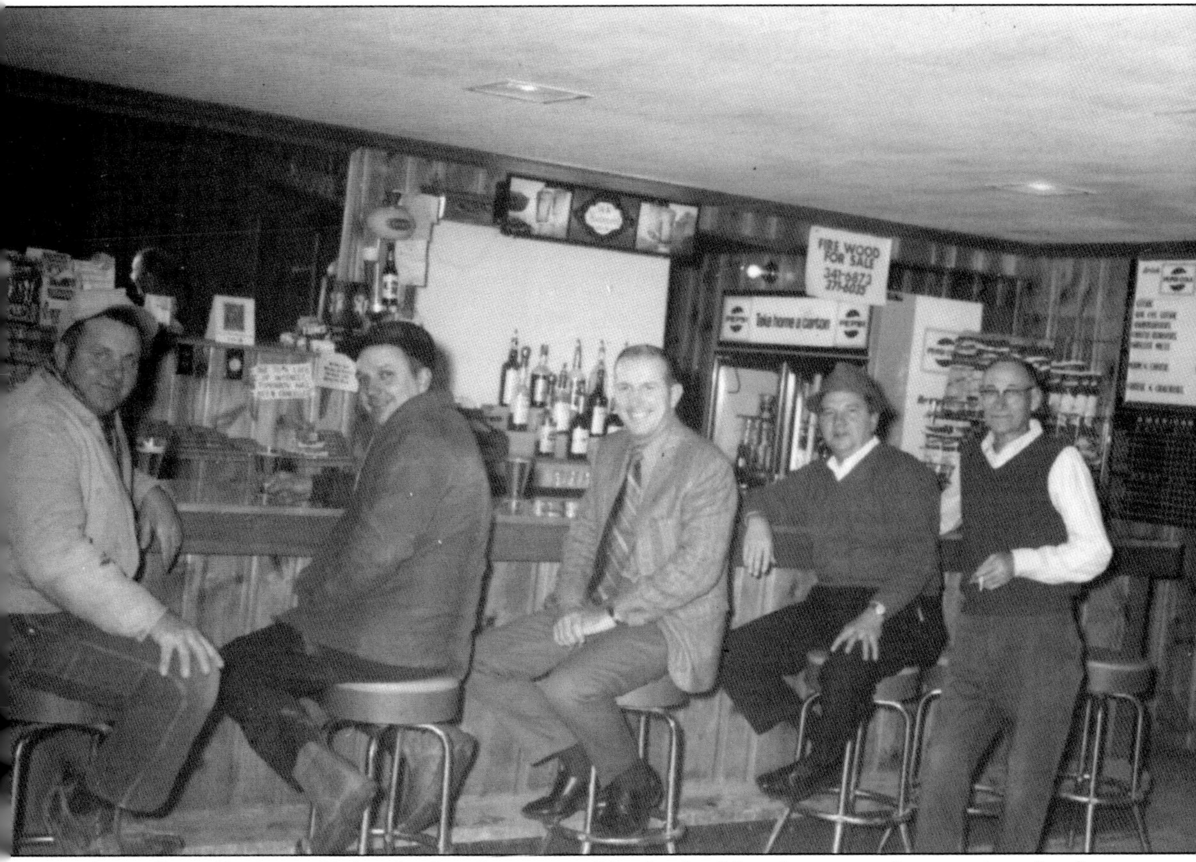

The Villa Hills Civic Club, which is known as "the Lodge," has been a gathering place for the entire community from the beginning. This early-1960s photograph shows, from left to right, Ben Krumpelman, Paul Schwarte, Nick Frohlich, Bert Melching, and Jerry Lohre enjoying drinks at the end of the day. (Courtesy of Barb Lohre Cooney.)

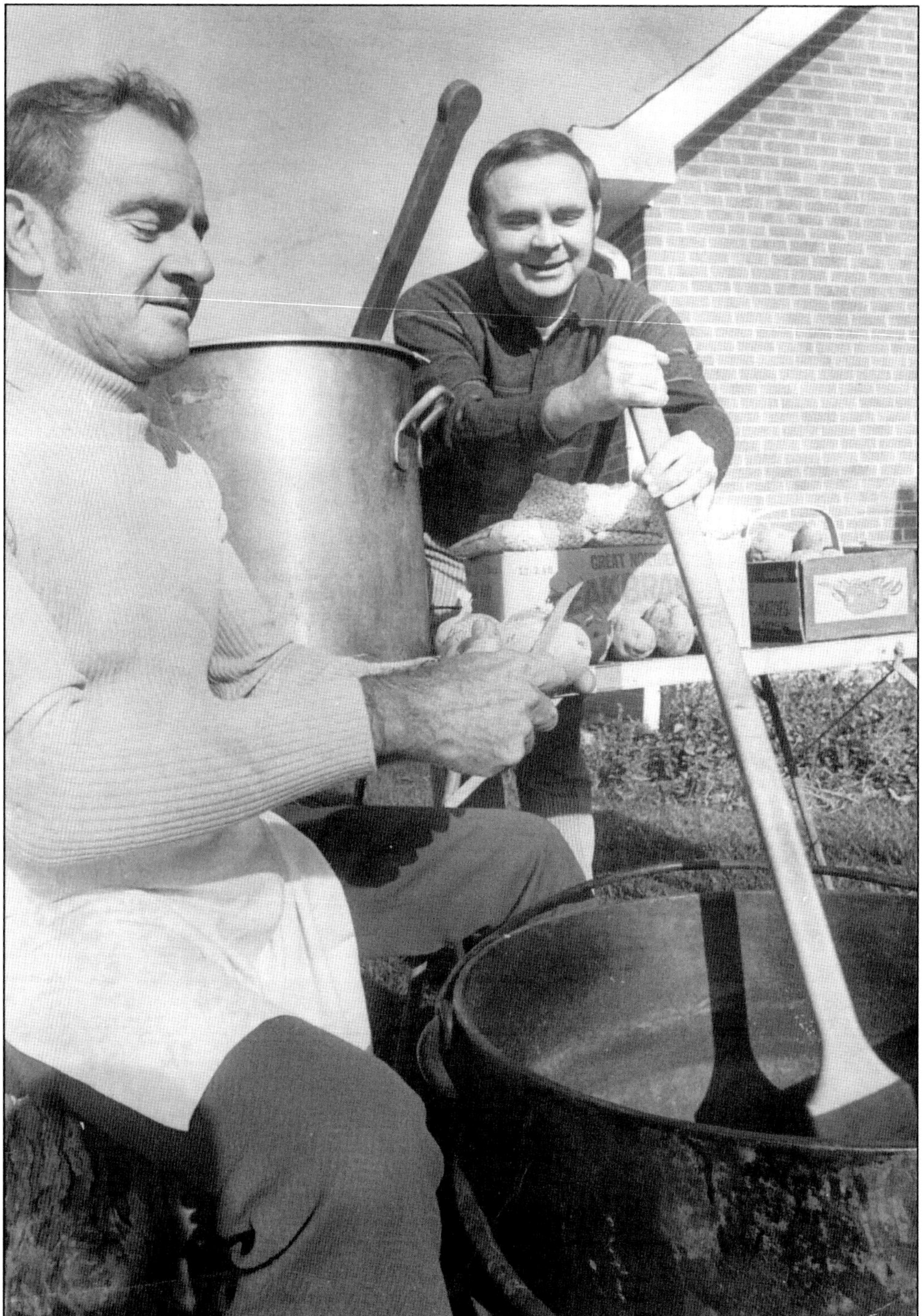

The Villa Hills Civic Club held festivals and turkey shoots through the years, and no matter what the event, the one constant was burgoo or mock turtle soup made by Rome Kremer. In this photograph from the early 1970s, Rome and Jack Wood cut up vegetables to be added to the pot. Organizers would gather at Rome's home on Collins Road the night before the event to chop vegetables for the next day's crowd. (Courtesy of Julie Kremer Bricking.)

The Villa Hills Civic Club sponsored the famous Skirt Game in the mid-1960s. The men dressed as women and played softball at the Franzen fields. This photograph shows, from left to right, Pete Goetz, Don Toebbe, Bob Huesman, and Skip Egbers enjoying refreshments after the game. (Courtesy of Bob and Pat Huesman.)

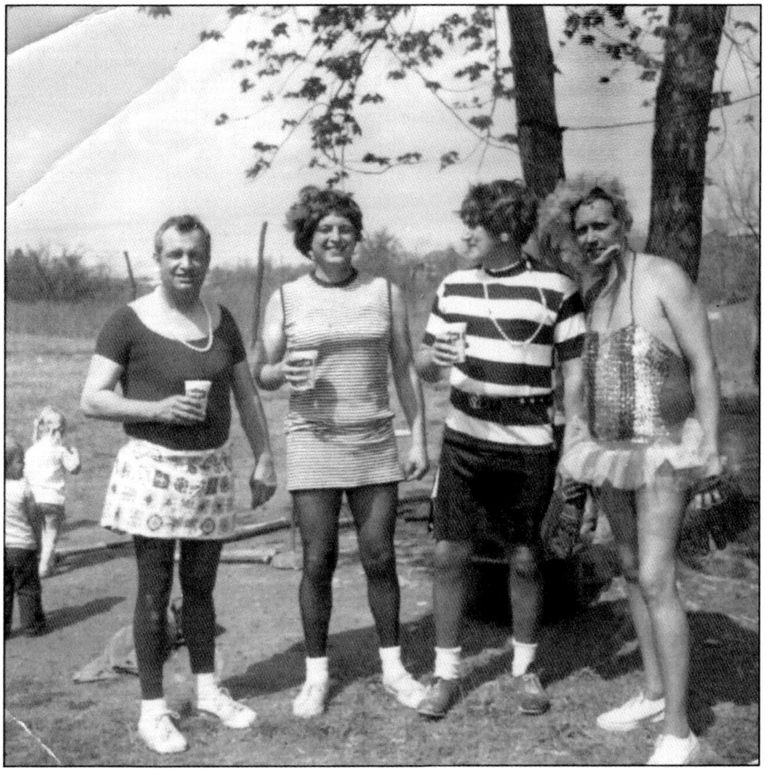

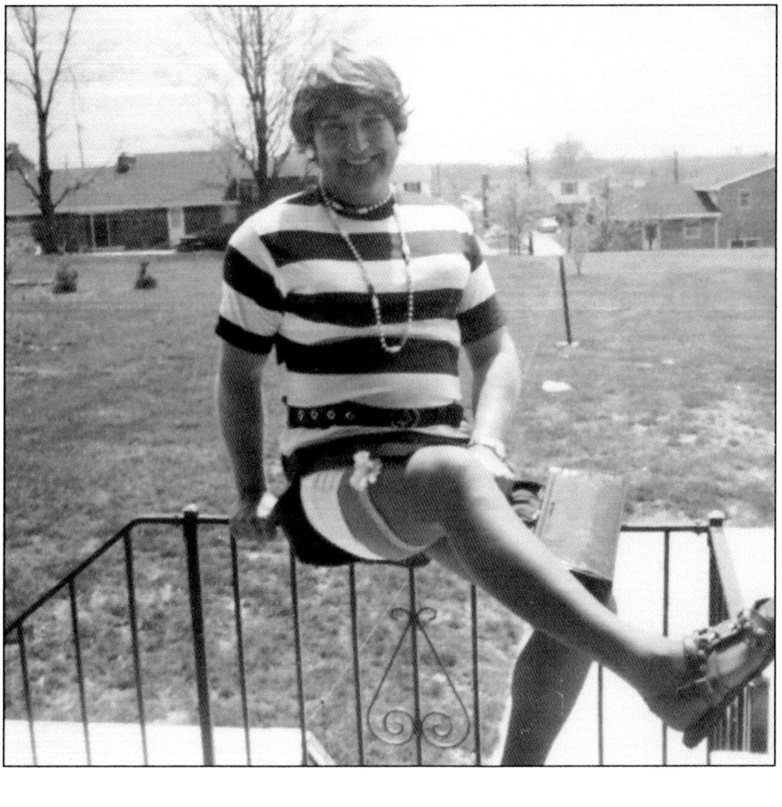

Although Bob Huesman was known as assistant chief of the Villa Hills Police Department, he was happy to participate in the Villa Hills Civic Club Skirt Game. This mid-1960s photograph was taken on the back porch of his home on Frank Street. In the back of his house were the homes on Buttermilk Pike, near Mary Street. (Courtesy of Bob and Pat Huesman.)

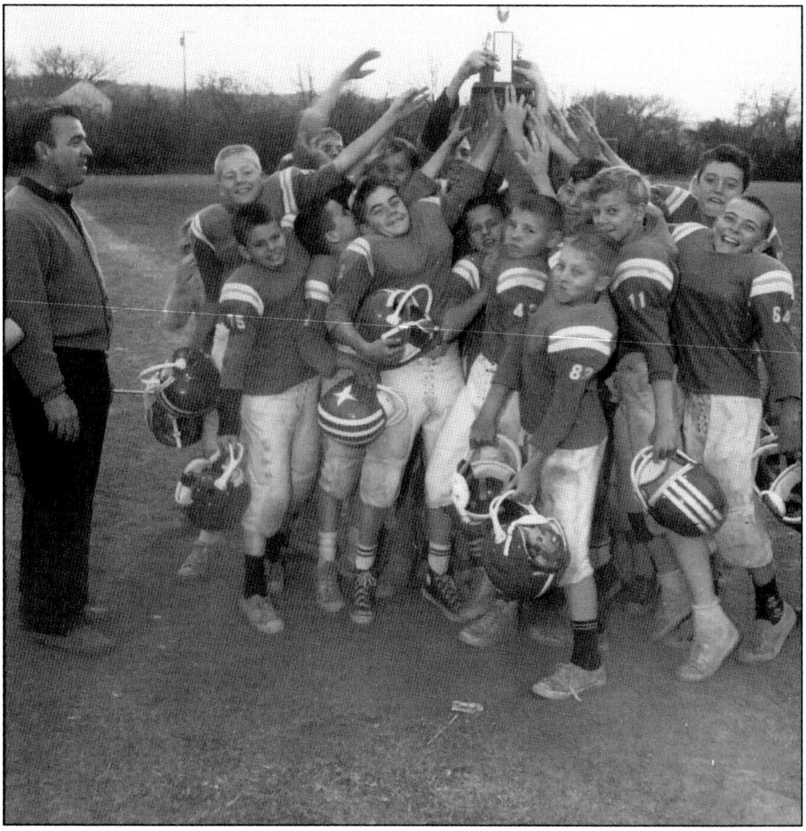

In the photograph at left, the Villa-Crescent pee wee football team, later known as the Villa Hills Spartans, celebrates their championship by hoisting the trophy, while coach Roger Nolting watches. Below are Harry Rigney, Tom "Red" Richardson, and Roger Nolting, (left to right) holding the trophy for the Villa Hills Spartans in the early 1960s. (Courtesy of Randy Nolting.)

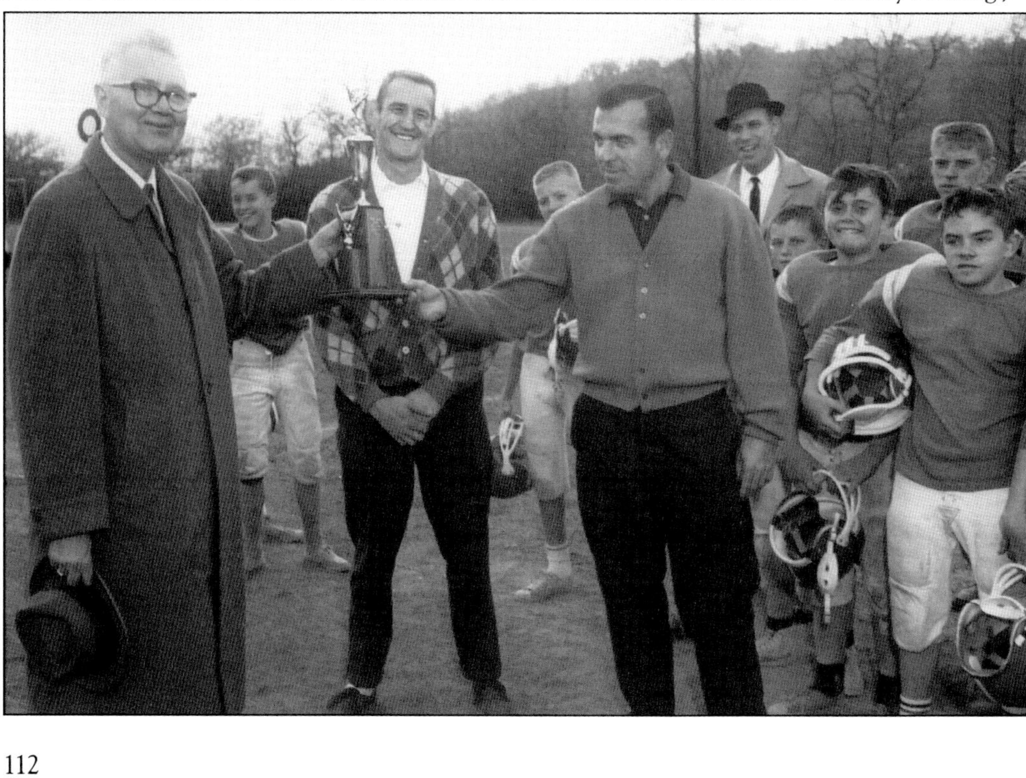

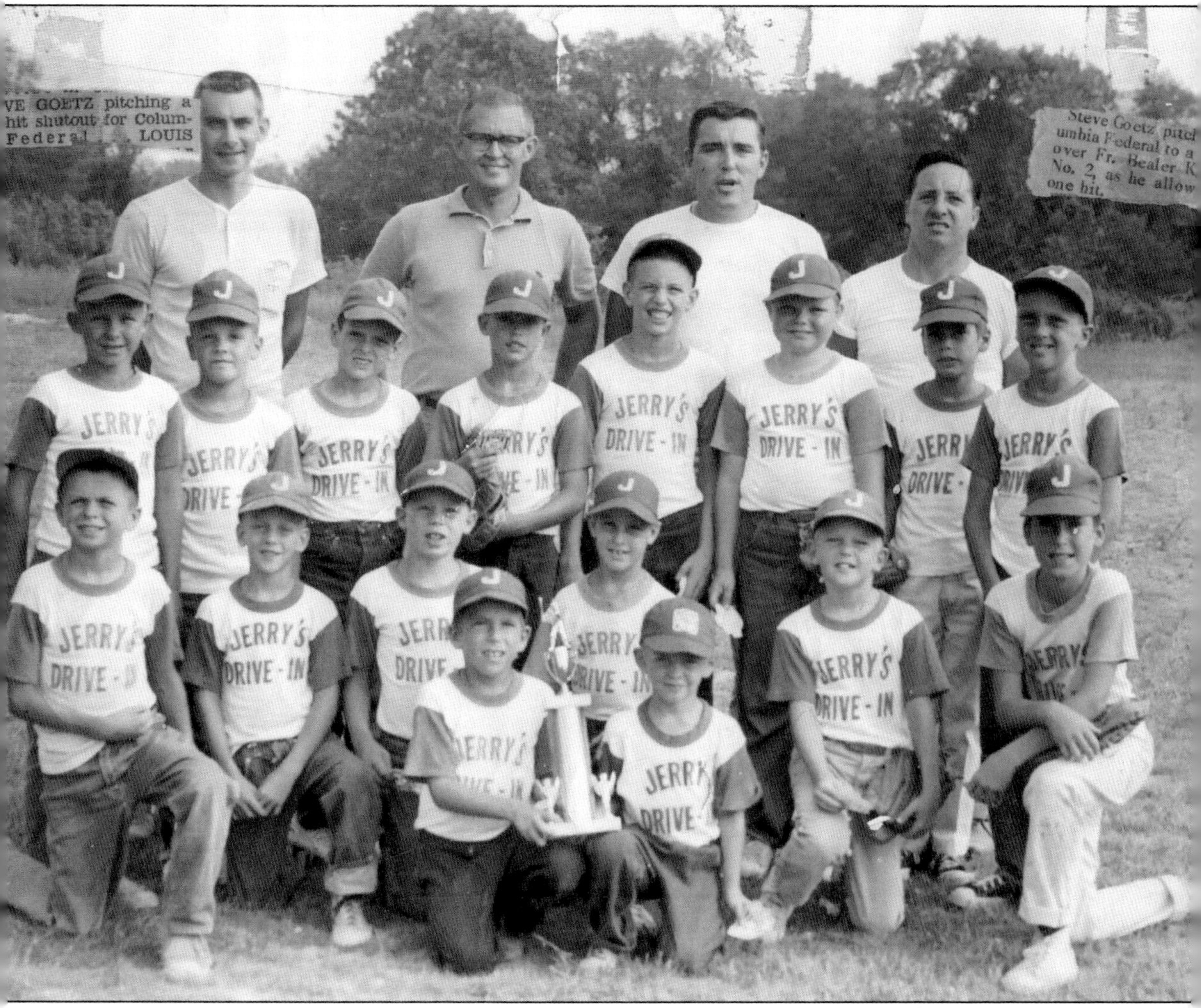

This photograph from 1965 is believed to have been taken at Franzen Field in Villa Hills. Some members of the team were Russell Klare, Tom Klare, Calvin Foltz, Jeffery Klare, Don Coyle, John Pflue, Mark Bowman, Mark Fieger, Tom Buenger, Jim Fauze, Tony Gronefeld, and Steve Goetz. The coaches in the back row are, from left to right, unidentified, Tom Buenger, Tom Klare, and Dave Bowman. (Courtesy of Andy Goetz.)

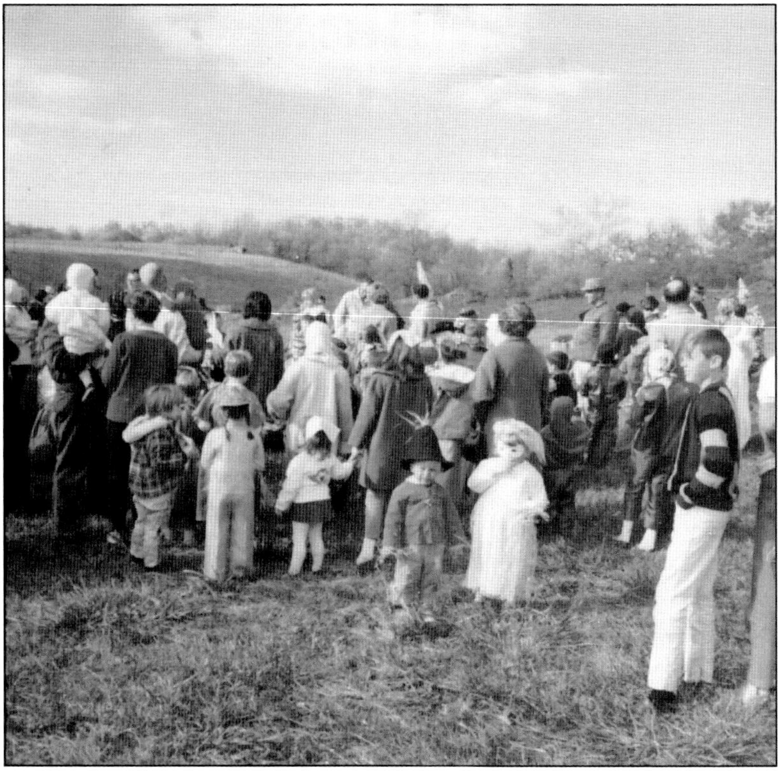

The community gathered at the Villa Hills Civic Club for Halloween parties every year. In this mid-1960s photograph, the Huesman children are facing the camera. In the background, Franzen's lake can be seen in the valley. Located beyond the valley was the hillside where the softball fields were created. (Courtesy of Bob and Pat Huesman.)

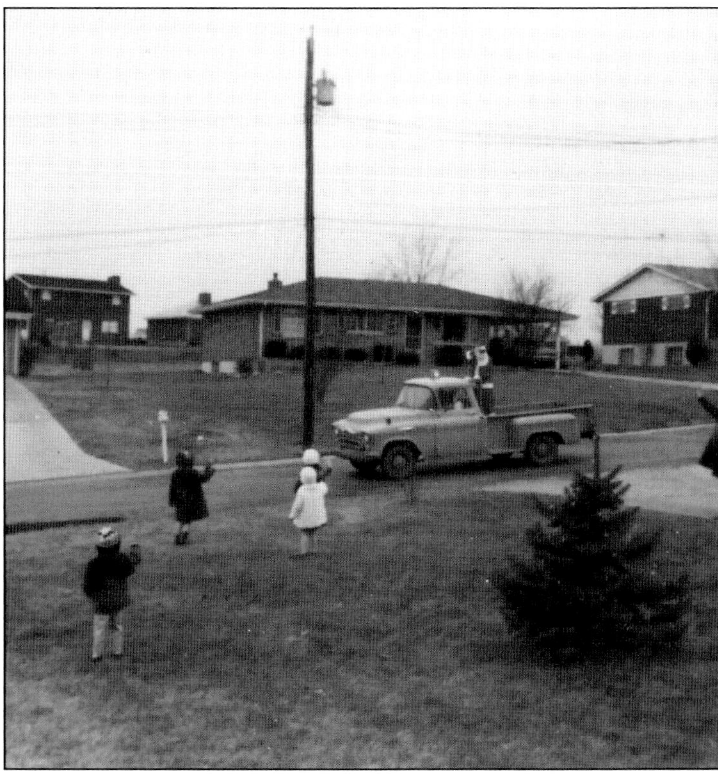

The Villa Hills Civic Club organized a visit from Santa each year. In this late 1960s photograph, Santa Claus arrives by pickup truck, throwing candy and waving to the Huesman family, who lived at 2531 Frank Street. Some years Santa patrolled the streets in the back of a truck and sometimes atop a fire truck, but residents knew when he was coming because it was always published in the *Voice of Villa Hills*. (Courtesy of Bob and Pat Huesman.)

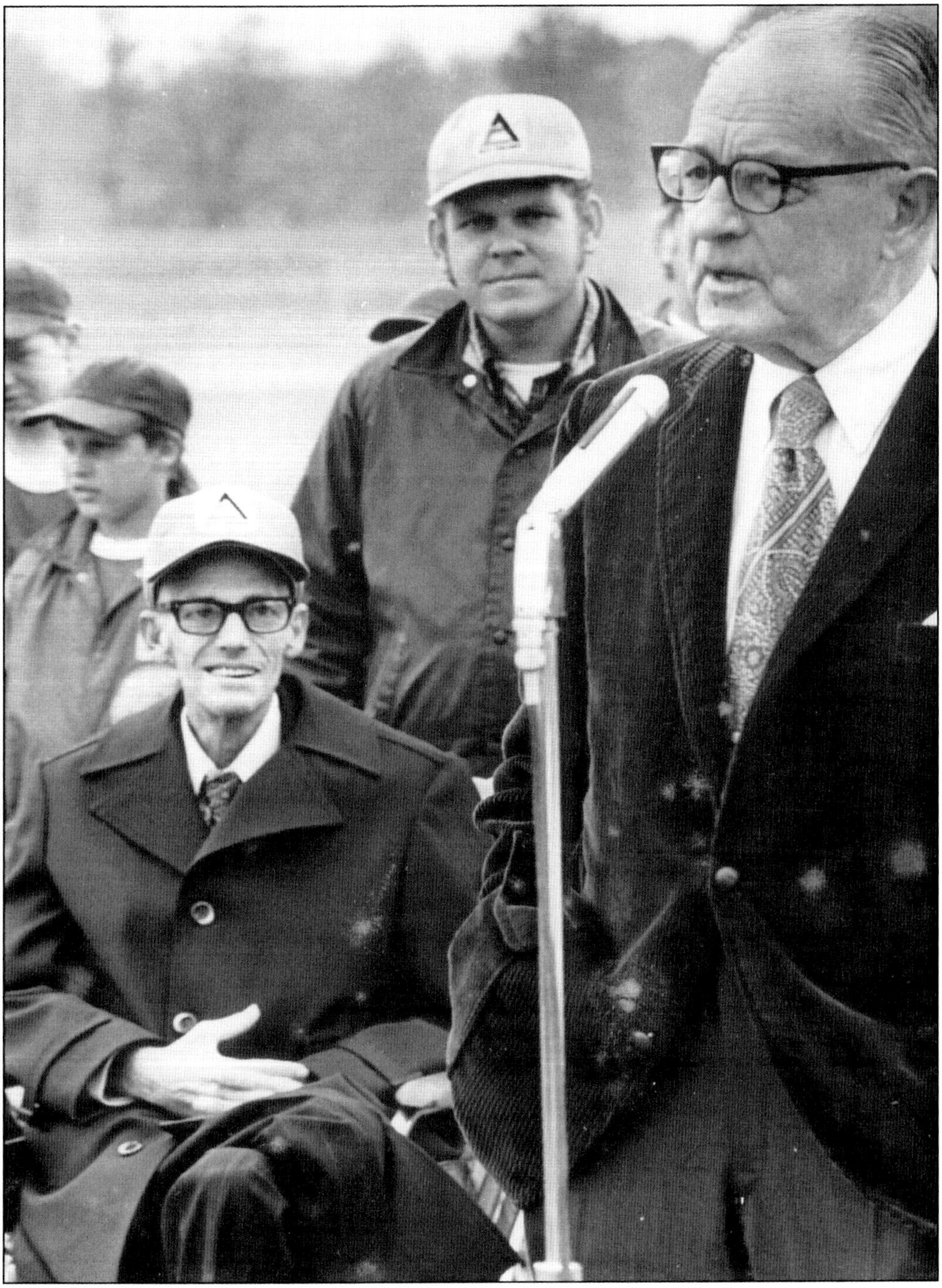

By the early 1970s, the growing city needed more recreation fields. The Crescent-Villa Athletic Association worked with the Sisters of St. Walburg to build baseball fields on 20 acres of the sisters' land on Amsterdam Road. An agreement was reached that the city would lease the fields from St. Walburg for $1 per year. On May 20, 1973, the city officially dedicated the three baseball diamonds, naming them Tom Braun Fields. In this photograph, Mayor Tom Braun (in the wheelchair, on left) and Randy Bising listen to former major league baseball player and Cincinnati Reds announcer Waite Hoyt at the dedication. Mayor Braun passed away about two weeks later. (Courtesy of Tom Braun and Loraine Braun.)

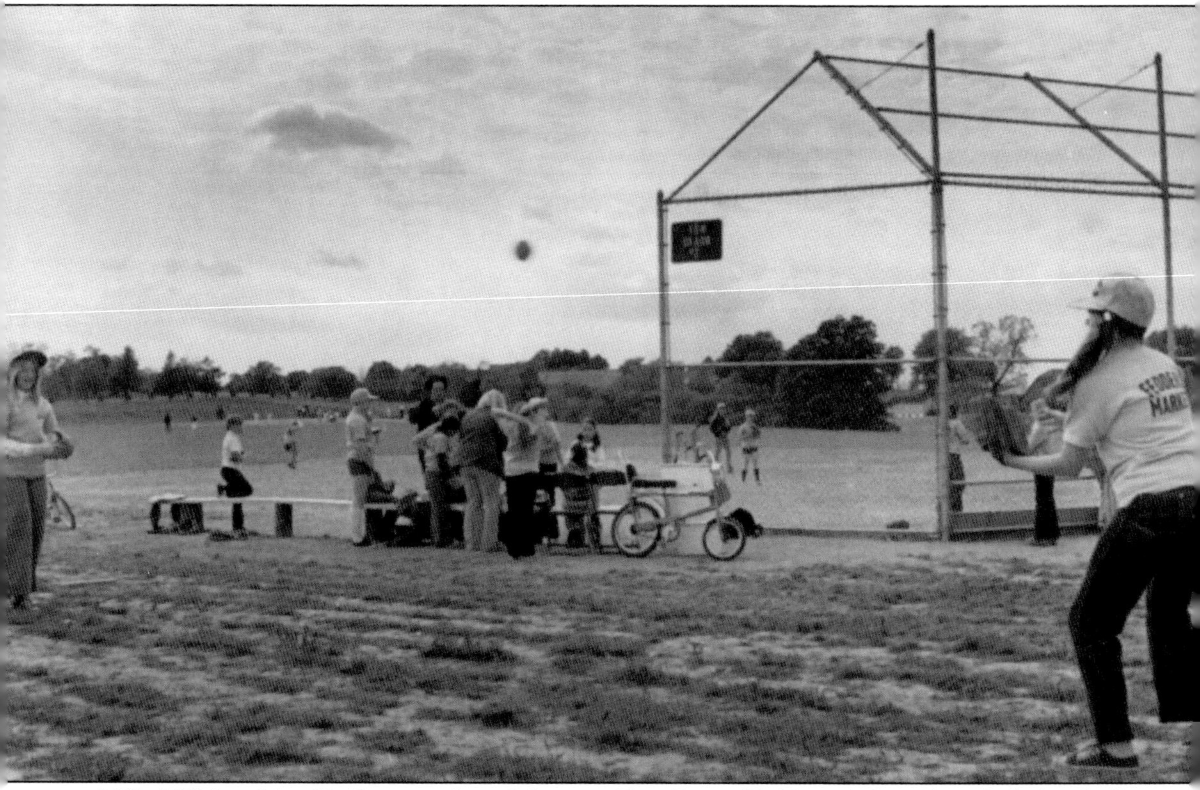

Villa Hills's girls' softball teams shared the new Tom Braun Fields with boys' knothole baseball. This 1973 photograph shows the Amsterdam Road field, looking toward Villa Madonna Academy. The teams were sponsored by local businesses; these girls were sponsored by Fedder's Market, which was the only grocery store in Crescent Springs at that time. (Courtesy of Tom Braun and Loraine Braun.)

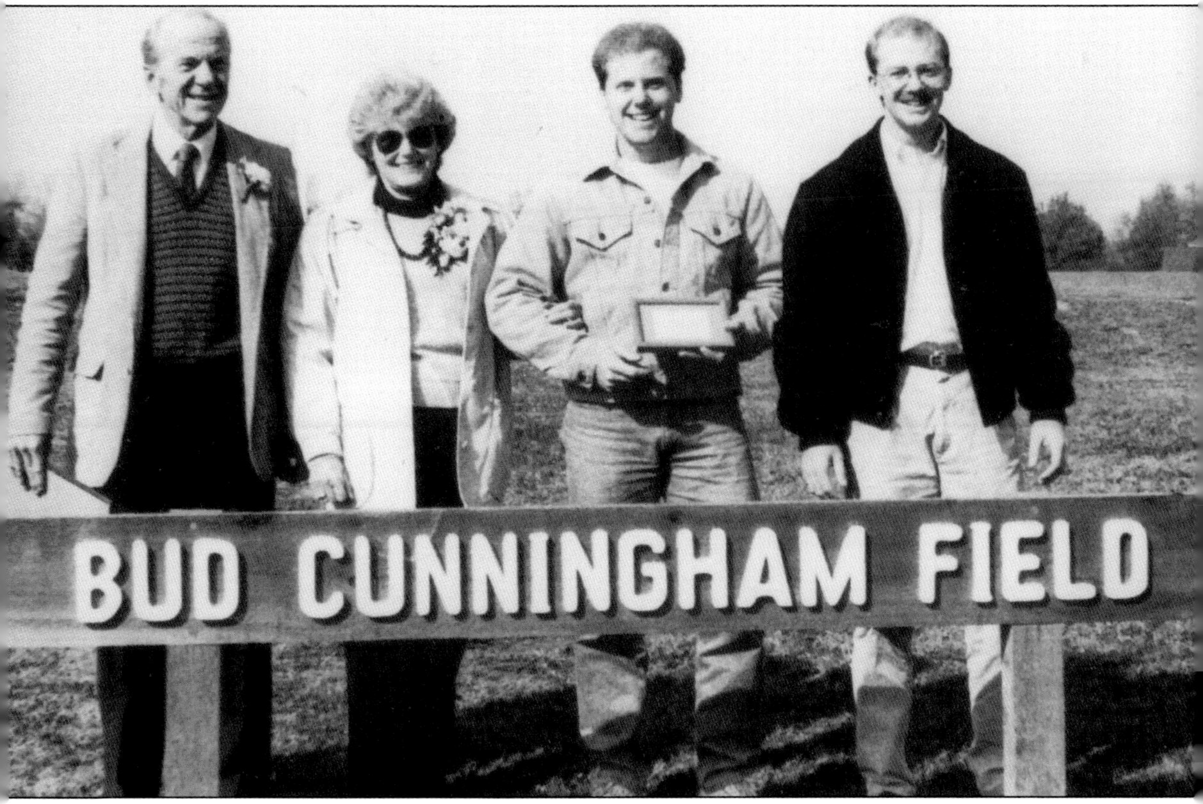

In the mid-1970s, Villa Hills added soccer to the list of recreational sports available. The sport had humble beginnings in Northern Kentucky. The teams had trouble finding enough balls, as local sporting goods stores did not even stock them. For uniforms, the team would bring a white t-shirt to the first practice and the coach would dye them all to match and then write a number on the back with a marker. Bud Cunningham, who was Villa Hills mayor at the time, reportedly constructed goals by inserting tall posts into the field and stringing a rope across the top. In this early-1980s photograph, Leroux "Bud" Cunningham (left) poses with his wife Mary Lou and sons Ron and Greg at the dedication of the Bud Cunningham Field, located on Amsterdam Road and on the grounds of St. Walburg Monastery, adjacent to Tom Braun Fields. (Courtesy of the Villa Hills Historical Society.)

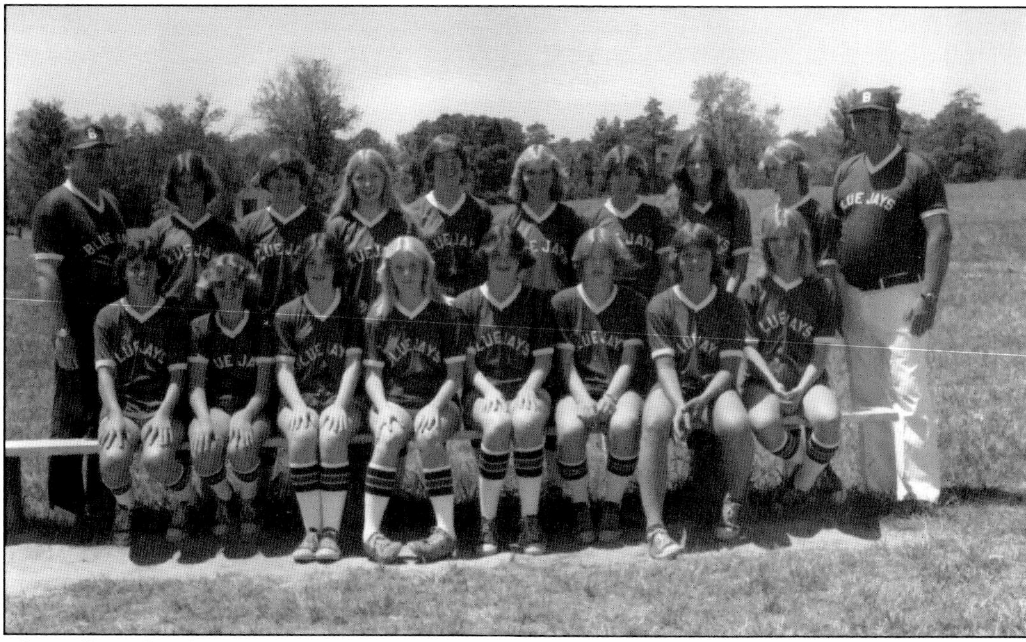

The Villa Hills Blue Jays were just one example of the many girls' softball teams in the city. This 1977 photograph, which was taken at Franzen Fields, included girls from Villa Hills and Crescent Springs. The Blue Jays finished sixth that year. Although the girls' last names were not noted on the photograph, they are, from left to right, (first row) Jenny, Denise, Melinda, Tami, Melissa, Linda, Dana, and Judy; (second row) Coach Ron Bising, Kim, Vicki, Susan, Lisa, Julie, Sandy, Debbie, Leslie, and Coach Bob Huesman. (Courtesy of Melinda Rogers Boesken.)

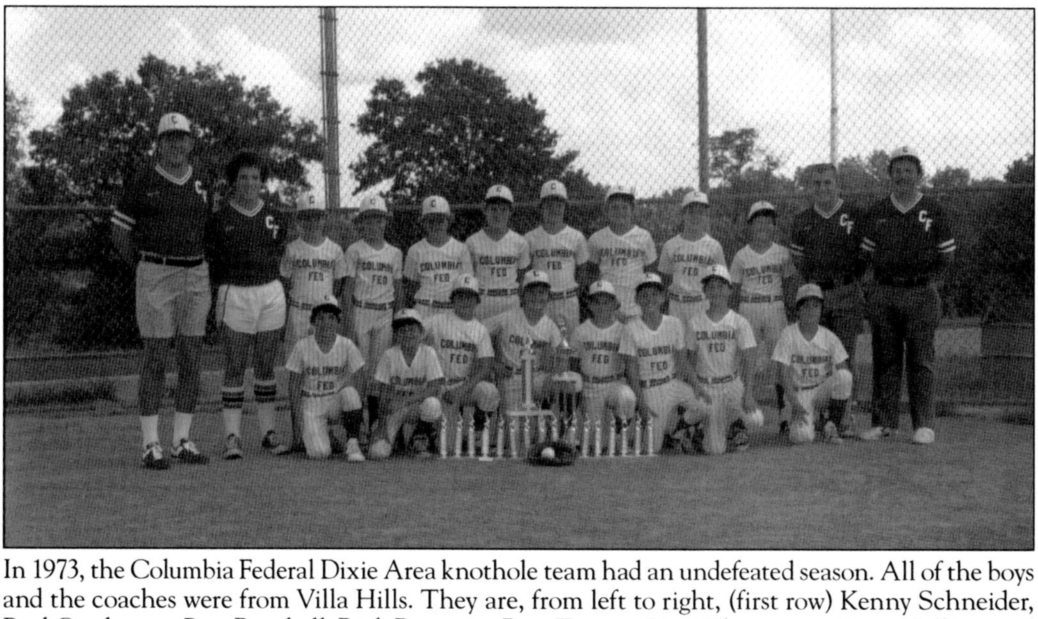

In 1973, the Columbia Federal Dixie Area knothole team had an undefeated season. All of the boys and the coaches were from Villa Hills. They are, from left to right, (first row) Kenny Schneider, Paul Castleman, Pete Ruschell, Rick Brennan, Ron Tormey, Kurt Thompson, Steve Collins, and Tim Huff; (second row) Coach Harry Beck, Coach Dan Boyle, Jim Collins, Jeff Kramer, Tom Board, Bob Beck, Paul Hennessey, Blake Mueller, David Noll, Tim Boyle, Coach Tom Thompson, and manager Larry Boyle. (Courtesy of Larry and Kathy Boyle.)

The *Voice of Villa Hills*, published first in June 1967, grew from a 3-page report to a 20-page newspaper and has been delivered free of charge to every resident every month since. This is the back page of an edition from the late 1970s. Notice the familiar businesses of times gone by. (Courtesy of the Grout family.)

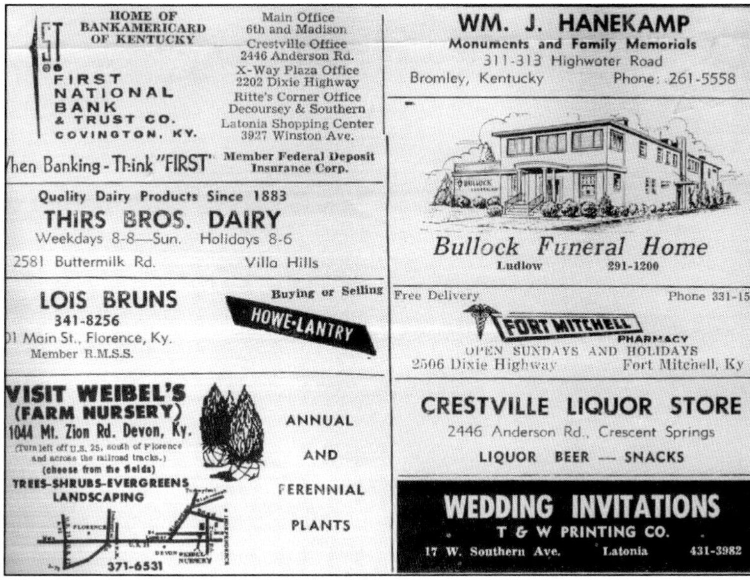

HOME OF BANKAMERICARD OF KENTUCKY
FIRST NATIONAL BANK & TRUST CO.
COVINGTON, KY.
Main Office 6th and Madison
Crestville Office 2446 Anderson Rd.
X-Way Plaza Office 2202 Dixie Highway
Ritte's Corner Office Decoursey & Southern
Latonia Shopping Center 3927 Winston Ave.
hen Banking - Think "FIRST"
Member Federal Deposit Insurance Corp.

WM. J. HANEKAMP
Monuments and Family Memorials
311-313 Highwater Road
Bromley, Kentucky Phone: 261-5558

Bullock Funeral Home
Ludlow 291-1200

Quality Dairy Products Since 1883
THIRS BROS. DAIRY
Weekdays 8-8—Sun. Holidays 8-6
2581 Buttermilk Rd. Villa Hills

LOIS BRUNS
341-8256
1 Main St., Florence, Ky.
Member R.M.S.S.
Buying or Selling
HOWE-LANTRY

Free Delivery Phone 331-155
FORT MITCHELL PHARMACY
OPEN SUNDAYS AND HOLIDAYS
2506 Dixie Highway Fort Mitchell, Ky

VISIT WEIBEL'S (FARM NURSERY)
1044 Mt. Zion Rd. Devon, Ky.
(Turn left off U.S. 25, south of Florence and across the railroad tracks.)
(choose from the fields)
TREES-SHRUBS-EVERGREENS LANDSCAPING
371-6531
ANNUAL AND PERENNIAL PLANTS

CRESTVILLE LIQUOR STORE
2446 Anderson Rd., Crescent Springs
LIQUOR BEER — SNACKS

WEDDING INVITATIONS
T & W PRINTING CO.
17 W. Southern Ave. Latonia 431-3982

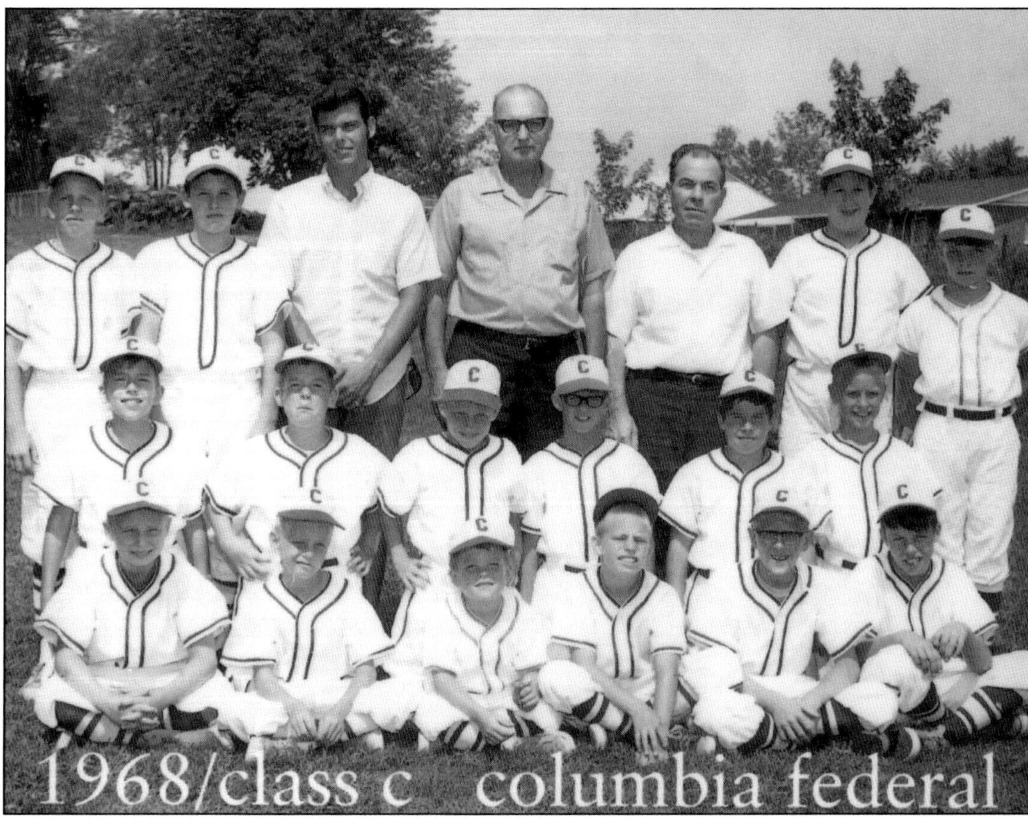

Columbia Federal Savings and Loan sponsored this 1968 Villa Hills baseball team. They are, from left to right, (first row) Steve Kleir, Chuck Brinkman, Mike Bennett, Tim Potter, Gary Brinkman, and Tom Goetz; (second row) Russ Klare, Fred Bennett, Wayne Siemer, Ken Potter, Tim Breetz, and Gary Luebbers; (third row) Greg Schulte, Jim Burger, Tom Burger, Coach Ed Burger, manager Howard Burger, Coach Kurt Kuhn, and Kevin Jansen.

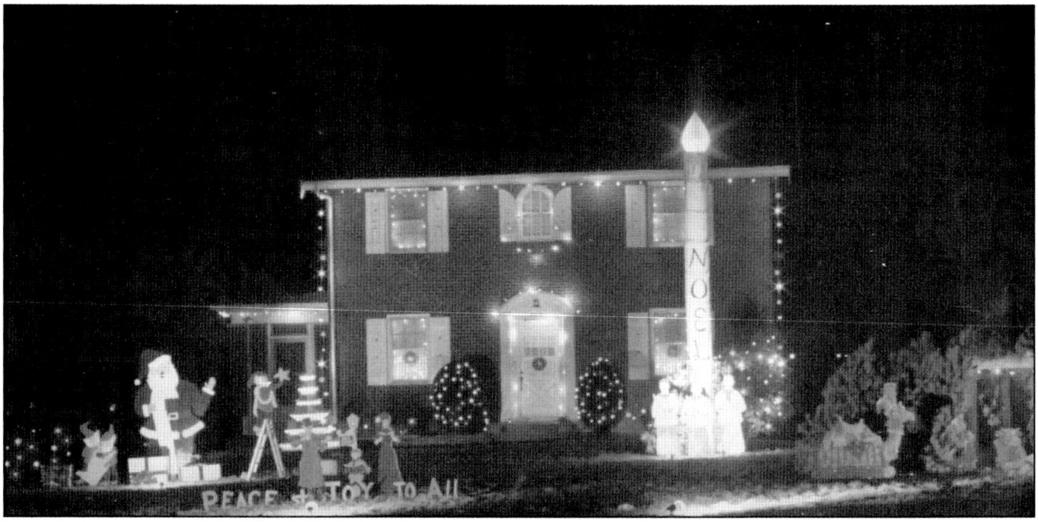

The Ed Grout family, who resided at 2519 Buttermilk Pike from 1963 until 1995, were well known in the city for their beautiful Christmas display. The family, which included 12 children, built the display and added to it every year. (Courtesy of the Grout family.)

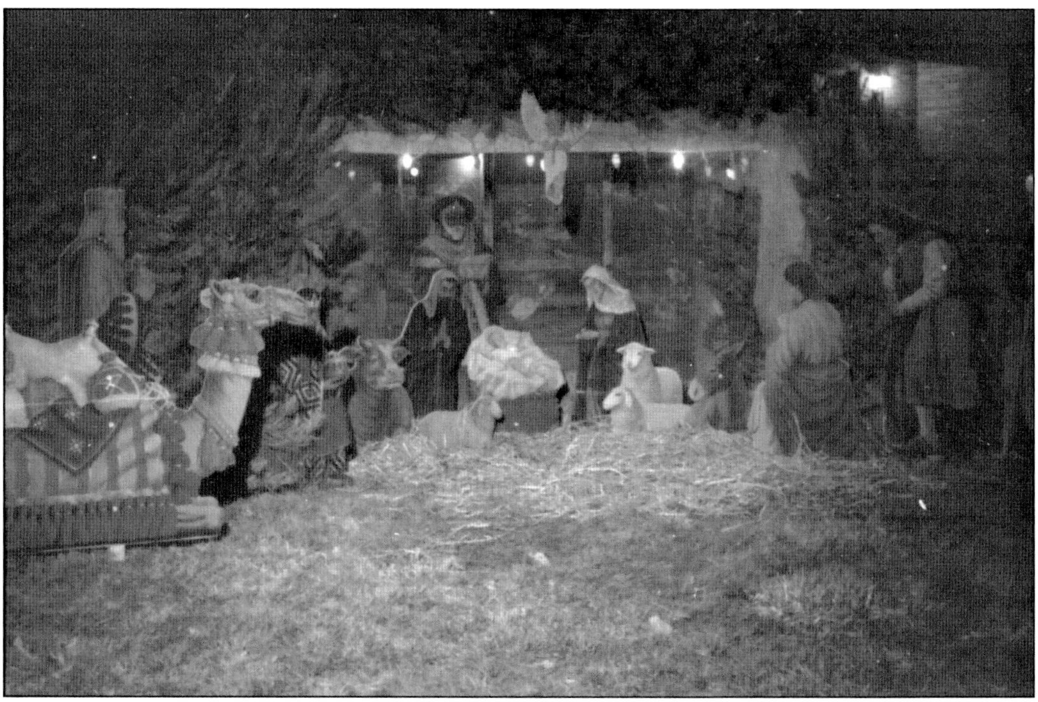

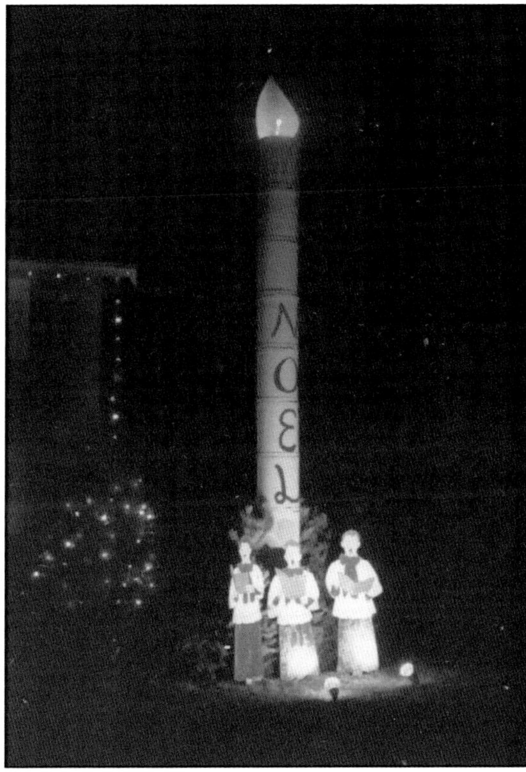

In the photograph at right, the giant candle, which was almost as tall as their house, was erected every year in the front yard of the Grout home. The photograph below shows the 6-foot sign that was built by the siblings and added to the Grout collection around 1980. After their parents sold the Buttermilk home, this sign was known to show up in the grown siblings' yards. The sign always appeared in the front yard of a recently bought Grout house at Christmas time. (Courtesy of the Grout family.)

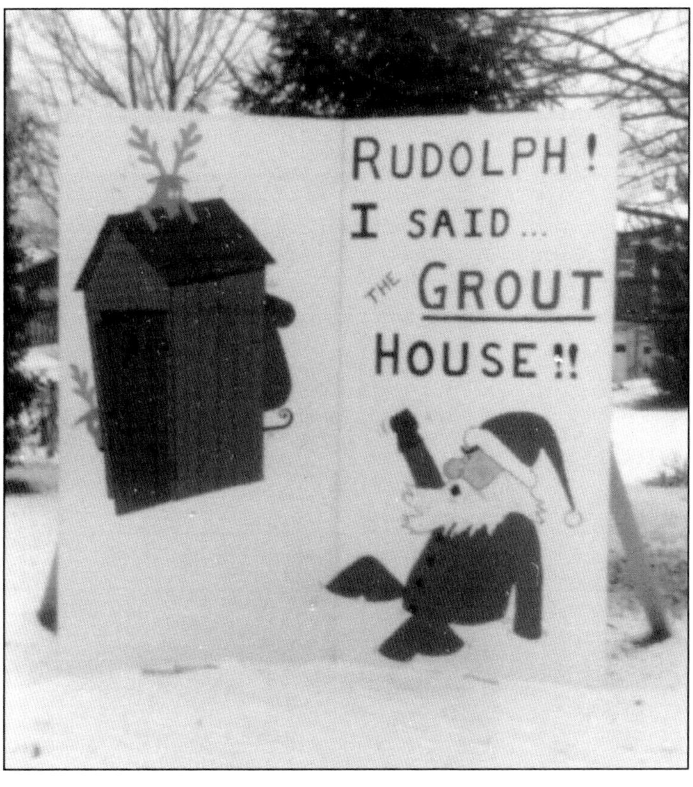

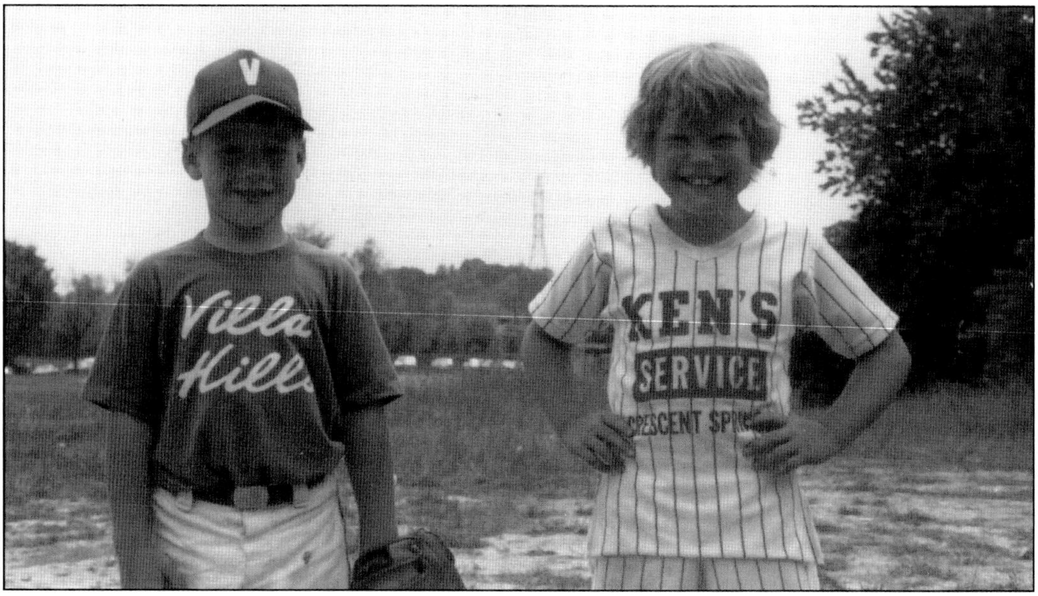

Villa Hills player Kevin Bresser (left) and his friend, who played for Ken's Service of Cresent Springs, pose for this 1979 photograph. The photograph was taken at Franzen Fields, looking toward the concession stand and parking lot. In the distance is Rogers Road. (Courtesy of Ken Bresser.)

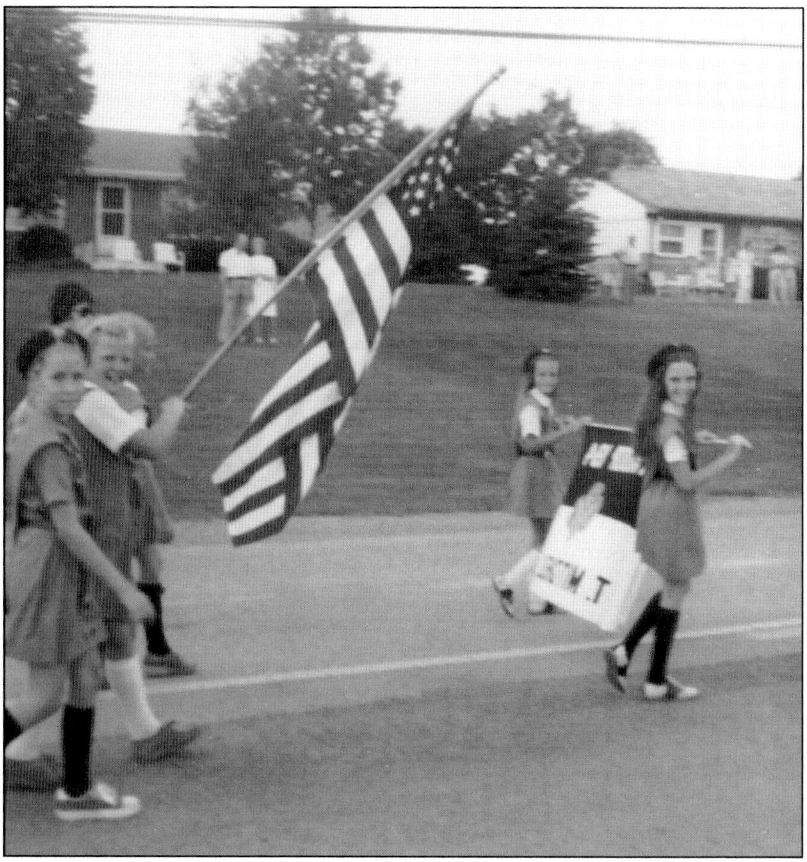

One of the many parades that wound its way through Villa Hills is seen in this late-1970s photograph. The Girl Scouts in this parade are heading north on Collins Road, toward Amsterdam Road. (Courtesy of Bob and Pat Huesman.)

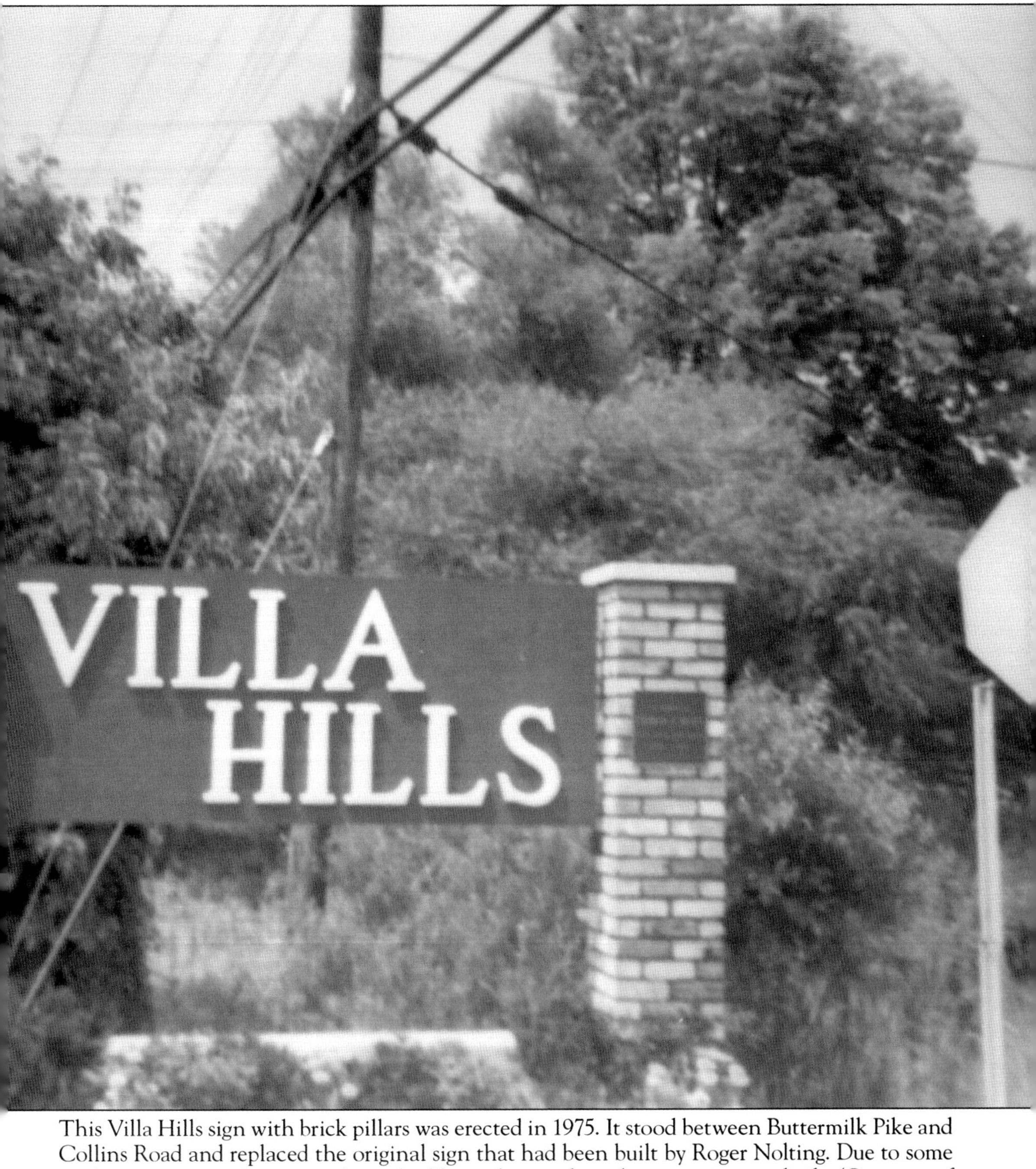

This Villa Hills sign with brick pillars was erected in 1975. It stood between Buttermilk Pike and Collins Road and replaced the original sign that had been built by Roger Nolting. Due to some road construction, the original sign had been damaged, so this new sign was built. (Courtesy of Virginia Feldhaus.)

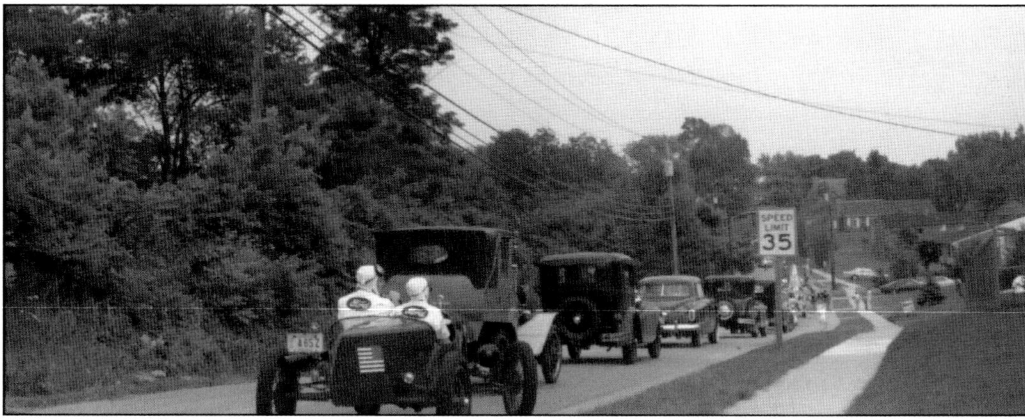

This undated photograph is of a parade of antique cars traveling down the hill on Amsterdam Road, just past Niewhaner Drive and going toward Rogers Road. The left side of the road is now the site of Stonewood Court. (Courtesy of Tom Braun and Loraine Braun.)

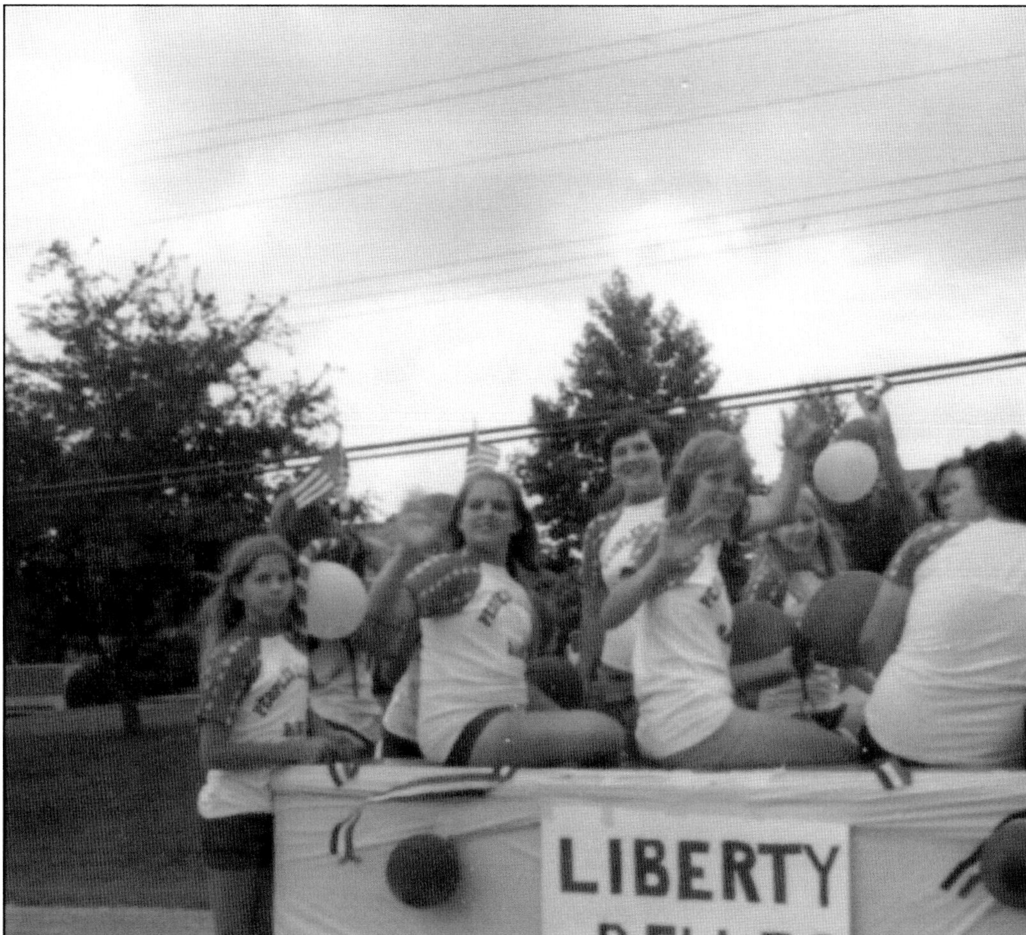

The Tom Braun girls' softball league was well represented in this undated parade photograph. Peoples Liberty Bank sponsored the team, the Liberty Belles. (Courtesy of Bob and Pat Huesman.)

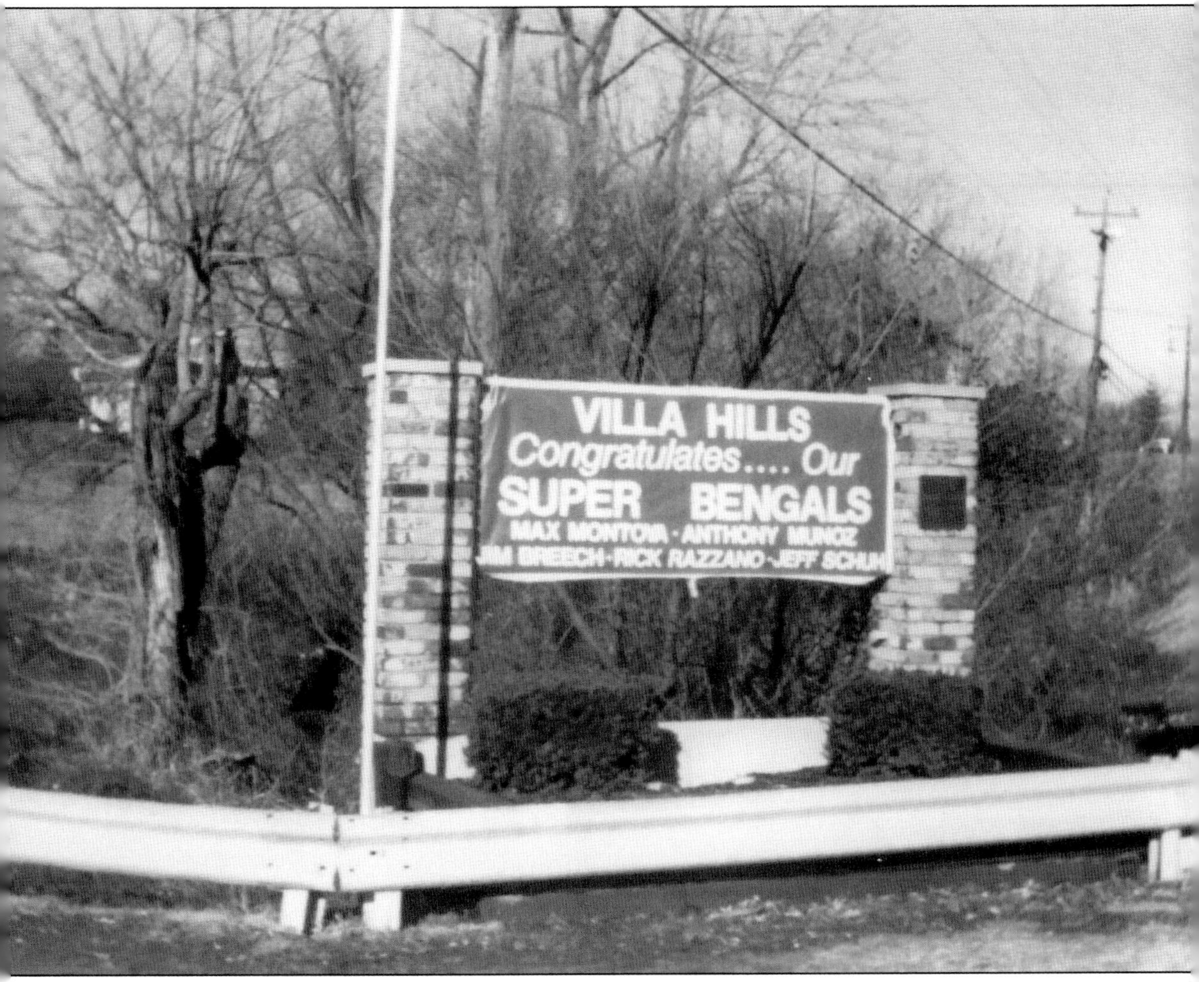

In January 1982, the Cincinnati Bengals were on their way to Super Bowl XVI in Pontiac, Michigan. Villa Hills was home to five members of the team, so the city sign was temporarily changed to congratulate residents Max Montoya, Anthony Munoz, Jim Breech, Rick Razzano, and Jeff Schuh. Although the team lost to the San Francisco 49ers, Villa Hills was proud of their American Football Conference champions. (Courtesy of Virginia Feldhaus.)

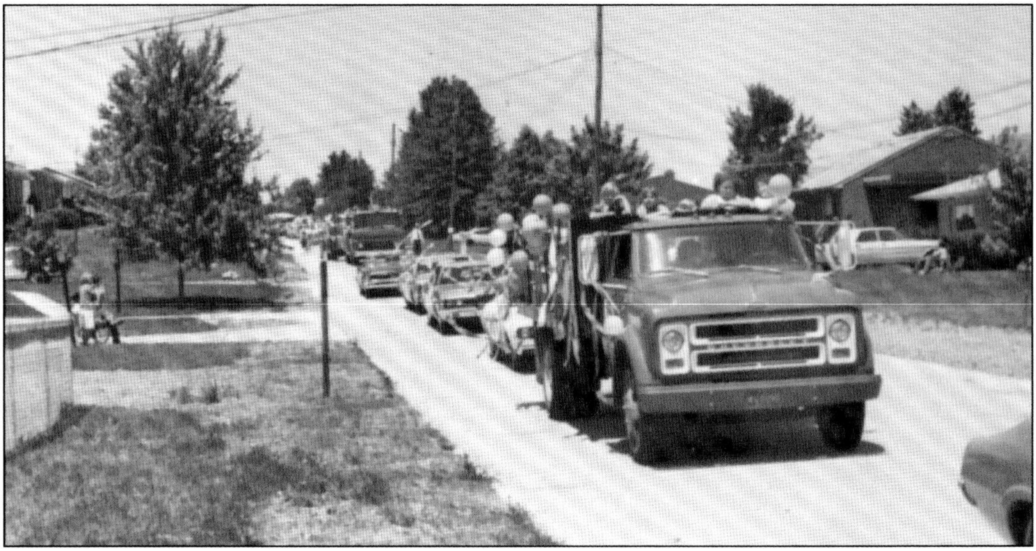

This photograph is from a very early Villa Hills parade, as the route comes down Sunglow approaching Buttermilk Pike. Those early parades included kids on bikes, residents in their decorated cars, fire trucks, tractors, and usually a garbage truck. (Courtesy of Tom Braun and Loraine Braun.)

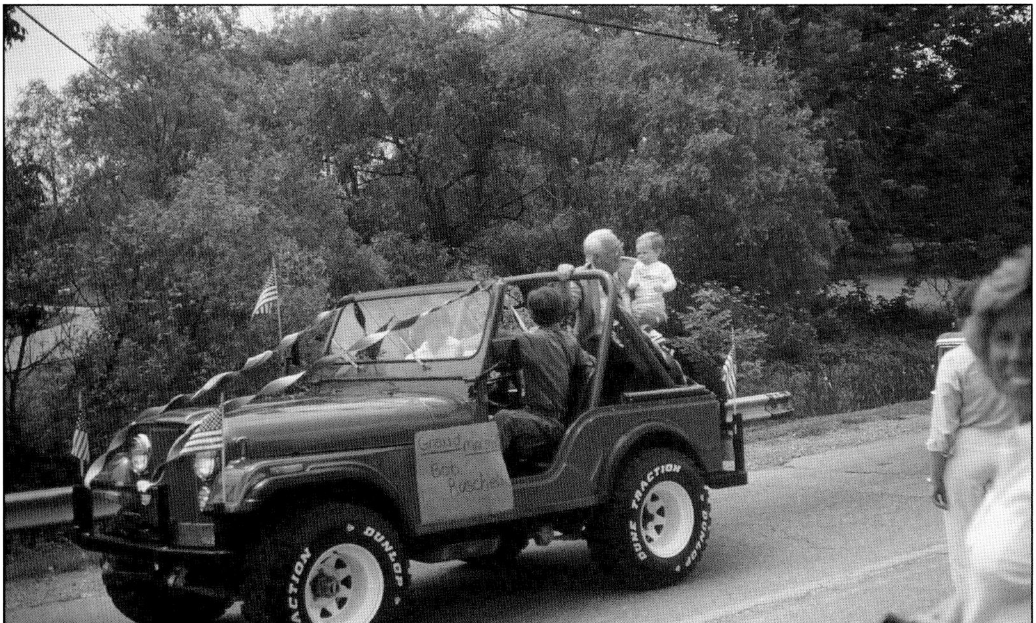

In order to celebrate Villa Hills's 20th birthday, the city held a parade in June 1982. The parade had some large floats, the Roger Bacon High School marching band, and the mandatory fire trucks, softball and baseball teams, and floats from local businesses. The grand marshal was Bob Ruschell, who lived on Sunglow Drive and had served as a Villa Hills councilman for almost 20 years. Ruschell is holding his grandson Kevin Weisenberger. In the front of the Jeep are Rushell's sons, Robert (driving) and Pete. (Courtesy of Paul and Peg Kohl.)

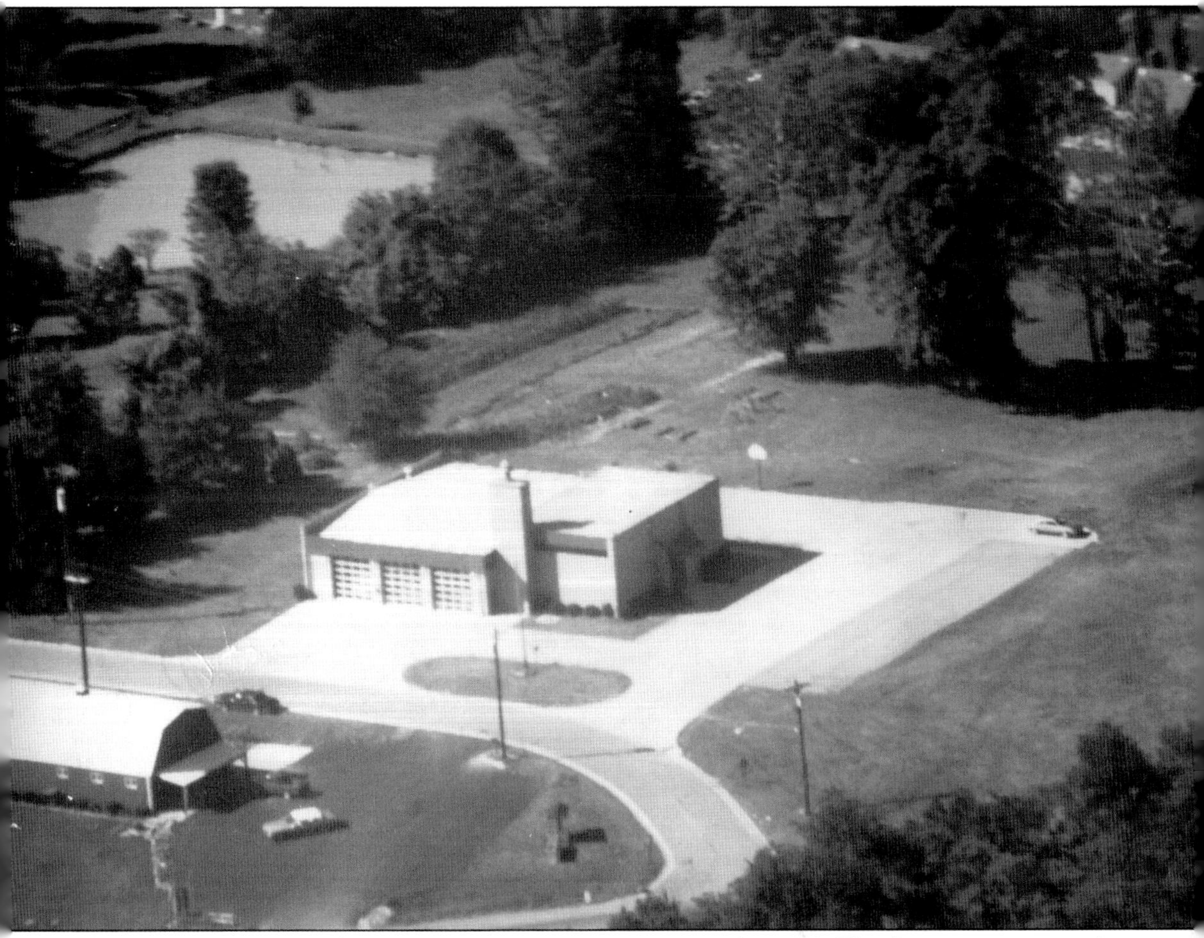

The Crescent Springs Volunteer Fire Department was organized in 1929. The department acquired hoses, equipment, and eventually trucks. Until a permanent firehouse could be built, they kept these items in residents' garages and barns. That first firehouse, which was located at the corner of Western Reserve and Erlanger Crescent Springs Road, was completed in 1934. The all-volunteer crew was made up of residents of Crescent Springs, Villa Hills, and Crescent Park, which is now part of Fort Mitchell. When the fire siren on top of the building sounded, these dedicated volunteers dropped what they were doing and came from all directions to go out on the call. This 1980 photograph shows an aerial view of the brand new firehouse, built on Overlook Drive in Crescent Springs. (Courtesy of the Crescent Springs/Villa Hills Fire and EMS Department.)

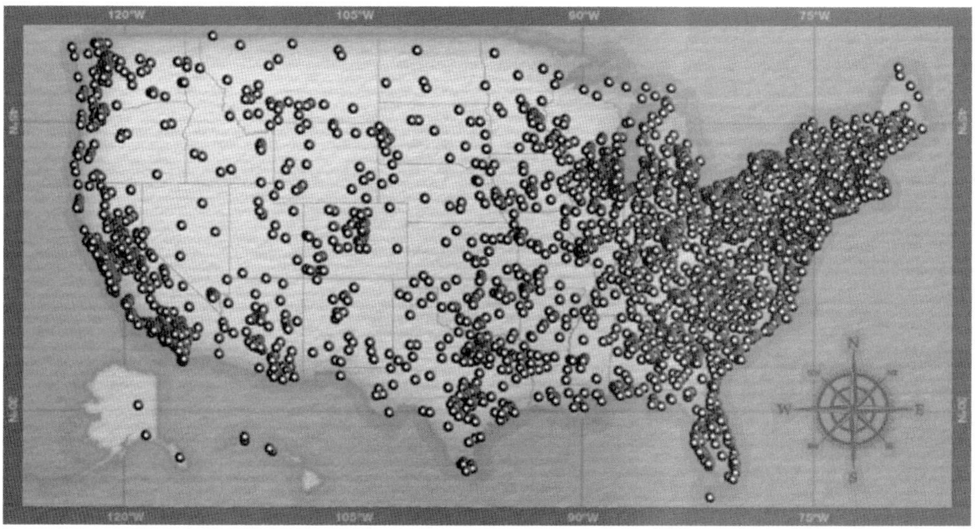